HOLLYWOOD'S STEPHEN KING

TONY MAGISTRALE

palgrave
macmillan

First published 2003 by
PALGRAVE MACMILLAN™
175 Fifth Avenue, New York, N.Y. 10010 and
Houndmills, Basingstoke, Hampshire, England RG21 6XS.
Companies and representatives throughout the world.

PALGRAVE MACMILLAN is the global academic imprint of the
Palgrave Macmillan division of St. Martin's Press, LLC and of
Palgrave Macmillan Ltd. Macmillan® is a registered trademark in
the United States, United Kingdom and other countries. Palgrave is
a registered trademark in the European Union and other countries.

ISBN 0–312–29320–8 hardback
ISBN 0–312–29321–6 paperback

Library of Congress Cataloging-in-Publication Data is available
from the Library of Congress.

A catalogue record for this book is available from the British
Library.

Design by Letra Libre, Inc.

First edition: November 2003
10 9 8 7 6 5 4 3 2 1

Printed in the United States of America.

Dedicated with great affection to the students at the University of Vermont who have helped to shape my own appreciation of the films addressed in this book.

CONTENTS

LIST OF ILLUSTRATIONS

ACKNOWLEDGMENTS

This book would never have reached your hands without the invaluable assistance of many people and institutions. Dawn Pelkey, Mary Findley, Eric Rickstad, Liz Paley, Sid Poger, Brian Kent, Bobby Haas, Corey Malanga, Mary Pharr, Allison Kelly, Keith Silva, Michael Stanton, and especially Hilary Neroni each read multiple drafts of successive chapters and supplied me with counsel that was both illuminating and encouraging. My editors at Palgrave, Kristi Long, Roee Raz, Debra Manette, Donna Cherry, and Erin Chan, were simultaneously nurturing and tough-minded with my writing—an important combination for any editor to possess. Early conceptual thinking about the horrors inherent in bathrooms in Stanley Kubrick's *The Shining* found its initial audience at Cecil Community College in Maryland, where I viewed the film for the first time on a theatrical-size screen and then presented a lecture to the college community; my thanks to Paul Haspel and Polly Binns for arranging this opportunity to explore such private places in public. The first half of chapter 5 is an expanded version of "Cronenberg's 'Only Really Human Movie': *The Dead Zone*," an article first published in a special edition dedicated to the films of director David Cronenberg in the journal *Post Script: Essays in Film and the Humanities* 15 (1996): 40–45. The Arts and Sciences dean's office of the University of Vermont provided me the opportunity to present "The Many Redemptions of *The Shawshank Redemption*," a lecture based on another section of chapter 5, when I accepted the Dean's Lecture award for 2003. Associate Dean S. Abu Turab Rizvi also supplied me with funds to travel to Bangor, Maine, to interview Stephen King. My appreciation to Steve King for taking time from his recuperation and busy schedule to indulge my request for this insightful interview, published for the first time in chapter 1. My respect for Stephen King as an artist and human being has been steadily enriched over the years because of similar examples of his immense generosity. Dear friends and family members—Larry Bennett, Ken Wagner, Annalee Curtis, Lynn Bessette, Kay and Norman Tederous, and Jennifer,

Daniel, and Christopher Magistrale—reminded me consistently that there is life beyond the computer screen, and these inimitable excursions, in turn, allowed me to return reinvigorated to the task of writing this book. One of the great joys of attaining tenure in academe is the freedom to teach courses that reflect a scholar's area of interest and capacity for imaginative design. In twenty years of teaching untraditional courses offered through the English department such as "The Films of Stephen King," "Poe's Children," "The Horror Film," and "The Literary Vampire," undergraduate and graduate students at the University of Vermont provided critical insights that have indelibly shaped, confirmed, challenged, and altered my understanding of Stephen King's films. My only regret is that I cannot thank all these students personally—there are just too many—but their sensitive and intelligent voices from classroom discussions and writing assignments most definitely resonate throughout these pages.

PREFACE

Several years ago, when I first began seriously thinking about authoring a book on the films made from Stephen King's fiction, I mentioned my intentions to a colleague in the English department. His initial response was an unenthusiastic "Why would you want to write about Stephen King's films? Especially when there have been so many *unremarkable* movies made from his fiction." Any volume entitled *Hollywood's Stephen King* must at least acknowledge the partial truth inherent in this negative opinion. After all, *Children of the Corn* in all its unnecessary permutations is a persuasive case in point. However, what is truly remarkable about the extensive body of celluloid work interpreted from King's novels, novellas, short stories, and teleplays—at this writing, an oeuvre that contains over seventy titles and is still growing—is just how many of these productions have turned out to be excellent films. For the sake of my skeptical colleague, even if we adopt a cruelly conservative estimate that only 25 percent of these movies are worthy of the specialized attention that a book such as this one seeks to provide, how many novelists, screenwriters, directors, or production companies would not be ecstatic with seventeen films that have proven to be both financially and artistically successful?

There is little doubt about Stephen King's marketability in Hollywood. When his name is connected with a film—either a theatrical release or a television miniseries—the production is virtually guaranteed to make money. New Line Cinema sought to capitalize on this nexus while advertising *The Lawnmower Man* (1992), a film that contained so little of King's original short story from which it was adapted that the author filed a lawsuit demanding that his name be removed from the credits. Bob Shayne, New Line Cinema's CEO, defended his company's position by insisting "that's what we paid for. . . . King's name was the most important thing we were buying [in purchasing the rights to the short story]" (Jones 75).

In spite of the obvious marketability associated with King's name, and ironically, sometimes because of it, the vast majority of films adapted from his fiction have failed to garner much formal critical attention over the years. In 1986 Michael R. Collings published *The Films of Stephen King,* the only book-length scholarly analysis ever published on King's movies. Collings's work, now out of print, is, of course, restricted to films released prior to 1986. Four other magazine-books, oversized and lavishly illustrated with movie stills, have been published since the Collings volume appeared: Jessie Horsting's *Stephen King at the Movies* (1986), Jeff Conner's *Stephen King Goes to Hollywood* (1987), Ann Lloyd's *The Films of Stephen King* (1993), and Stephen Jones's *Creepshows: The Illustrated Stephen King Movie Guide* (2002). Each of these texts is primarily concerned with satisfying the average fan's curiosity about the making of King's movies—cataloging technical data, plot line evolution, credits, budgets, on-location gossip, King's own evaluation of the finished product—essentially, the data behind the production history of each film. While certainly valuable and interesting on their own terms, none of these recent publications offers much by way of serious film interpretation.

The majority of the King films that are released through conventional Hollywood theatrical premieres attain critical notice in the popular press—e.g., newspaper and periodical reviews of current cinema—but these five-to ten-paragraph reviews differ substantially from the type of focused and comprehensive analyses found in academic film journals and books. The notable exceptions, *Carrie* and *The Shining,* have received considerable and consistent attention in various scholarly publications. The reason for this, I suspect, has little to do with these films as adaptations of Stephen King novels and everything to do with the fact that Brian De Palma and Stanley Kubrick respectively directed them. *Carrie* (1976) and *The Shining* (1980) have obtained their critical due because they are part of larger directorial oeuvres that have nothing to do with Stephen King. On occasion, an insightful reading of an individual picture has appeared in popular fanzines devoted to the genre of the horror film, such as *Cinfantastique* or *Fangoria,* and sometimes one of King's movie adaptations is the subject of a critical article published in an obscure academic journal, an independent essay in a collected volume dealing with a larger topic to which the film somehow relates, or a chapter in a book committed to analyzing King's literary fiction. Generally speaking, however, the academic world has tended to view cinematic versions of Stephen King with the same level of dubious disaffection with which it treats his published prose. It is notable, for example, that no film journal has ever produced a special issue devoted to critical readings of various Stephen King movies (or, for that matter, *any* film adaptation of one of his books), even as the corpus of distinguished work that now exists would appear to make such a publication highly attractive to both the film specialist and a broad general audience.

There are a myriad of explanations for why most of King's cinematic canon has been so conspicuously ignored critically, but here are several of the most important:

- The films, like the books that have inspired them, are linked to an enormously popular writer, arguably the most successful author in the history of publishing. Despite the diverse thematic range and nuanced skills of this writer, his popularity has called his artistic seriousness into question, at least in the minds of academic snobs. Moreover, King's popularity likewise affiliates him with children and young adults, who have always constituted a large portion of his audience and the major demographic for the horror genre in general. For certain teachers and critics, the same issues that make him attractive to adolescents serve to weaken the gravity of his fictional and cinematic art. Indeed, regarding this issue, the writer has often been his own worst enemy. At a 1999 party at Tavern on the Green to celebrate King's twenty-fifth anniversary as a published author, an event that was attended by many important members of the New York literati and publishing worlds, the host ended the evening by screening a highlight tape of the bloodiest scenes from his film canon. Sometimes Stephen King, the serious artist, comes into direct conflict with Stephen King, the mischievous kid.
- The seventy-plus films that have been released since 1976 make the King adaptations a true cultural phenomenon worthy of deeper interpretation and understanding as independent works and as a collection. Unfortunately, some of these films are, as my English department colleague reminds us, similar in quality to *Children of the Corn* and *Maximum Overdrive:* difficult for an adult to watch— much less appreciate—and nearly impossible to write about. Many critics have unfairly repudiated the entire King canon after viewing one or two of these celluloid disasters.
- Several of the best examples that have successfully made the transition from printed page to screen include *The Dead Zone* (1983), *Stand by Me* (1986), *The Shawshank Redemption* (1994), *Dolores Claiborne* (1995), *Apt Pupil* (1997*),* and *The Green Mile* (1999*).* It is remarkable how many people, both in and outside of universities, still fail to associate these films with Stephen King. Because his reputation was established around predominant subject themes in the

fields of fantasy, horror, the supernatural, the bizarre, and the occult, pictures such as *The Shawshank Redemption, Apt Pupil,* and *Dolores Claiborne,* which are devoid of the requisite supernatural monsters and concerned instead with the monsters of everyday reality, are not readily linked to him. Despite the tremendous commercial potential of King's name, Hollywood producers will often downplay his connection to a "mainstream film" in order to avoid typecasting a movie that does not belong to the "horror genre."

- As a corollary to this preceding point, academics tend to associate King with the gothic genre exclusively, and many scholars—ironically in spite of the wealth of superb critical attention applied to the genre (horror films in particular) over the past thirty years—still continue to view horror art as too unsettling to their aesthetics or, worse, dismiss it categorically. Robin Wood's generalizations on horror film can be accurately applied to our discussion of King: "The horror film has consistently been one of the most popular and, at the same time, the most disreputable of Hollywood genres. . . . They are dismissed with contempt by the majority of reviewer-critics, or simply ignored" (29–30).

- Scholarship does not occur in a vacuum; it relies on a history of dialogue among different minds to stimulate opinion and debate. There simply has not been sufficient scholarly attention paid to Stephen King's films to foster such an environment. It is my hope that this book will establish at least an initial context for viewing many of these films, and that this will spark further critical discussion. While it is difficult to locate the highly varied King films neatly under the comprehensive umbrella of any single poststructuralist paradigm, individual pictures inspire a range of theoretical readings. For example, *Carrie* has long attracted psychoanalytical feminist criticism (see the work by Barbara Creed and Shelley Stamp Lindsey) because it at once addresses the abjection of the female body and its eventual empowerment. Additionally, as Fredric Jameson posits, *The Shining* lends itself to a Marxist critique of class warfare between the ruling hegemony ensconced at the hotel and Torrance's working-class positioning (serving as the Overlook's "caretaker"). The present volume frequently relies on the influence of both Marxist and feminist theory in interpreting other cinematic texts.

In the last analysis, this writer must admit to being as baffled as King himself (see the chapter 1 interview) in explaining to complete satisfaction how a diverse body of work that has garnered such enormous popular attention and generated so many millions of dollars continues to be so critically unexamined. Hollywood itself has clearly recognized the outstanding merit of several of these films, nominating *Stand by Me* for an Academy Award for Best Screenplay Adaptation, *The Shawshank Redemption* for seven Academy Awards, and *The Green Mile* for another four; acknowledging the acting contributions of Sissy Spacek and Piper Laurie (*Carrie*) in nominating both for the same Best Actress Award; as well as Kathy Bates (*Misery* and *Dolores Claiborne*), who was also twice nominated for Best Actress, winning the Oscar for *Misery*.

Notwithstanding the dearth of critical attention paid to films from Stephen King's fiction, Hollywood has fortunately not required the imprimatur of the academic world to appreciate the value of translating his writing into visual images. What Michael Collings maintained in 1986 still holds true today: "The simple fact is that King's stories and novels have provided a wealth of material for filmmakers. Almost every novel published under King's name has been produced as a film, is in production, or has been optioned" (1). King's novels, short stories, screenplays, and teleplays have been adapted for both the theatrical screen and television. Yet because his name is so recognizable in the popular imagination and has generated such enormous revenue, his novels and films also have inspired disappointing sequential films that typically have little or nothing to do with anything King himself has actually written or authorized, as in *The Lawnmower Man* and *Children of the Corn* sequels, *A Return to 'Salem's Lot* (1987), *Pet Sematary Two* (1992), *Sometimes They Come Back . . . Again* (1995), *The Rage: Carrie 2* (1999) and *Firestarter 2: Rekindled* (2002).

But why have Stephen King's titles proliferated on celluloid while other famous horror authors, who have composed their own share of outstanding work—Peter Straub, Clive Barker, Dean Koontz, Joyce Carol Oates, and Anne Rice spring to mind immediately—have not? Compared to King, only a very small percentage of their published titles have been optioned into movies, and except for Barker's *Hellraiser* (1987) and Rice's *Interview with the Vampire* (1994), none of these has been particularly noteworthy. Most assuredly, Hollywood is a business, and its business is making money. Between box office receipts and film rental distribution around the world, the Stephen King movie business is now worth well in excess of a billion dollars. This is a staggering bottom line, and it makes adapting the novels of other authors—even from the list of best-selling authors just mentioned—a high-risk proposition when compared to King's name recognition, cinematic reputation, and proven track record.

Filmmakers are also drawn to Stephen King's world because of his inimitable ability to tell an interesting story. King himself has often acknowledged that the best fiction is plot driven, comprised of characters the audience identifies with and cares about. It is certainly no surprise that these are likewise the same fundamental traits that all good movies share in common. Many of King's commentators have already noted that the author's published work is readily suited for presentation on the screen because he writes extremely visual, action-centered narratives. And certainly movies themselves have impacted King's authorial vision and narrative style; his novels frequently allude to specific titles from horror cinema, and the particular brand of terror he usually unleashes has a filmic quality to its unfolding. King's nonfiction book *Danse Macabre* (1981) chronicles the history of horror films as well as the classics of horror literature. It is evident throughout his analysis that movies such as *Night of the Living Dead* (1968) and *Alien* (1979) have proven to be at least as influential on King's own work in the genre as has the literature of H. P. Lovecraft and Edgar Allan Poe: "The real movie freak is as much an appreciator as the regular visitor to art galleries or museums," King insists. "For the horror fan, films such as *Exorcist II* form the setting for the occasional bright gemstone that is discovered in the darkness" (210). Born in an era of visual media—television as well as theatrical films—King is a novelist who often writes like a screenwriter, although, as Bill Warren cautions, "Stephen King is not the best possible person to adapt Stephen King to the screen" (139). Warren's point underscores the curious fact that the most successful cinematic interpretations of King's work have emerged from screenplays written by other people.

What I have undertaken in this volume is not so much an analysis of the films of Stephen King but an analysis of the films of a variety of producers, directors, and screenwriters who have adapted Stephen King's fiction. Some of these cinematic artists have been extremely faithful to King's primary source material (Cronenberg's *The Dead Zone* and Garris's *The Stand*), while others have imposed their own creative vision on King's original text to create an inimitably different work of art (Kubrick's *The Shining* and Hackford's *Dolores Claiborne*). Another way to put this is that this is a book more interested in what other people have done with their skills in making movies that use King's stories and themes as a basis for filmmaking than it is an exegesis of King's fiction per se. On the other hand, since the films treated in this volume all share at least a genesis in King's authorial creation, they must necessarily possess important elements of similarity, and I try to explicate these elements in relationship to one another by assigning them to relevant chapters. Thus, while this book endeavors to view the individual films as distinctive works of art—bearing the artistic markings of *auteur* directors and original screenwriters—these films also embody something of King's perspective on the world. Stephen King's literary vision intersects with the possibilities for film in allowing for a kind of cross-pollination with talented screenwriters or directors. It cannot be over emphasized that King's fiction uniquely lends itself to such cross-pollination. His contribution, even to those movies with which he is only nominally affiliated, transcends his popularity and reputation as a "bankable writer" in Hollywood; it confirms his status as a great storyteller and versatile artist capable of producing narratives so compelling that that they translate well into a variety of mediums.

Brian Kent posits that King has always written for those who pursue leisure entertainment for "pleasure without an iota of concern for what critical theory is currently carrying the day in the halls of academe, or what social significance is inherent in the particular manifestations of King's monsters" (40). Most certainly Kent's portrait of the "typical" King reader, whom he playfully labels the "literary slob," spills over into the same audience likely to go to a Stephen King film adaptation. People tend to appreciate horror art obsessively or not at all. Although Kent further believes that King's heart is with these "literary slobs"— spending their money in pursuit of the entertainment factor above all else—King's "remarkable accomplishment is that he has [also] carved out a sizable audience of scholarly-academic readers, while maintaining and expanding his massive popular appeal" (40). I believe that to appreciate fully both the fictions and films of Stephen King, it is necessary to abandon the threadbare and specious distinctions used to separate high and low definitions of art. The reason is that in King's literary and visual texts, art does not always appear as art—at least not what contemporary educators and critics have taught us to value as art: a composition that is complex, subtle, fiercely unsentimental. Rather, King's brand of art is classically American—aggressive and violent, vital and unrefined. The best movies based on his fiction embody the essence of King's own aesthetic sensibility: emotional and messy, at the edge of being out of control. But these are also the very qualities that make these films so tremendously engaging. Like the rock music that he both listens to and enjoys playing, Stephen King has always preferred raw to refined, the irrepressible and compulsive to the balanced and ordered, the juvenile and subversive to the rarefied austerity of the sophisticated and culturally sanctioned. When Andy Dufresne (Tim Robbins), arguably the most urbane and highly educated of all King's protagonists, decides to "get busy living" and tunnel out of Shawshank prison, he is traveling in the footsteps of generations of American cinematic rebels, from James Dean and Steve McQueen to Jack Nicholson and Mickey Rourke. Two mainstream American institutions—the judicial and penal systems—have failed Andy miserably on two separate occasions. His prison break and appropriation of the warden's illicit monies is thus as much a repudiation of these corrupt and oppressive institutions as it is a bid for freedom and a personal claim to the rest of his life. As Andy acknowledges, fully aware of its implicit irony, to his friend Red (Morgan Freeman), "On the outside I was an honest man, straight as an arrow. I had to come to prison to be a crook." What other national cinema could make a hero out of a man whose criminality appears not only justified but also is duly rewarded?

This book seeks to provide a coherent overview of Hollywood's major cinematic interpretations of Stephen King. His film canon has expanded to the point where it is impossible to address comprehensively all his movie adaptations in a single volume. Consequently, I have tried to select a sample that is both representative and indicative of the artistic vision that Hollywood has applied in translating King to celluloid. In doing so, my choices reflect a personal bias—these are also the King pictures that I admire the most and feel to be the most successful as works of cinematic art. This volume does not pretend to analyze this cinema with sufficient attention to the technical aspects of filmmaking. I am still very much a novice in the art of understanding film's nuanced language of technique, and I leave the task of interpreting these films from such a perspective to a scholar more adept at this specialized undertaking. As someone who has not received formal training in cinema studies, what I bring to this exegesis, besides a literary critic's close attention to the details of a narrative text, is a desire to view these films according to shared similarities of themes, characters, motifs, and narrative designs. This book consequently divides King cinematic corpus into individual chapters designed to highlight these features.

Despite King's frequent snip that he feels as if he needs a passport each time he travels to Los Angeles, his deepening and specialized involvement with Hollywood over the years has made him a savvy commentator on the movie industry. This fact is never more evident than in the chapter 1 interview that explores King's thirty-year relationship with the movie business and his attitude toward, and obvious appreciation of, a wide variety of Hollywood productions. Chapter 2 includes a wide sampling of films where children and issues relevant to their physical survival, psychological development, and memory of childhood figure prominently. In addition to exploring the supernatural capacities inherent in many of King's children, this chapter also includes discussion of the "normal" adolescent protagonists in his films who must remain continually vigilant in the face of innumerable "adult" assaults against their innocence, identities, and friendships. Chapter 3 focuses on King's cinematic females and the evolving roles they have come to assume as Hollywood has followed King into an examination of the horror tale from within a domestic context. As with the children in his canon, King possesses an idealized attitude toward mothers, and the establishment of a feminist consciousness in his canon is sometimes compromised and sometimes enriched in his portrayal of the selfless bonds mothers share with their children. Chapter 4 scrutinizes the roles of fathers and father figures in those films where secret male covenants create unhealthy barriers between men and their families. Unlike King's maternal archetypes, the fathers in these cautionary tales indulge in experimental and self-indulgent behavior that is insidiously isolating and self-destructive. Manipulated by intangible malevolent forces they once sought to control, these protagonists are victimized by their own highly masculinized desire for power and manipulation. Chapter 5 counterpoints the failings enumerated in the preceding chapter and posits a definition for heroism and moral progress in King's universe. The unassuming central characters highlighted in the three films examined in this chapter emerge as prototypical King heroes who rise above their personal sorrows to emphasize what is good and enduring in the human spirit. Chapter 6 is less about human beings than it is about the machinery humans have created—and the relationship forged between this technology and those who seek to exploit it. King's fascination with portraying the inhuman forces of technology is translated into tactile extensions of human and supernatural evil. The monstrous machinery featured in this chapter underscores the sentiment that as man becomes more reliant on his technological creations, he comes to resemble them at the expense of his humanity. The last chapter of this book, the longest, examines the most important made-for-television films that have either been adapted from King's novels or produced and written explicitly for television by King himself. Uneven in quality but embracing a chronology nearly as long as Hollywood's involvement in major theatrical releases of King movies, these miniseries range from the incoherent final editing work performed on the video butchering of *'Salem's Lot: The Movie* (1979) to the brilliantly disturbing resolution of *Storm of the Century* (1999).

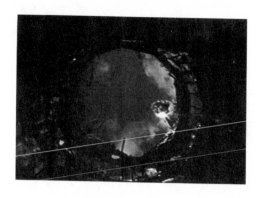

CHAPTER 1

STEVE'S TAKE: AN INTERVIEW WITH STEPHEN KING

MAY 31, 2002

This book begins with a journey east across U.S. Route 2. Over the northern ridges of the Green Mountains of Vermont, through the White Mountains of New Hampshire, and into Maine, where the topography finally begins to flatten out. New England's northern tier consists of scattered towns, rolling meadows, impenetrable woods and bogs. This is Stephen King's country. Lancaster, New Hampshire, or Skowhegan, Maine could seamlessly be transformed into the sets for movie remakes of *'Salem's Lot, IT,* or *Stand by Me.*

Fewer cars pass me now, mostly trucks, many of them hauling loads of timber and heating oil. This is a land where winter never really loosens its hold on the imagination, even late in May. There are also fewer radio stations, especially as I ascend into the mountains. Long stretches of static are occasionally punctuated by country music and heavy metal rock. I have lost all contact with classical music.

The first road sign that points the way to Bangor, Maine, appears incongruously at the Vermont–New Hampshire state border. Immediately following it is another sign welcoming travelers to New Hampshire and the Great North Woods, and then, one more sign, as if as an afterthought, "Brake for Moose—It Could Save Your Life." About this point it occurs to me that *Dracula*'s Jonathan Harker and I share some things in common: We are both traveling east through rugged mountains on a strange journey that may prove to be as terrifying as it is beautiful.

Bangor is a small town. Like most New England places, it is difficult to know; it keeps its secrets to itself. On one hand, there is the Bangor of charming downtown boutiques and quaint canals cut through solid blocks of granite. The Bangor Opera House on Main Street is the epicenter of town. But there is also Bangor the blue-collar city. A downtown that—except for the teenagers assembled in the parking lot of a Dunkin' Donuts—is completely deserted at ten o'clock on a Friday night. A place of abandoned factories and concrete oil storage tanks that appears to have more in common with Baltimore or Buffalo than with its upscale coastal cousins, Kennebunkport and Portland. At dinner my first night in town, the waiter, a Bangor native, informs me that the population of his city is 35,000 "and shrinking. We're at the end of the line here."

Stephen King lives on unequivocally the most elegant street in Bangor, composed of large, rambling houses that once belonged to nineteenth-century timber barons. King's house is the largest and most rambling one on the block, a restored Victorian mansion that is ten times as long as it is wide. Yellow surveillance cameras hang from underneath the wide eaves of the structure's first floor, like the suspended nests of giant bees. Lovely landscaping that is now in full bloom graces the front yard. A high black iron gate, similar to what might be found along the perimeters of a cemetery, demarcates King's property lines. The message is clear: This is a well-tended, lovely place, but don't bother ringing the doorbell unless you have an invite.

Stephen King's business office is located on the other side of Bangor, behind an airport runway of the Bangor International Airport and next door to a towering blue General Electric power plant. In a one-floor nondescript, prefabricated concrete building—resembling more a barracks than an office—off to the right of a dead-end street overgrown with weeds pushing through cracked asphalt, America's Storyteller conducts his daily affairs.

The contrast between King's office and home is stunning, but also instructively symbolic. The Victorian mansion is heir to King's own Horatio Alger–like achievement of the American dream. It is a monument to his enormous literary, cinematic, and financial success. His unassuming office, however, speaks to King's working-class origins and ethics. It is a comfortable but unpretentious space where the humble heroes and heroines who populate his narratives—the Dolores Claibornes and Stu Redmans and Johnny Smiths—would likely feel very much at home.

Magistrale: I spent most of this morning in downtown Bangor, just walking around. There were a couple of moments down there when I could have sworn I saw a clown, but I might have imagined that. Can you tell me something about the role Bangor has played over the years in helping you to visualize settings for novels and screenplays?

King: We moved here in 1979. At that time, when we decided the kids would be needing more contact with other kids rather than just the woods—we had been living down in Lovell—we had two choices: There was Portland and there was Bangor. Tabby wanted to go to Portland, and I wanted to go to Bangor because I thought that Bangor was a hard-ass, working-class town—there's no such thing as nouvelle cuisine once you are north of Freeport—and I thought that *the story,* the *big* story that I wanted to write, was here. I had something fixed in my mind about bringing together all my thoughts on monsters and the children's tale, "Three Billy Goats Gruff," and I didn't want it to be in Portland because Portland is a kind of yuppie town. There had been a story in the newspaper about the time we decided to move up here about a young man who came out of the Jaguar Tavern during the Bangor Fair. He was gay and some guys got to joking with him. Then the joking got out of hand, and they threw him over the bridge and killed him. And I thought, that's what I want to write about. Tabby did not really want to come here, but eventually we did.

Before I started writing *IT,* I did just what you did today: I walked all over town, I asked everybody for stories about places that caught my attention. I knew that a lot of the stories weren't true, but I didn't care. The ones that really sparked my imagination were the myths. Somebody told me something that I still don't know if it is true or not. Apparently, you can put a canoe down into the sewers just over across from here at the Westgate Mall and you can come out by the Mount Hope cemetery at the other end of town. It's one of the stories that you say to yourself, if it isn't true, it ought to be. I like very much the idea of a Plutonian canoe race. This same guy told me that the Bangor sewer system was built during the WPA and they lost track of what they were building under there. They had money from the federal government for sewers, so they built like crazy. A lot of the blueprints have now been lost, and it's easy to get lost down there. I decided I wanted to put all that into a book and eventually I did. But there was one image that remained with me through all this. Whenever I would walk through the two beautifully kept cemeteries that are on this side of town, where the ground slopes down into the woods I would notice these four-foot-deep drifts of dead flowers. This is stuff that came off the individual graves and washed down into the gully, and I thought to myself, This is the truth of the dead, this is where the dead end up. This is what we don't see aboveground.

Eventually, at least in the geography of my mind, Bangor became Derry. There is a Bangor in Ireland, located in the county of Derry, so I changed the name of the fictional town to Derry. There is a one-to-one correlation between Bangor and Derry. It's a place that I keep coming back to, even as recently as the novel *Insomnia*. And the same is true of Castle Rock. There was a piece that appeared last week in the Sunday *Telegram* called "Stephen King's Maine." The writers said that Castle Rock was really Lisbon Falls, which is where I went to high school, but it's not. Castle Rock is a lot more fictionalized than Derry. Derry *is* Bangor.

TM: There are also the civic landmarks that you have appropriated, such as the Paul Bunyan statue and the Standpipe water tower.

SK: And don't forget the Bangor Auditorium, which is called the Derry Auditorium in the books. It figures very large in *Insomnia,* where a guy turns a plane into a missile and tries to kill everybody inside.

TM: Before we get much further into this interview, I'd like to tell you something about the scope of the book I am writing. It's divided into chapters that contain close readings of three to five films that share much in common thematically. But I'm not trying to cover *all* the films that have been made from your work. Ultimately, perhaps about half.

SK: I hope that in the course of your study you intend to pay some attention to the films that haven't been "done to death." You might find some worthwhile things in these movies that will encourage others to have another look [at these films].

TM: To be honest, with the notable exception of Kubrick's *The Shining,* which carries with it a critical bibliography as large as all the other interpretative work done on your films combined—and I think this is primarily because Kubrick directed it—I can't think of any other King movie that has been analyzed sufficiently, much less "done to death."

Michael Collings wrote an excellent introduction to Hollywood's earliest films adapted from your novels, up to and including *Silver Bullet,* but his book was published back in 1986 and is long out of print. After that, you can find the occasional critical essay on a single film in an academic journal, a chapter in a scholarly book dealing with the particular King adaptation that belongs to the canon of a specific director (e.g., David Cronenberg or Stanley Kubrick) or is associated with a topical issue. Then there are the oversized "fanzine" magazine-books that try to say something about everything that has appeared on celluloid associated with your name. Unfortunately, these magazine-books are big on glossy stills and production history, which are interesting and sometimes helpful to know, but short on serious film analysis. In addition to the seven-paragraph reviews published in newspapers and popular periodicals shortly after a film is released, that's what is out there in the libraries right now.

SK: I wonder why this is. Why haven't these movies received more extensive and serious critical attention? Do *you* know why? I hope you will address this issue somewhere in your book because, quite frankly, I don't have a clue to answering this question and I would be very curious to understand it.

TM: From the eighteenth century to our own era, the horror genre has always maintained a wide popular interest. Do you feel that the reasons for the genre's popularity changed over time, or has horror sustained a consistently constructed audience?

SK: I think that the appeal of horror has always been consistent. People like to slow down and look at the accident. That's the bottom line. I went out this past week and picked up a copy of *The National Enquirer* because I wasn't supposed to. They featured a story about Dylan Klebold and Eric Harris, the Columbine shooters. This issue of the newspaper, which was censored in some places, had death photos of these two boys. There were also several sidebars that accompanied these photos explaining, no, justifying why *The National Enquirer* was doing the country a real service in running these photographs. Well, that's bullshit. It was all just an attempt on the part of the publishers to justify running the pictures of those two boys lying in a pool of blood. And of course I picked up a copy because that's what I wanted see: I wanted to see the photographs of those two boys lying in a pool of blood.

Now, over the years I have had to answer a lot of questions regarding the scrapbook that I kept about Charles Starkweather when I was a kid. I would argue that there was a constructive purpose behind my scrapbook: It was proof, at least to myself, that the boogeyman is dead. But there is something else at work here as well. There is always the urge to see somebody dead that isn't you. That was certainly the central premise behind the journey those kids take in *Stand by Me*. And that urge doesn't change just because civilization or society does. It's hard-wired into the human psyche. It's a sign of low taste, perhaps, but it's a perfectly valid human need to say "I'm okay," and the way I can judge that—the yardstick, if you will—is that these people are not.

TM: In *Danse Macabre*, you say that the horror genre has often been able to exploit "national phobic pressure points. . . . Such fears, which are often political, economic, and psychological rather than supernatural, give the best work of horror a pleasing allegorical feel—and it's the sort of allegory that most filmmakers seem at home with." When you look back at how Hollywood has treated your own work, which films have been most successful at capturing and allegorizing "national phobic pressure points"?

SK: *Carrie.* It is a film that covers everything that we are afraid of in high school. Also, it explores the feelings we all had in high school: That everybody is laughing at us. The bottom line is Piper Laurie's warning, "They're all going to laugh at you." We're all afraid of that, in high school, and even after we graduate from high school.

TM: Margaret White's (Piper Laurie) vision of the world thoroughly warps Carrie's once the bucket of blood comes crashing down. Mother's intrusive voice becomes a dominating presence in the cataclysmic scene when Carrie burns down the gym. However, Mrs. White is wrong; not everyone is laughing at Carrie. [Director Brian] De Palma makes that very clear. The gym teacher feels great compassion toward Carrie's humiliation—you can read this in her face—and so do the majority of Carrie's other classmates, except, of course, that wretched Norma. I've always thought that one of the most unnerving moments in the film is that everyone gets punished, the empathetic as well as the evil pranksters.

SK: Well, in the book they all do laugh at her, but it's a reaction brought on by hysterical horror. To return to your question, I would say that in addition to *Carrie*, Cronenberg's *The Dead Zone* manages to present strongly developed elements of political allegory, and *'Salem's Lot: The Movie* talks about small-town life as vampiric culture. *Dreamcatcher,* a film that has not yet been released but I have seen it, has a scene in it where there is a group of bewildered Americans who are locked behind barbed wire in a detainment camp. I sometimes think I wrote this entire novel just to be able to have this one woman in the group identified by her Blockbuster video card. There is a terrifying fear of the government that runs throughout *Dreamcatcher*, and that's something that runs through many of the films—*Firestarter, The Stand*—the idea that they would rather kill all of us than tell us the truth. This is something we should all remain afraid of.

TM: Could you make some comments from the perspective of a novelist about the production process that takes place in the transformation of a literary text into a film? How much do you get to work with the directors and screenwriters?

SK: Pretty much as much as I want to. I've had a deal for years with Castle Rock Entertainment that goes back to *Stand by Me*. I have told them that you can have my work for a buck. What I want from you is script approval, director approval, cast approval, and I want to have the authority to push the stop button at any point regardless of how much money you [the production company] have invested, because none of the money you have put in has gone into my pocket.

What I get on the back end, if things work out, is 5 percent from dollar one. This means that for every dollar that is spent at the box office, I get five cents of it. In most cases, that hasn't amounted to a whole hell of a lot, because most movies made from my work haven't made tremendous amounts of money. But still, even on a movie such as *Needful Things,* which didn't succeed very well, I do okay. Its domestic gross was only twenty million dollars, and out of that sum I got half a million dollars. Now, that doesn't sound like much, especially if I had decided to sell the rights outright, but then, sometimes a picture comes along like *The Green Mile,* and I make twenty-five million dollars, and that makes up for all the rest.

TM: And you also have an investment regarding your reputation. To this end, I can see why you would want approval over a film's cast and director. Perhaps at this point in your career this issue may be more important to you than the money?

SK: That's right. But I think I have developed a reputation in Hollywood as a "bankable writer." Castle Rock has had better luck than any one in decoding what it is that I do. That is, with the exception of *Needful Things.*

That movie was a special case. The first cut was shown on TNT. I have a copy of it, and the length of this film was four hours long. As a four-hour miniseries, it works. When edited down to "movie length," it is almost indecipherable because it doesn't have time to tell all the stories and do all the setups. It's a complicated book.

TM: The same thing happened to *'Salem's Lot.* As a miniseries in 1979, it held together pretty nicely. But when it was cut apart and re-released as *'Salem's Lot: The Movie,* it was pale reflection of its former self (no vampire pun intended).

SK: And none taken. When Tobe Hopper finished this movie, there was a lot of serious talk about buying it back from CBS and releasing it as a feature-length motion picture instead of a miniseries. The reason this never happened is that they couldn't cut it in a way to make it decipherable.

The opposite thing happened with a Danish miniseries called *Kingdom Hospital* directed by the Danish filmmaker Lars von Trier. I saw this when we were in Colorado remaking *The Shining,* and it scared the hell out of me. I thought, This is a wonderful thing; we have to get it and show it on American television. As soon as *The Shining* came out and did well in the Nielsen ratings, I went to ABC and told them I wanted to adapt *Kingdom Hospital* as a miniseries. Well, by then Columbia Pictures had it, and they didn't want to give it up. Their intention was to make a feature film out of it. They paid for four different scripts, and every one of them had the same problem. It's what I call the hotel towel problem: You steal all the towels in the hotel room and you try to get them into a single suitcase. You sit on it and move the towels around, and it still won't shut because you are working with too much material. It's a problem that all moviemakers have when they buy novels. In a way, film producers are like the sharks you see in horror movies. They are eating machines that buy and option titles, and then these projects sit on their desks while they wonder what the fuck to do with them. Columbia tried to make a motion picture out of *Kingdom Hospital,* while I was praying, Please let it all fall through. I mean, if they get it made, it will be just another piece of garbage that will be out for two weeks, put on video release, and then forgotten. And we could really do something with it.

Finally, Columbia Pictures came back to me and asked if I would trade something of mine for theatrical release if they gave me *Kingdom Hospital.* Ultimately, this is the way a lot of what goes on in the movie business gets done. It's the barter system; it's just beads. So I traded them *Secret Window,*

Secret Garden from *Four Past Midnight.* Nothing was happening to it. Now Anthony Minghella, who directed *The English Patient* and *The Talented Mr. Ripley,* is going to make it into a movie. My novella is the right length— it's small, and it's in one place. Columbia now has the chance to make a great feature. Castle Rock made a great feature out of *Misery* because it's short and all in one place. The same thing is true of *Gerald's Game,* which is a property that I have decided to hold on to. We've had a lot of offers on *Gerald's Game,* but I have refused. I'm thinking eventually, if I get a chance in my retirement, I want to write the screenplay for *Gerald's Game.*

Now that I have the rights to *Kingdom Hospital,* ABC wants it to be a television series. I think that might work. I want to divide it up into a fifteen-hour series, and that would give ABC two or three seasons of airtime. You see, what everybody wants when they do a TV series is something similar to *CSI* or *Seinfeld.* The magic moment occurs at the end of the fifth season, when a program gets somewhere in the neighborhood of a hundred and fifty episodes. Then the show gets syndicated and everybody gets really, really wealthy all at once. My idea is to take *Kingdom Hospital* and expand it. If you have a short story you can always expand it, whereas if you are working with a novel, you are always thinking of taking stuff out. This is not to say, however, that filming a novel can't be done.

Getting back to your original question, because I knew as soon as you asked it that this is where we would be spending most of our time. I love the movies. I have always loved the movies. And one of the reasons that my work gets bought in the first place is that I write cinemagraphically. Producers pick up my stories because they are cinematic. They are able to take my stories around to directors, and sooner or later a director says, This really pushes my buttons. I really want to do that. This is what happened with the novel *Dreamcatcher.* The first-draft screenplay that Bill Goldman did of it was good, but probably not good enough to justify an eight-million-dollar budget. Lawrence Kasden [the film's director] broke it open because he understood what Castle Rock has for years, that this is not a novel about space ships, or interstellar war, or the end of the world. It's a story about four guys who go up to a cabin every year and make "guy food." The definition of "guy food" is that you can't use the oven; everything you eat has to be done on the stove burner. You have a hunk of butter, and you have shit in cans. Maybe you use a little ground beef, but you are talking really basic cooking.

In the first half of the screenplay for *Dreamcatcher,* nothing much happens. But you need to remember that the best fears, the ones that really work in horror stories and movies, are the ones that have not been articulated, that are still looking for some manner of expression. One of the things that I discovered after my accident was that I was having a lot of problems with narcotic drugs and their effect upon my body. Your whole system gets clobbered into the middle of next week, and everything falls out of sync. Things that I had taken for granted, especially about going to the bathroom, changed radically. And I got to thinking about these things. In 1956, in *Peyton Place,* we finally got to see beyond the bedroom door. Since then, graphic sex is just something we take for granted in the movies. I don't know if you have seen *Unfaithful* yet, but it's a terrific film. It is a sexually candid movie and it operates on a number of interesting levels. But I thought to myself that no one in novels, let alone in movies, talks about one of the primal fears that we have: That one day we will stand up from taking a shit only to discover that the toilet bowl is full of blood. This event could signal many things: It could just be a hemorrhoid, or it could be colon cancer. We don't talk about this because it is a function that we are raised not to discuss in polite society. But I thought, If we have gone behind the bedroom door, let's go behind the bathroom door and talk about what is there. In Bill Goldman's script of *Dreamcatcher,* these guys find blood in the woods that leads up to the bathroom door of the cabin where they are staying. This is all very effectively rendered in the rough cut of the film that I have seen. You see the trail of blood going from the bedroom, which is empty—and that's symbolic in a way, because in my story the bedroom stays empty, as I don't care what goes on in the bedroom, only the bathroom—and these guys are standing in front of the bathroom door wondering what to do. All this time, the audience is getting more and more nervous about what is happening behind that bathroom door. And then one of the guys says, "I don't think I want to see this." For me, that's the point where the horror story begins to do its work. The audience is in the dark, particularly if it's a theatrical situation, the suspense has been building steadily, and we are faced with exactly the same issue: Do we want to see what is behind that closed door? The audience is perfectly suspended over this point: The desire to look, the repulsion against looking.

When it comes to films, I want people to try to go beyond what we have seen already. I'm willing to let a director try anything, including Tobe Hooper with *The Mangler.* I knew it wasn't a good idea. The screenwriter that he selected looked like a college sophomore, but he was awfully eager for the chance, and you never know what someone like Tobe Hooper is going to do. *Texas Chainsaw* is still one of the scariest movies ever made. Now, there's a film that did wonderful things with the hidden terror that lurks behind closed doors. So, my idea is always to give a director the chance, because I am not very personally invested in these things once they are out of my word processor and downloaded from my head and onto the page. Once you move from a single artisan working in his hut to the Hollywood film, the writer is no longer the one in control, and you discover a situation where complications arise exponentially. In the making of a film, you are suddenly dealing with four hundred artists in the studio. Then it becomes a lottery. All you can do is try to pick the best people possible; sometimes it works, sometimes it doesn't.

TM: In *On Writing* you say: "What I cared about most between 1958 and 1966 was movies." You go on to recall that your favorites were "the string of American-International films, most directed by Roger Corman, with titles cribbed from Edgar Allan Poe." You even had a name for these movies—Poepictures. To what extent did these movies influence your writing? Were you influenced more by Poe's written work or by movies based on his work?

SK: Poe influenced me plenty, but not so much through the Poepictures. The best of the Poepictures was the last one, *The Masque of the Red Death.* It was choreographed beautifully, like a Kabuki play. The big scare moments of these films I still treasure. I remember when they discovered Vincent Price's wife in the iron maiden in *The Pit and the Pendulum.* All you see are the horrified eyes of Barbara Steele gazing out through a small opening in the contraption that encases her. She can't talk because she is sealed up to her eyes in the device. She has this horrified, frozen expression that she conveys directly to the audience. And then the picture ends. Brilliant. I've been trying to do something like that ever since.

TM: The merging of horror and humor characterizes some of the most memorable cinematic adaptations of your work. I'm thinking of films such as *Carrie, Misery, Stand by Me.* Why do these apparently oppositional elements appear to work so harmoniously with each other in these films?

SK: We can only speculate here. I think that what happens is that you get your emotional wires crossed. The viewer gets confused as to what reaction is appropriate, how to respond. When the human intellect reaches a blank wall, sometimes the only thing left is laughter. It is a release mechanism, a way to get beyond that impasse. Peter Straub says that horror pushes us into the realm of the surreal, and whenever we enter that surreal world, we laugh. Think of the scene with the leeches in *Stand by Me.* It's really funny watching those kids splash around in the swamp, and even when they try to get the leeches off, but then things get plenty serious when Gordie finds one attached to his balls. Everything happens too fast for us to process. We all laugh at Annie Wilkes because she is so obviously crazy. But at the same time, you had better not forget to take her seriously. She's got Paul in a situation that is filled with comedy, and then she hobbles his ankle. Like Paul Sheldon himself, the viewer doesn't know what to do. Is this still funny, or not? This is a totally new place, and it's not a very comfortable place. That's the kind of thing that engages us when we go to the movies. We want to be surprised, to turn a corner and find something in the plot that we didn't expect to be there.

What Billy Nolan and Christine Hargenson do to Carrie is both cruel and terrifying, but the two of them are also hilarious in the process. [Actor John] Travolta in particular is very funny. His role as a punk who is manipulated by his girlfriend's blow-jobs suggests that he's not very bright. But a lot of guys can appreciate Billy Nolan's predicament: He's got a hot girlfriend who wants to call all the shots. He's the one character in De Palma's film that I wish could have had a more expanded role. He's a comic character who behaves in an absolutely horrific manner.

The character of Roland LeBay in *Christine* starts off to be a funny character, almost a caricature, but if you watch him carefully through his time on the screen, you'll note that he grows ever more horrific, getting uglier and uglier all the time. When I wrote *Christine* I wanted LeBay to be funny in a twisted sort of way. He's the same blend of horror and humor that you find in the car itself. Christine is a vampire machine; as it feeds on more and more victims, the car becomes more vital, younger. It's like watching a film running backwards. The whole concept is supposed to be amusing but scary at the same time.

TM: In the "Walking the Tracks" section of the DVD edition of *Stand by Me*, you indicate that [director Rob] Reiner's film was the "first completely successful adaptation" of one of your books. Have there been other films that have satisfied you to the same degree?

SK: *Shawshank* did. I thought *Shawshank* was a terrific piece of work, and it is not a one-to-one adaptation. There are a lot of things in that film that are not in my book. The scene where Andy is playing the opera music in the yard is a good example. It's a film about human beings—and human beings are not secondary to the theme of horror. That's an important thing to remember: You cannot scare anyone unless you first get the audience to care about these make-believe characters. They have to become people with whom you identify. After all, they are only as thick as the screen, which means about as thick as your thumbnail. We go to the movies with the understanding that we are watching people who are not real. But if we come to like them, and we recognize that the things they are doing are also part of our own lives, if they are reacting the way in which we would react under similar circumstances, then we become emotionally invested. Once this happens, it is possible to frighten the audience by putting the character in frightening situations.

When Sissy Spacek was cast as Carrie, people wondered how she could play the role of ugly duckling convincingly. I really didn't give a shit what she looked like before the prom, as long as she could appear transformed into a beauty when she got to the dance. It never really mattered to me exactly what she looked like, because I never had a clear picture of her. But I always had a clear picture of her heart. That's what remains important to me. I want to know what my characters feel and think, and I want the reader to know these things, too. De Palma did such a good job in this film because he was interested in these things as well.

I would have to say that I was delighted with *The Green Mile*. The film is a little "soft" in some ways. I like to joke with [director] Frank [Darabont] that his movie was really the first R-rated Hallmark Hall of Fame production. For a story that is set on death row, it has a really feel-good, praise-the-human-condition sentiment to it. I certainly don't have any problem with that because I am a sentimentalist at heart.

TM: This is a good place for me to ask you this next question. Spike Lee, among other commentators, has been critical of John Coffey's character in *The Green Mile*, arguing that his portrayal is insulting to blacks because his role is essentially to suffer for the sins of white people. According to Lee: "You have this super Negro who has these powers, but these powers are used only for the white star of the film. He can't use them on himself or his family to improve his situation." How accurate is this criticism?

SK: It's complete bullshit. Coffey was black for one reason only: It was the one sure thing about his character that was going to make certain that he was going to burn. That was the situation I was trying to set up. It was completely plot driven and had nothing to do with black or white. I've heard this same argument advanced by Toni Morrison about the so-called "magic Negro." If you want to get me on this, then you should talk about Mother Abigail in *The Stand*. The reason I made Mother Abigail black is because I wanted a character that was old enough to remember slavery. And I wanted to write a song to celebrate their moment of emancipation while Randall Flagg lurked behind the drapes. All this got cut out of the original published version of *The Stand* and then got reinstated in the uncut edition. But in the case of Coffey, who is obviously a Christ figure, he's black because his color makes certain that he will fry. As far as using his powers to help his race, he has no family; he's a total loner. Whatever past he has is completely lost, and that's crucial to the story. And the other thing that is crucial to the story is that he is a Christ figure. Christ figures are supposed to do good to them that revile you, to turn the other cheek to those who strike you. By doing good for white people—and particularly the wife of the warden, the man who is going to put Coffey to death—he is basically exhibiting his saintliness. You ask most people what was Christ's race, and they'll say white, god damn it.

I am not surprised that this is Spike's reaction. It's a knee-jerk reaction of a man who sees everything in terms of his race. And for an artist of his stature, it's a hobbling factor in his creative life. If I took my pants down right now in front of you, you would see that my right leg is withered where there used to be muscle. This is a result of my accident. But the muscles in my left leg are bigger than ever because that leg has had to do all the work. This is the way it is with Spike. He sees things exclusively in racial terms. It has made him a spectacular artist, but the idea of Coffey being a superman is just plain wrong.

TM: Does John Coffey have to be black? What happens to the film's meaning if he is a white character?

SK: In most cases you can cast a character in either race. Morgan Freeman in *Shawshank* could have been cast as a white man. But in the case of John Coffey, he's supposed to be black because that puts him in a situation where the minute he gets caught with those two little blond girls in his arms, he's a doomed man.

TM: But isn't that at least part of what Spike Lee is trying to argue? What chance does Coffey, a black man in Depression-era Louisiana weeping over the dead bodies of two little blond girls, have to save himself in spite of his redemptive powers? In one sequence the warden's wife asks Coffey, "Who hurt you?" Why does he have so many wounds, and where did they come from? Much of this seems suggestive, at least to me, of the legacy of being a black man in America.

SK: I am going to ask you a question now. Can you visualize a giant of a white man in that same situation? A dimwitted white man living in the

South, knocking around low-paying jobs, a gentle giant riding the rails that is not able to hurt anybody? But a white man who bears the same scars as Coffey—can you visualize this person?

TM: Maybe bearing the same physical scars, but not the same psychological scars as Coffey. The internal wounds he carries are particular to his race. If John Coffey is a Christ figure, he's also a *black* Christ; his suffering, it seems to me, becomes all the more profound because he is black and a victim of wounds that are particular to his racial history.

SK: I think your answer represents an imaginative failing on your part. Remember Steinbeck's Lenny in *Of Mice and Men*. He's white and he bears similar scars of suffering.

TM: Have you been satisfied with the televised miniseries that have been done of your work? Do you feel that your novels are better suited for the miniseries genre? What are the limitations of the televised miniseries? Do you have a favorite Stephen King miniseries?

SK: I think my novels are much better suited for miniseries presentations. I didn't care very much for *The Tommyknockers* because it just didn't seem that the people doing it got behind the project sufficiently and felt the story. As with a feature-length film, again it's a crapshoot to have all the different parts to fall into place. My favorite made-for-television production is *Storm of the Century*. I love that as a piece of work, and I am still very proud of it. In my mind, it is as good as the best of the novels. Everything worked the way it was supposed to: The setting of the harbor town, the convincing sense of snow piling up, and Colm Feore was terrific in the role of Andre Linoge. ABC's Standards and Practices was so obsessed with whether they would see blood on the faces of the some of these children that they totally ignored the fact that the bad guy wins and takes the sheriff's son away with him. *The Storm of the Century* is fairly hard-edged for television. It's not like any other miniseries that you'll see on any of the other networks—you know, the happy-time, everything-works-out-happily-in-the-end program. It's very realistic. And everyone who was involved with that show—from my screenplay, to the director, to the set designer, to the producer—we all did *Rose Red,* and *Rose Red* is just not as good.

TM: This is good place to ask about the group decision in *Storm of the Century* to sacrifice the child, Ralph Anderson. Besides the destruction of

Molly and Mike Anderson's marriage, what are the other consequences—especially to the town of Little Tall Island itself—that occur as a result of this sacrifice?

SK: Everybody that takes part in that decision is a worse person, a smaller person as a result. Whatever flaws they have are worse afterward. The sheriff's wife is in therapy; she remarries, but she is not very happy in her new marriage. One of the guys commits suicide. The sheriff ends up on the other side of the country, and he is the one person who has a chance at rebuilding his life. He knows that he was the one person who stood up for what was right. Everybody else pays a price for the town's collective lapse in moral judgment.

TM: Why did the citizens make this choice? Why was the sheriff the only one who stood up for what was right? I keep thinking of Shirley Jackson's short story "The Lottery," and how much you admire it.

SK: Let's put it this way: In all of our lives we are faced with situations in which we are tested. Generally, it isn't until years later that we find out that we actually failed the test. We come to understand that our morals gave out a little here, or our sense of right and wrong slipped, or our misplaced sense of expediency got the better of our morality. I've always been fascinated with the story of Job. The sheriff tells a version of the story of Job in *Storm of the Century*. He faces God and says, You took my kid, you wrecked my crops, and you ruined my marriage and left me alone to wander the earth. And God says, I guess there's just something about you that pisses me off.

We all have a duty to look at our lives. What do we see? Children falling down wells to die, we send our loved ones off to work and crazy people hit their office towers and we never see them again. I was in New York for a screening of *Hearts in Atlantis* at Columbia University the week after the twin towers were destroyed. My taxi driver wanted to show me something. He took me down about four blocks from Ground Zero. He said, "Do you see all those cars in that parking lot?" There were several hundred parked cars all covered with white dust. He told me that the city doesn't know what to do with those cars. They belong to the people who drove in from New Jersey to work at the twin towers the day of the attack. They are never going to come back and claim their cars. The people who escaped the tragedy, who are still alive, came and drove their cars away. You could see by the empty spaces in the parking lot that God had decided to let that one live, but that other poor bastard who parked in the spot next to him is never coming back. God had moved His finger and decided who would get to live a while longer. And you could look inside these remaining cars and see the toys that belonged to their children, the McDonald's coffee that was maybe half drunk the morning of the last morning of their lives.

TM: The September 11 event challenged many of our assumptions and added to our neuroses as a society and as individuals. How will the post-September 11 climate change the shape of horror? Is there anything on the page or screen that can equal in terror what we witnessed on our living room televisions?

SK: Why should it? Think of how many references you have heard to this event over the past several months. You'll be watching a talking head on television discussing the *Star Wars* movie and somebody will begin a question to George Lucas, "In light of September 11, do you feel . . ." The event has totally pervaded the American consciousness. I read a lot of new fiction in galleys, and I have noticed the first ripples of awareness in the artistic consciousness—not conscience, it's too early for conscience, that comes much later—that represent the first droplets of a rainstorm that will continue for years.

TM: On several levels, the terrorist bombing of the World Trade Center was very much a "cinematic event." The planes were timed to hit at least twenty minutes apart from one another so that after the first plane plowed into the first tower cameras would be already in place to record—from a variety of angles and perspectives—the second plane's explosive arrival. And of course, the world learned of the tragedy through its graphic visualization on film. I suppose that is the goal of any terrorist action: To make it as visual and as personal as possible.

SK: And don't forget the desire to traumatize as many people as possible, which occurs when singular events in time are recorded on film and then televised to millions. In *The Stand,* my own rendering of cataclysmic proportions is always brought down to the individual, personal level. Franny Goldsmith trying to bury her father, and saying to Harold Lauder when he shows up in a car, "I'm just so tired." To me, one of the great scenes in the television miniseries is when Harold and Franny are sitting around listening to records. These two people sitting at the end of the world, drinking warm lemonade, and listening to records for what may be the last time in their lives. As an artist, I can show you the end of the world on a microcosmic level, but no one can deal with it the way it actually comes down from the sky.

TM: Your cameo appearances in your films have become something that fans enjoy and anticipate with each new film. Is this something you inherited from Hitchcock? How much control do you have over your cameo? The most original and humorous may have been your role as a weatherman on the broken TV in *Storm of the Century.* Was this your decision?

SK: I generally pick the cameo. I picked, for example, the pizza guy in *Rose Red,* the weatherman in *Storm of the Century.* I gave myself a bigger role in *The Stand.* It's fun. And yes, I'm playing Hitchcock here; I'm just a frustrated actor.

TM: I'd like to spend a few minutes with you talking about the eclipse scene in *Dolores Claiborne.* You told me once that you labored hard to get that scene written right for the novel. Do you feel that the film did it justice?

SK: I loved the way they did that; it's probably my favorite scene in the film. I didn't notice this the first time I saw the movie, but the filmmakers of *Dolores Claiborne* actually flip-flop our ordinary perceptions of the world. That is to say, we generally view what is going on right now as bright and colorful, crisp and clear. The past has a tendency to be a little bit misty, even as there are certain things that stand out among all the other things that are faded and fading, just as the color red is the last thing to fade in a photograph. This is how the human mind and its capacity for recollection work. But Taylor Hackford shoots his movie so that everything in the present is dull and monochrome, even the clothes are dull. In contrast, every moment in the past is bright and the colors really jump. It's the best color photography I've seen since the *Godfather* films, particularly *Godfather II,* which is filmed like no other movie before it. It's the difference between a color photograph and one that has been hand-tinted. I think *Dolores Claiborne* is a remarkably beautiful film to watch, if simply as an exercise in cinematography and the technical possibilities of using a camera and colors as active vehicles in the presentation of a story.

TM: As horrible and as violent as the moments leading to the eclipse are, the actual scene of Dolores gazing down into the well where she has just committed murder with the eclipse at her back is actually almost transcendent, beatific. Is this right?

SK: Yes. If there is anything wrong with *Dolores Claiborne,* it was the decision on the part of the filmmakers to try to tack on this artificial reconciliation between Dolores and her daughter. It's a very human desire, and it's understandable that producers would want to cater to it.

When you go to the movies and put down your cash to see a film, I don't think it out of line to ask for people up on the screen to behave a little bit better than they do in ordinary life; certainly we expect people to look a little bit better than in ordinary life. This urge to make things a little bit nicer than in real life has a tendency to carry over into other aspects of the movie. I have always been interested in emotions. And the difference between books and movies is that when I have you in one of my books I want to move you emotionally, to establish some kind of intense emotional reaction—terror or laughter or serious involvement. But because I am one person and I do everything myself, the creative instrument I use is like a scalpel, it cuts deftly and deep. With films, every time you add another layer of production, the surface gets blunted more and widens. So that when you consider a big Hollywood production such as *Pearl Harbor,* you get a beautifully produced, eye-popping spectacle that does absolutely nothing to you emotionally or spiritually because what should be a hypodermic point has become blunted into a sledgehammer. All you can do is to swing it as hard as you can.

Unfortunately, *Dolores Claiborne* is a film, like Kubrick's *The Shining,* that is nearly overwhelming because of its beautiful photography, but the story that surrounds the photography is flawed.

TM: I think I have a good spot for us to end. Your film *Maximum Overdrive* has a lot in common with *The Terminator* and *Blade Runner* insofar as these are films about the general paranoia our culture has about our overreliance on technology and machines. Were these conscious considerations as you were writing and directing *Maximum Overdrive?*

SK: I had a very clear image of technology having totally overrun our ability to control it. You know, when Bram Stoker wrote *Dracula,* all the men who were part of the Crew of Light were technological men. Seward compiled his medical records on a phonograph; Van Helsing was one of the first doctors to pioneer the use of transfusions. All this fascinated Stoker; these men were his heroes, and their technologies were used to help defeat the evil of a supernatural past embodied in Dracula himself. But look at what has become of technology now. Think of the situation right now between India and Pakistan. These are two countries that do not have very highly developed skills and attitudes about problem solving. They may have a long religious history, which I would argue is in itself very dangerous to the modern world, but they also possess nuclear weapons. That's really what I was thinking about when I did *Maximum Overdrive*. Technology may be its own dead end.

The problem with that film is that I was coked out of my mind all through its production, and I really didn't know what I was doing [as the director of the film]. I learned a lot from the experience, however, and I would like to try directing again some time. Maybe I'll direct *Gerald's Game*.

TM: *Gerald's Game* remains one of my favorite books. I have always presented it to students as an appropriate bookend to *Misery:* Its limited setting, the gender conflicts, and the bedroom as a battlefield.

SK: I had all these things in mind when constructing both these books, and I've always thought to myself that *Misery* was a kind of trick. You have two people fighting it out in a cabin. That's all it is. *Gerald's Game* is kind of a trick on the trick: one person in a room fighting it out with herself. I've been telling people that the third book in the trilogy will be called *Sofa,* and it's just going to be a sofa in a room.

CHAPTER 2

THE LOST CHILDREN:
CARRIE, FIRESTARTER, STAND BY ME,
SILVER BULLET, HEARTS IN ATLANTIS

The cinemagraphic children of Stephen King are simultaneously blessed and cursed, but mostly they are lost. They may live with parents who supply them with material comforts, but they seldom experience love from these people. They may appear psychologically adjusted on the outside, but their young lives are often terribly troubled. They inhabit a landscape of dread, loneliness, and a primal fear of abandonment. Some of these children, such as Carrie White (*Carrie*), Charlie McGee (*Firestarter*), and Danny Torrance (*The Shining*), are gifted with supernatural abilities; others, such as Gordie Lachance (*Stand by Me*) and Marty Coslaw (*Silver Bullet*), are endowed with imaginative capacities that make them exceptional beings, particularly when they are compared to the adults against whom these children must alternately flee and combat. Almost every Stephen King adolescent is under siege; many of them must undergo rites of passage in which the innocence of adolescence must confront adult realities, a journey that is always fraught with violence and danger. King's children cling to their youthful idealism and romantic vigor, but these elements are always imperiled by random moments of violence and oppressive codes of behavior imposed from the outside—from families, social institutions, cruel and abusive peers, immoral and mentally unbalanced adults, and the various supernatural creatures who come, like the clown/spider in *IT* or the ghosts in *The Shining,* seeking to enrich their malefic energies by challenging and subsuming the power of youthful imaginations. If these children are to survive—morally as well as physically—they must somehow find a way to resist the prevailing values of a society (often by connecting to individual adults who are outsiders themselves) that is dead or dying and has transformed its adults into monsters.

King's kids are not responsible for their parents' divorces or for governmental errors in judgment, but they are nonetheless forced into coping with the consequences of such events. His children, like the female protagonist in an eighteenth-century gothic novel, appear as perfect victims—their confrontations with evil are initially overwhelming—and their plights elicit intense sympathetic responses from the film viewer. To offset the oppressive nature of their relationships with adults and social authority, King endows his young protagonists with tremendous energies; indeed, they often possess imaginative capacities or supernatural abilities so potent that the children who wield them must learn to "grow into" their powers. As novelist and critic Clive Barker has opined, "In King's work, it is so often the child who carries the wisdom; the child who synthesizes 'real' and 'imagined' experience without question, who knows instinctively that imagination can tell the truth the way the senses never can" (63). As King's children come to discipline their attributes, they evolve as human beings, slowly maturing into child-adults who exhibit traits of adaptability, survival skills, and, most important, a level of sensitivity seldom present in King's adults. (When King does supply an adult with these qualities, as in the case of Johnny Smith in *The Dead Zone* or Uncle Red in *Silver Bullet,* usually the adult has not progressed far beyond the realm of adolescence and maintains childlike loyalties, significant bonds with children, and a romantic faith in life.) His heroes and heroines are orphans and castaways, unloved sons and daughters, and disenfranchised younger siblings of cruel and unsupportive brothers who must overcome the indifference of their families and the malignancy of the larger world to find a way to survive.

King's children embody the full spectrum of human experience. Many of these youthful protagonists are at the centers of the films that feature them, and from them all other actions seem to radiate. Some represent the nucleus for familial love. They are often healing agents, as in the first halves of *Firestarter, Pet Sematary, The Shining,* and *Cujo,* enabling parents in unstable marriages to hold their union together. Moreover, many of the films that center on children test the moral capacities of their adolescent protagonists; most of King's child-heroes represent a Wordsworthian ideal of goodness struggling against the forces of a corrupt world. King may have achieved his reputation by writing about threatening and disconcerting subject matter, but this does not necessarily impose a corollary that his vision is hopeless. Perhaps the most misunderstood opinion of those who have never actually read King or seen the films adapted from his work is that he lacks a sufficient moral base to counterpoint the human and supernatural evil that the popular imagination associates with his art. In fact, *Carrie* may well be the single notable exception to the axiom that children represent the most viable spirit of hope in the frequently desolate landscape of Stephen King's universe.

Carrie was the first Hollywood adaptation of a Stephen King novel. King's book told the story of a young woman's supernatural powers, specifically the ability to move things telepathically. The novel is a fragmented, experimental narrative featuring a blend of pseudodocumentary elements, diary entries, and frequent flashbacks to Carrie's youth all in an effort to present the young woman's history through the eyes of other observers. We learn her history through the commentaries of Sue Snell (Amy Irving) and others, through the occasional newspaper clipping or scholarly article published in an effort to explain Carrie's extraordinary talents, or through third-person narrative renderings of events from her past. King constructs his portrait of Carrie as if she were the object of a Cubist painting or sculpture: The reader is meant to view her from multiple perspectives, but she herself is not permitted to contribute to her own experience, which in itself effectively underscores the degree of her victimization. In short, the novel *Carrie* is not only Stephen King's first published book; it is also representative of the author's fascination with experimental narrative stylistics (William Faulkner remains one of King's favorite novelists) and a harbinger of future efforts in this vein.

Brian De Palma's film rendition abandons the book's pseudodocumentary perspective, as well as its efforts to provide a history of Carrie White's (Sissy Spacek) telepathic experiences. Instead, De Palma focuses exclusively on a relatively short span of Carrie's life—roughly two weeks—and concentrates on events leading up to and including the climatic night of her high school senior prom. The eternal scapegoat who is always mocked because of her drab clothing and because she is "different than the other kids," Carrie is victimized by both her classmates and her mother. Mrs. White (Piper Laurie) is a fanatical blend of evangelical Protestantism (her literal reliance on scripture and belief that every woman and all forms of sexual expression are inherently sinful) and Catholicism (the cathedral-like environment she constructs in her home, from the overabundance of votive candles to the shrine of the martyred figure of St. Sebastian that Carrie confronts inside her prayer closet). All of her life Carrie has been forced to conform to her mother's warped social and religious perspectives, but early in the film the girl discovers— simultaneous with her first menstruation—that she possesses telekinetic powers, and this awareness instills in her an ephemeral confidence to stand up and briefly challenge her mother.

Poised as the good mother in opposition to Mrs. White, the gym teacher, Miss Collins (Betty Buckley) encourages Carrie to dress and act like the other girls in her school. Feeling guilty because of her involvement in the torturing of Carrie, Sue Snell persuades her boyfriend, Tommy Ross (William Katt), to take Carrie to the senior prom in her place. Fueled by her emerging desire to fit in, her growing defiance of her mother, and by Tommy's and Miss Collins's steady encouragement, Carrie agrees to go to the prom and is crowned its queen. At the moment of her triumph, however, Carrie is drenched by a bucket of pig's blood, a final wicked trick pulled off by Chris Hargenson (Nancy Allen), the school's beautiful and evil cool girl and Carrie's most vicious nemesis. In response to this final indignity, Carrie goes ballistic. While none of the other promgoers is actually laughing at her plight, except for Chris's vile friend and co-conspirator Norma (P. J. Soles), Carrie automatically perceives them from the perspective of her mother. Their imaginary laughter sparks Carrie's telekinetic wrath, and in a scene inspired by the Old Testament, Carrie punishes everyone in the Bates High School gymnasium—the innocent as well as the guilty. She then exits the burning building and walks home to wash off the pig's blood. There mother waits to murder evil daughter ("Thou shalt not suffer a witch to live"), while all the pathetic Carrie seeks is her protection and sympathy. Rejected by the outside world represented by the school, Carrie is literally stabbed in the back by her inner world at home. Before her mother can complete the job, however, Carrie crucifies her with kitchen utensils in a prolonged death throe that is a comically grotesque mixture of agony and sexual ecstasy. As Mrs. White dies, Carrie collapses their home down upon both her mother and herself.

De Palma's *Carrie* initiates a cycle of teenage film comedies—*Animal House* (1978), *Porky's* (1981), *Fast Times at Ridgemont High* (1982)—that celebrate the physical grossout, the adolescent body out of control. These are films whose humor come at the expense of raging male hormones, gross toiletry, and fetishized female body parts. But *Carrie* also begins a cycle of teenage horror flicks featuring the adolescent body under vicious assault in films such as *Halloween* (1978), *Friday the 13th* (1980), and *Nightmare on Elm Street* (1984). *Carrie* presents itself as a unique blend of both teen genres, highlighting the disturbing links between adolescence as a time of silly misadventures and encroaching violence, between the teenage body reveling in its hormonal potential and as a site of abject terror. It is a film that manages to create a dramatic tension between humor and horror, even if its horror aspects eventually end up dominating the screen. De Palma himself has commented on this blend: "I sort of put everything into *Carrie*: I had the romantic story between Tommy Ross and Carrie White; I had all the visual suspense elements, and the terror elements; and I was using everything I knew, including comedy and improvisation, from all the other pictures I had made" (Brown 58).

In light of any discussion of *Carrie* as a teenage genre film, it is worthwhile to note that, like *American Graffiti* (1973), many of *Carrie*'s scenes feature its young actors filmed through car windows. Chris and her toughguy boyfriend Billy Nolan (John Travolta) are, for example, almost exclusively pictured together inside a car (often engaged in some form of highly sexualized activity), or from a perspective that is constructed to resemble closely the interior of a car. Even when they are lurking surreptitiously underneath the stage in the gymnasium the night of the prom, the camera frames them together either in upper-body silhouettes or in an enclosed headshot created by the rectangle formed by two steps leading to the platform. The effect in both cases is the same: They appear to be inside a car interior. Beginning with *American Graffiti* and *Carrie*, the connection between the automobile and adolescence became a ubiquitous presence on the landscape of the American teenage film genre. Since these films, kids in cars have been used to highlight the last fleeting moments of childhood innocence (cruising as a form of play) and the conflicting transition into adulthood (the car as illicit bedroom and illegal barroom, site of unsupervised behavior). In *Carrie*, as in *American Graffiti*, the automobile is backdrop and character, the locus of adolescent overindulgence and the sobering introduction to adult codes of behavior, a transitional place on the American highway where comedy often blurs into tragedy. These contrasting admixtures are definitely evoked in *Carrie* when Billy Nolan and Chris Hargenson are viewed from the interior of Nolan's car cruising down a boulevard to the music of Martha and the Vandellas' song "Heat Wave."

This sequence juxtaposes slapstick comedy in the couple's fumbling sexual misadventures with a disturbing undercurrent of violence that surfaces periodically throughout the shot to dispel the comic ambiance. The scene is a brilliantly balanced fluctuation between adolescent play and rape, sexual titillation and manipulation, heterosexual attraction and repulsion.

In June 1999, Stephen King delivered the keynote address for the Vermont Library Conference. This speech, entitled "The Bogeyboys," was composed shortly after and in response to the murderous assault that took place at Columbine High School in Colorado. King's address chose to examine that tragedy, focusing particularly on the motivation for the boys who decided to commit the assault, in the context of his own life and fiction:

> My stories of adolescent violence were all drawn, in some degree, from my own memories of high school. That particular truth, as I recalled it when writing as an adult, was unpleasant enough. I remember high school as a time of misery and resentment. In Iroquois trails of manhood, naked warriors were sent running down a gauntlet of braves swinging clubs and jabbing with the butt ends of spears. In high school the goal is Graduation day instead of a manhood feather, and the weapons are replaced by insults, slight, and epithets, many of them racial, but I imagine the feelings are about the same. The victims aren't always naked, and yet a good deal of the rawest hazing does take place on playing fields and in locker rooms, where the marks are thinly dressed or not dressed at all. The locker room is where *Carrie* starts, with girls throwing sanitary napkins at a sexually ignorant girl who thinks she is bleeding to death. (5)

Carrie starts with what has become one of the most famous opening sequences in Hollywood history. Behind the credits that begin to appear on the screen, we witness a girls' volleyball game in session. In the background, an authoritative voice proclaims, "Game point," while another, younger voice commands, "Hit it to Carrie. She'll blow it." Meanwhile, the camera makes a slow but steady zoom toward a blond adolescent girl playing the top corner position. Her hair hangs down in her face while another girl, who is obviously trying to limit the blond girl's access to the game, is slowly pushing her toward the extreme corner of the court. Inevitably the ball comes to the blonde on whom the camera is focused. She takes a lame swat at the ball with her right hand, only to miss it completely. As the camera zooms in on Carrie White and she is pushed deeper into the upper corner of the volleyball court by her unsupportive teammate, we note that the square shadow of a basketball backboard looms directly behind her. Not only is the unfortunate girl cowed into the most exterior section of the court itself and compelled to hide behind the wall of her hair, by the end of the scene she also stands inside the only shadow cast on the volleyball court's surface. Boxed into a shadowed corner, swatted in the face for her athletic failings, and told to "eat shit," Carrie retreats alone into the girls' locker room.

If we study these opening frames in the film, De Palma initiates the positioning of Carrie's body through increasingly restrictive external movement. Throughout the film, these initial images of Carrie portrayed in shadowy isolation and boxlike enclosures are restated in an effort to dramatize forcefully her own experience in high school as "a time of misery and resentment." Her mother locks Carrie into a dark prayer closet; even her own cloistered bedroom, demarcated by an angular ceiling that disrupts sharply the viewer's perspective, is located in a corner of the attic. But perhaps the most persuasive reemployment of such imagery occurs at the end of the opening sequence itself. Once more isolated from the other girls in her class, Carrie indulges her body in a warm shower. The other girls are shown romping through the locker room in various stages of nudity and partial dress. Only Carrie lingers in a deserted shower stall. It is here that she discovers the advent of her period. Terrified by the sudden appearance of her own blood, Carrie seeks help from her more worldly classmates, who respond by pushing her naked, bleeding body back into the corner of the shower and pelting the now-hysterical girl with tampons and sanitary napkins. All through this protracted opening sequence Carrie is without language, her voice only a high, plaintive groan of distress. Carrie is boxed in and isolated by the physical assault posed by her cruel classmates, by the aggressive chant—"plug it up, plug it up"—that they all engage, and by the presence of the camera itself as it zooms in to record the full extent of her humiliation, relentlessly pressing Carrie into yet another corner, just as it did on the volleyball court.

Although she is naked throughout this scene, Carrie does wear a single key on a string around her neck. The key operates on several semiotic levels simultaneously. Since it appears to be the key to her gym locker, she apparently wears it around her neck so as not to lose it, and thus it signals Carrie's emotional immaturity—especially in light of the other girls in the locker room who do not wear keys around their necks and, in further contrast, are viewed applying lipstick, fixing their hair, and zipping up high-heeled boots. Carrie's key also reminds us of the fact that she is "locked up," emotionally and physically; she has not been open to society, open to her own sexuality, open to understanding the changes a girl goes through on her journey to womanhood, open to self-knowledge. As the key symbolizes that part of Carrie that has been padlocked up and contained, separated from the rest of the world, it thereby connects with the visual images of enclosure and confinement that are found throughout the film's opening sequence. But the key may also be viewed as signaling the dramatic change that is about to occur to Carrie, for she holds the key to unlocking herself from the bondage of her past and the opportunity to view, however ephemerally, the possibilities of an emancipated future.

In a seminal essay entitled "Visual Pleasure and Narrative Cinema," Laura Mulvey has maintained that the camera's perspective, as it is usually directed and literally operated by men, reflects accordingly a gender-biased perception. This bias is especially apparent when the object of the camera's focus is a woman. According to Mulvey, this male gaze objectifies the woman, so that the gazer both controls and punishes the woman by fetishizing the female body in whole or part. Women are reduced, in other words, to body parts and clothes, and this effectively limits and contains them so that they become less threatening, more manageable. The camera embodies the anxiety of the heterosexual male confronted by an autonomous female sexuality he neither comprehends nor can control. As a result, the movie audience—both men and women—tend to view the cinemagraphic image of the female from this deliberately restrictive perspective and come to accept its positioning as natural.

In *Carrie,* Mulvey's theory is particularly applicable. As Carrie's classmates romp through the girls' locker room in the opening scene, the camera caresses their towel-wrapped and naked bodies in slow motion and soft focus. The scene has little in common with the realities of a woman's locker room, as the nubile women on screen reflect the male gaze—in fact, appear to play to it as in soft-core pornography. As soon as the camera introduces the blood of Carrie's menstruation, however, not only does the accompanying romantic violin music stop abruptly and the slow-motion camera resume normal speed, but also the fantasy projection of the male gaze turns into something more problematic and disturbing. The camera continues to focus on the women exclusively, but now it is made to reflect less the erotic qualities of the objectified female body and to center on its more abject and horrific elements. In other words, Mulvey's theoretical male gaze operates consistently throughout this opening scene; it just shifts in its orientation from woman as erotic object to woman as object of disgust.

Like *The Exorcist* (1973), a film that parallels *Carrie* especially in its fierce attention on the female teenage body possessed by a force it can neither control nor comprehend, it is not only threats *to* the flesh but also threats *of* the flesh that complicate these films. How else to explain why Carrie's schoolmates pursue her humiliation with such a relentless ferocity? They are unconsciously motivated by their own hatred of the female body—the open wound that reveals its monthly "curse"—a misogynistic self-loathing that reflects the extent of their own acculturation of patriarchal values and judgments. The locker room scene in which Carrie's menstruation is realized and abjectified is so unsettling in part because it is orchestrated by women who also menstruate but have been so molded by patriarchal norms that they will forcibly reject that which threatens their social standing, even if it is an essential facet of being a woman. When Chris dangles a clean tampon from its string and announces gleefully, "Hey, Norma, Carrie's having her period," she is mocking both Carrie and all women who must submit to a monthly bleeding. One could even argue that the throwing of tampons and sanitary napkins on the ignorant, prone and bloodied Carrie is a further expression of patriarchal oppression of the feminine, as all of these items are arguably uncomfortable, bleached, and disposable *stoppers* of that which is most innate to womanhood.

If Chelsea Quinn Yarbro is right in her interpretation of the Cinderella myth as a vehicle for programming women to accept their social role and obligation in Western culture (47–49), then Carrie's classmates torture her to reaffirm their own unstable positioning as emerging women. In Carrie's ignorance of traditional femininity, she poses a threat to the other girls who, it must be remembered, have only recently become women themselves and are still inculcating what this means. In light of this argument, it is important to note that Carrie becomes acceptable to these same women only when she attends the prom, after she has brought her appearance and behavior into alignment with their own.

Chris's obsessive attention to her mouth—compulsively darkening it with lipstick, employing it as a manipulative aid for persuading Billy Nolan to help her further humiliate Carrie, licking her lips wantonly before pulling the cord that releases the bucket of blood—merely relocates the horror of Carrie's menstruation to another part of the female anatomy. Female orifices in this film are uniformly perceived and projected as untrustworthy. They remain so terrifying because they operate outside the bounds of rational control, not only in their refusal to be subjugated to the will of male authority but additionally by the manner in which the women of this film fail to exert a sufficient measure of self-discipline over their own bodies. It is well worth noting that the tragic destiny of *Carrie* is set in motion because Chris, after receiving her humiliating slap from Miss Collins on the athletic field, is unable to follow Sue Snell's sobering advice to "just shut up" and practice some self-discipline.

With the notable exception of pornography, horror remains the most physiological of genres. And often, as Barbara Creed has pointed out in her book *The Monstrous Feminine,* abject horror focuses on the feminine. The female form is in and of itself considered a perpetually worthy subject of horror art. This is why the horror film—delving always into the abject as a means for terrorizing audiences with everything from bodily excrement (blood, sweat, vomit) to sexual perversion and sexualized, violent death—relies so heavily on the female character, be she in the role of besieged heroine or monster, in order to subvert further the comfort level of the viewer. All through *Carrie* the female body becomes the site where the monster and the victim converge and blur. In the shower scene, De Palma's camera juxtaposes extreme close-up headshots of the women who torment Carrie with the naked, fetal-positioned body of Carrie herself.

According to Carol Clover in her book *Men, Women, and Chainsaws: Gender in the Modern Horror Film,* "Although the camerawork of *Carrie* repeatedly invites us to take the perspective of Carrie's sadistic tormentors (a familiar feature of Brian De Palma's direction), the majority position throughout, and certainly the position that prevails in the final phase, is Carrie's own" (8). I would disagree strongly. Part of what makes this comedic horror tale more horror than comedy is that Carrie is never allowed to shed the role of victim, even when she occupies that of the monster. At the prom itself, it is the voice of her mother ("They're all going to laugh at you") and Mrs. White's point of view—not Carrie's—that motivates Carrie's wrath. This helps explain why the camera literally fragments into multiple—and wildly distorted—images of the other promgoers compelling Carrie to commence her last dance of destruction. The initial, objective view of the camera reveals quite unambiguously that with the exception of the dreadful Norma, no one else inside the gym laughs at Carrie's expense. She hallucinates the crowd's taunts; at the point when the blood descends, her mother's distorted perspective usurps both the extrinsicality of the camera and Carrie's own objectivity. The *only* time in this film that Clover is right and Carrie's perspective prevails is at the moment when she chooses to defy her mother and go to the prom, and the dire consequences of that minor rebellion make her mother's judgment appear infallible and Carrie's choice ridiculous. The camera's positioning always belongs to others rather than to Carrie herself—from her sadistic classmates, to her paranoid mother, even, finally, to Carrie's alter ego, Susan Snell.

With its emphasis on prom queens, menstruation, tampons, dating, clothes, makeup, and hair, women are located at the center of *Carrie.* The camera's gaze may often embody Mulvey's gender prejudices in the objectification of these women, but the females in this film also occupy positions of power that would appear to extend and qualify Mulvey's thoughts on the misogyny of the cinemagraphic gaze. For as much as this movie focuses on the objectification of women, it also insists that women wield the real power. Consider, for example, the role men play in *Carrie.* The English teacher, Mr. Fromm (Sydney Lassick), and the school principal, Mr. Morton (Stefan Gierasch), are ineffectual and easily manipulated; Morton also represents the general male anxiety associated with specific discussions of menstruation. Early in the film, while Miss Collins discusses the incident that took place in the locker room, there is a shot in which Morton's eyes drift uncomfortably toward the stain of Carrie's blood on the gym teacher's white shorts. Even Morton's language in this scene reflects the unspeakable nature of femininity in a patriarchal culture: He skirts the issue of Carrie's menstruation and never actually refers to it directly.

These two buffoon-authority figures, Morton and Fromm, are another element that *Carrie* shares in common with other adolescent genre films such as *Animal House* and *Porky's.* Since these males presumably represent the adult models for masculine behavior, perhaps this helps to explain why the film's adolescent boys—Tommy Ross, Billy Nolan, and even Norma's boyfriend Freddy (Michael Talbott)—prove so easily susceptible to the wills of their respective girlfriends. A good portion of the film is spent detailing the methodologies that Sue and Chris employ to get their boyfriends to join them in deepening their own involvement with Carrie. The women utilize differing strategies that reflect their inimitable personalities, as Sue chooses to rely on homework and a stony silence as her means of persuasion while Chris is more orally proactive in her approach. Nevertheless, both women understand intuitively that they occupy the central positions of power in their relationships with their boyfriends, while the males are shown having little choice other than to obey their girlfriends.

None of this is to imply, however, that either of these women employs her prodigious powers responsibly. In the end, both Chris and Sue have more in common with Carrie than either girl would ever care to admit: All three women are in possession of prodigious energies that they wield capriciously and without much respect for those whom they directly affect. In the opening shower scene, the camera briefly shifts its attention from an exclusive focus on Carrie's plight to include Sue as a figure under scrutiny. Snell is the first girl that Carrie encounters when she emerges wet and bloody from the shower; she comes to Sue directly in her desperate search for assistance. Carrie grabs the sleeve of Sue's white blouse with her right hand, literally marking her with the menstrual blood. But Sue chooses, at least at this point, to reject Carrie's avatar. For it is Sue who leads the group in their collective torture, opening the sanitary napkin dispenser, passing out pads to the other girls, and commencing the actual airborne assault on Carrie. When Miss Collins arrives on the scene, Sue is deliberately singled out for her actions: Even though she is part of a larger group, the gym teacher calls only her name, shakes Sue by the shoulders, and asks directly: "Sue, what are you doing?" At this point something happens to Sue Snell; Miss Collins forces her to confront her own behavior. The camera scans the young woman's face, and it is clear that she is experiencing a dark epiphany. While the other girls exit the locker room giggling and snickering in the aftermath of their warped fun, Sue lingers in a corner created by the sanitary pad dispenser, her face drained of emotion, and she is the last to leave the locker room. From this point on, Sue's role changes dramatically as she seeks exculpation. Each of her well-intentioned efforts toward Carrie, however, is incapable of diverting the disaster that appears destined to take place. (The reproduction of Da Vinci's "Last Supper" that hangs on the dining room wall of Carrie's house underscores the film's larger themes of doom and destiny, as Jesus conducts the supper already aware of his fate and, most of all, that He has already been betrayed by one of his disciples. Similarly, Carrie will be betrayed by her own mother, knifed in the back when she returns from her telekinetic prom where she wrongly believes herself deceived by Miss Collins and her classmates.)

When Miss Collins forces Sue to exit the gym, wrongly believing that the latter may be planning yet another trick on Carrie, the scene closely resembles the opening shower scene where Carrie is isolated from the larger group and unjustly punished. Even Sue's boyfriend refuses to offer her any degree of recognition when he observes her from atop the prom platform. His sense of confusion is mixed with revulsion as he, like Miss Collins, condemns Sue's intrusive presence with his gaze. From the end of the shower scene on, Sue's choice of action estranges her from her female friends, her teachers, even her boyfriend. By the film's conclusion, Sue has transformed into a version of Carrie herself. (In King's novel, the intimate bond that Carrie and Sue share is made even more explicit, as just before dying Carrie shares a psychic experience with Sue that leaves the latter invested with Carrie's history of pain and suffering.) Bereft of her fellow classmates, aware that she is inextricably linked to Carrie's final dousing in pig's blood and the consequences that follow (Sue's fingers literally touch the clothesline connecting the suspended bucket and Chris's hands), and trapped in a deathless cycle of torment and penance, Sue spends her afternoons dreaming restively under her mother's anxious watch. The last scene of *Carrie* therefore echoes the first: Sue, like Carrie, wanders alone amid a barren landscape, as the lyric score of a single flute is displaced by the abrupt intrusion of a brutal reality simultaneously accompanied by a slow-motion dream sequence that collapses into nightmare. By the time this final sequence of slow-motion lyricism occurs, the audience anticipates the inevitable modulation into blood—be it the blood of a menstrual cycle, of a slaughtered pig, or of violent death. Indeed, the bloodied hand that reaches up to grab the dreaming Sue from the carbon remains of the Whites' house is the same hand that marked her in the girls' locker room. And once again, Sue is incapable of rendering it any real assistance. Like Carrie herself in the opening shower scene, Sue's character exits the film in an endless scream.

Carrie and Charlie McGee (Drew Barrymore), the young girl in possession of pyrokinetic abilities in *Firestarter* (1984), are separated more by mere chronology than either chromosomes or destiny. Both films link the supernatural powers of each protagonist to their hormonal cycles (Charlie's fire starting intensifies in the course of the film and is associated with the development of her pituitary gland, while Carrie's telekinesis commences at the advent of her menstruation), and other similarities between Carrie and Charlie are indeed striking: Neither is permitted the luxury of a near-normal childhood, each has parents who have either abandoned her or have been forcibly removed from interaction with her, even their respective supernatural powers serve only to isolate each of these girls further from a normal mainstream. In short, *Firestarter* takes place in the same social siege atmosphere of *Carrie*. Carrie's life is irrevocably distorted by a warped religion imposed by her mother, while the zealotry of an intrusive government that ends up murdering her parents likewise complicates Charlie's life. In both cases, the violence initiated by Carrie and Charlie is directly related to adult manipulation and abuse. Violence constitutes the last resort for these children stripped of their opportunities for normal life and forced to conform to behavior that is arbitrarily imposed. Many of the more obscure scenes in *Firestarter* feature Charlie performing acts that are typical of a ten-year-old girl, but the near-ecstatic enjoyment she takes from feeding chickens with Norma Manders (Louise Fletcher), horseback riding, or fishing with her father, Andy McGee

(David Keith), highlights the fact that Charlie, like Carrie, is operating under too much stress imposed from outside forces that are totally unaffected by her aborted childhood. At one point in the film, Charlie mourns her loss of a normal childhood, confessing to her father that what she really wants is to go back to school, yet also aware that "It's never going to be over."

The primary reason that Charlie is trapped in this state of arrested development is because of her pyrokinesis. Before she was born, Charlie's parents were involved in a secret government-sponsored "Lot Six" experiment; both her mother (Heather Locklear) and father were given dangerously strong hallucinogens. As a result of this irresponsible tinkering of biological phenomena neither understood nor respected by the gothic scientists in charge of the research, Charlie becomes a contemporary version of the creature in Mary Shelley's *Frankenstein,* the unwitting recipient of a genetic mutation that has endowed her with the ability to start fires spontaneously. As is often the case in Stephen King's world, her supernatural gift is in reality a curse; she must struggle to exert constant control over her emotions so as to restrain this dangerous force that threatens to overwhelm both her and those around her. The Shop, a covert governmental agency similar to the CIA, wants to employ Charlie's capabilities for its own nefarious goals, even if this means murdering her mother and pursuing Charlie relentlessly. The scientist who supervised the Lot Six experiment speculates that when Charlie reaches adolescence, she may come to possess the ability to "crack the very planet in two like a china plate in a shooting gallery." Consequently, half the film, which adheres closely to King's 1980 novel, follows Andy and Charlie on the run from suit-and-tie agents from The Shop, while the second half explores their incarceration at a Shop compound in Virginia where Charlie is forced to participate in a series of closely observed pyrokinetic experiments. Led by Captain Hollister (Martin Sheen), a sinister bureaucrat who will resort to any level of manipulation necessary to produce Charlie's compliance in her own research, The Shop hopes that the child's energies might be harnessed and refined into a powerful weapon for their own use. The Shop is a visible manifestation of the post-Vietnam/Watergate skepticism engendered in many Americans of King's generation. King himself in *Danse Macabre* summarizes the political backdrop for this novel and subsequent film concisely:

> We had just witnessed the sorry end of the Nixon administration and the first presidential resignation in history, we had been resoundingly defeated in Southeast Asia, and we were grappling with domestic problems, from the troubling question of abortion-

on-demand to an inflation rate that was beginning to spiral upward in a positively scary way.... These were changes enough to try and cope with, but on top of them, the America I had grown up in seemed to be crumbling beneath my feet ... it began to seem like an elaborate castle of sand unfortunately built well below the high-tide line. (372)

Consequently, King's treatment of politics and the workings of governmental agencies in *Firestarter* focuses on the estrangement of individuals caught in the machinery of social institutions no longer adequate to human needs. The same bureaucracy responsible for the misadventure of Vietnam now turns its vast resources and cold-war morality toward complicating and harassing the lives of a little girl and her hapless father. Rather than learning some cautionary lessons from the disastrous experiment that altered the chromosomes of Charlie's parents, The Shop desires to extend its genetic research—even if it comes at the expense of Charlie's childhood.

In all fairness, the most interesting character in *Firestarter* is not the besieged Charlie but her surrogate father, John Rainbird (George C. Scott). Although he appears to operate outside the perimeters of The Shop, Rainbird, the psychotic Native American who believes that by murdering Charlie he will assume her supernatural gifts in the afterworld, actually epitomizes the warped and unethical values that guide the government agents of this organization. Both Rainbird and his employers seek to manipulate the girl's terrible powers to make themselves stronger. He befriends Charlie while she is held prisoner at The Shop compound, but his friendship and artificial vulnerability are actually only ruses that he employs to gain the child's trust. Everything Rainbird does in this film is a lie, and he exploits Charlie's confidence without conscience. Unconcerned about the girl's personal welfare except insofar as it furthers his own selfish ends, Rainbird has no loyalty to the people he works for and has no intention of serving their needs. He represents the purest evil in this film of unscrupulous male behavior; indeed, he possesses all the unsavory attributes of a Shakespearean villain: He is as arrogant as Edmund, as duplicitous as Iago, as ruthless as Macbeth.

Rainbird labors under the delusion that he is, in contrast to the various secular bureaucrats and scientists who work for The Shop, a deeply spiritual man. He criticizes Hollister for not recognizing that Charlie possesses "forces beyond your comprehension. Forces that belong to the gods alone." And yet even as he levels this condescending remark, Rainbird drinks The Shop's expensive liquors from Waterford crystal and views Charlie strictly as a means for elevating himself to the godhead in the afterlife. Rainbird's spirituality and personality are as false as his very identity as a Native American—in reality, he resembles more his "white man" identity, the "John" prefix of his name (and his role is played by a Caucasian actor), which actually perverts the forces of nature embodied in his Indian name and heritage. At the end of *Firestarter*, it is because of Rainbird and his obsession with Charlie's supernatural gift that Andy McGee is murdered and Charlie is forced to burn her way to freedom by destroying The Shop's compound in a final conflagration. Rainbird leaves Charlie to contemplate an uncertain future of fear and flight; even exposing her sordid tale to the *New York Times* is no guarantee that the government will abandon its quest to aggravate further the supernatural fury conceived by its own carelessness.

Both *Carrie* and *Firestarter* detail the dire consequences of youths who, for whatever reasons, are precluded from feelings of acceptance and a collective identity with other children. Carrie's plight appears on the verge of radical improvement when she begins to assert herself against her mother's will. Her decision to attend the prom with Tommy must be viewed as a tremendous risk on her part, and undertaking it is both laudable and significant. But it also leads to the most poignant horror moment in the film. Just when Carrie appears on the verge of discovering an alternative identity, she has it violently and unfairly stripped away. The desperation that definitively marks Carrie's and Charlie's isolation from their peers is less obvious an issue in Rob Reiner's film adaptation of King's novella *The Body*, retitled *Stand by Me*. The four principal characters—Gordie (Wil Wheaton/Richard Dreyfuss), Chris (River Phoenix), Teddy (Corey Feldman), and Vern (Jerry O'Connell)—seemingly possess such a close-knit bond with one another that it is easy to overlook the fact that these boys, like Carrie and Charlie, are estranged from their families, from the community of Castle Rock, and even, to a very real extent, from one another.

The title *Stand by Me* suggests a parallel to the words of the famous song: That this will be a film about undying friendship and commitment in the face of all obstacles. And yet it is noteworthy that its title song is more a plea than it is an assurance, with its implied question "Stand by me?" left decidedly unanswered. In spite of the male bonding that is clearly in place among these four boys, *Stand by Me* is a film that continually stresses the theme of betrayal. In fact, the degree to which these boys are betrayed (and betray one another) establishes perhaps its closest parallel to *Carrie* than to any other King film. Undercutting the film's jocularity and moments of adolescent male bonding are a myriad of scenes where older brothers punish younger brothers for the mere fact of their existence, where school authorities betray students for petty cash, where alcoholic parents burn the ears of unsuspecting children on woodstoves—or simply choose to ignore the needs of their offspring in favor of tending the sour gardens of their own private grief—and where "best friends" elect to abandon one another at the sight of a switchblade knife wielded by a sociopathic punk.

Set at the end of summer 1959, the social-historical context for *Stand by Me* places it on the cusp of radical change. The United States is emerging from the conservative security of the Eisenhower administration and is about to enter into the tumultuous Age of Aquarius. The musical score, which contributes greatly to the ambiance of this film, also signals the cultural shift about to take place: The lyrical do-wop songs of *Stand by Me* will soon give way to the hard edge of rock. Just as the film is set on the edge of great historical change in America, it also signals a moment of great personal change in the lives of these four boys. Each of them verges on puberty, so discussions of Mighty Mouse and Superman and punches to the bicep for "flinching" are punctuated by talk of penis size and girls' breasts. Moreover, the four boys in this film are down to the last precious hours of their summer vacation, due soon to report to the new experience of junior high school, where, as Chris informs Gordie, the class distinction will begin separating those destined to take shop classes and those who will go in quite another direction toward college-prep studies. At the film's end, when the boys return to Castle Rock, Vern and Teddy literally walk away from Chris and Gordie in opposite directions, and Gordie's voice-over informs us that this journey marked the last time he remembers the four boys together: "As time went on, we saw less and less of Teddy and Vern, until eventually they became just two more faces in the halls. It happens sometimes, friends come in and out of your life like busboys at a restaurant." So their choice to make an overnight journey to find the dead body of twelve-year-old Ray Brower, a boy who is the same age as the protagonists, and who was "knocked out of his Keds" when he was hit by a train while collecting blueberries, may begin as an end-of-the-summer lark to "get our pictures in the papers," but it assumes multileveled significance as the film unfolds.

The entire film is essentially a flashback, narrated from Gordie's point of view as an adult. With children of his own and a career as a professional writer, Gordie is inspired to write this tale of adolescent memory upon learning of Chris's death—the latter stabbed in the neck during a knife attack while trying to break up a fight between two other men in a restaurant. In retrospect, the search for Brower's body becomes both a literal and symbolic journey toward death. The four boys walk the train tracks, following in the exact footsteps of Ray Brower, to view his dead body but also, unconsciously, to view their own deaths: The death of their friendly foursome, the death of their summer, and, most important, the death of their own childhoods. In his Jungian analysis of "The Mythic Journey in *The Body,*" Arthur Biddle imbues the journey with elements of the mythic quest wherein Gordie undergoes a series of archetypal "adventures that promise a spiritual transformation through a dying and a rebirth" (87).

Stand by Me is a coming-of-age story, but not only do these children stand to lose important aspects of their lives, they also gain new things to replace what they have lost. The narrative commences with Chris in the role of the group's titular leader; but it ends with Gordie usurping this position. Early in the film we learn that Gordie's brother, Denny, has recently died. Gordie still grieves for him, and he clings to the last gift his brother has given him, a Yankees baseball cap. A gang of town bullies led by Ace Merrill (Kiefer Sutherland) steal the cap off Gordie's head, and because Ace and his gang are older, bigger, and more ruthless than Gordie, the latter has no choice but to relinquish it. The film's climax is a revisitation of this early scene, only now the stakes are higher: Instead of stealing a baseball cap, Ace and his gang want to take Ray Brower's body from Gordie and his friends. When Chris refuses to capitulate to Ace's bullying, insisting "You're going to have to kill me," Ace is more than willing to comply by slitting his throat with a switchblade. Before he can do so, however, Gordie fires a pistol into the air and then aims it directly at Ace's face. When the older punk asks if Gordie intends to shoot his entire gang, Gordie retorts coolly, "Just you." Left with little choice than to retreat, Ace and his gang threaten a severe payback later (which occurs in King's novella but not in the film).

The confrontation over Brower's body not only represents the climax of the film, it also signals the onset of Gordie's maturation into manhood. Throughout the movie, Gordie's own body comes under scrutiny and attack. He is forced to run from the infamous Chopper, "the most feared and least seen dog in Castle Rock," who commences his canine assaults with the command "Chopper! Sic! Balls!"; he must undergo quiet humiliations in front of both his father and the male owner of a local deli, both of whom compare him unfavorably to his dead brother, the star quarterback; Ace and his gang demean Gordie and his friends by referring to them as "ladies," "girls," "pussies," and "faggots"; and when the boys stray from the railroad tracks and stumble into a swamp, Gordie faints at the sight of his own blood when he must remove a huge leech that has attached itself to one of his testicles. In a dream sequence where his brother's casket is lowered into the grave, Gordie envisions his father whispering, "It should have been you, Gordon," undoubtedly a reflection of the man's truest feelings, but also an indication of the guilt and inferiority that Gordie still carries inside.

At the end of the film, Gordie's firing the pistol and his willingness to use it against Ace is a repudiation of all the symbolic acts and language of emasculation mentioned above. The pistol is nothing less than a phallic object, and Gordie uses it to assert his identity as a man, while abandoning forever his status as impotent boy-child. He even assumes the bravado of male potency when he tells Ace to "suck my fat one, you cheap dime store hood" while pointing the gun directly in his face. In his confrontation with Ace and the older boys over possession of Brower's corpse, Gordie declares his independence from the tyrannical premise that the weak must always remain subordinate to the strong. When he stands up to Ace, he reestablishes the rule of justice and sympathy that have been abandoned in Castle Rock. And this spirit continues in the choice Gordie and his friends make in electing not to claim credit for finding Brower's body but instead to alert the police through an anonymous call. His behavior at the site of Brower's body is representative of Gordie's maturation and an acknowledgment of the bond of respect that he now shares with the dead child. He was, after all, the first to recognize that "Going to see a dead kid, maybe it shouldn't be a party."

At the same time that *Stand by Me* is about Gordie's journey toward selfhood and maturation, it is also reflective of his efforts to escape the wasteland of Castle Rock, a rural town in Oregon. Indeed, the four adolescents are as much in flight from their homes and community as they are curious about seeing Brower's corpse. Castle Rock is a place that is demarcated by alcoholism (Chris's father gets drunk and beats him, while Ace and his gang are seldom seen without open bottles of beer), easy violence and madness (Teddy's father is currently incarcerated in an asylum, while Vern lives in absolute terror of his older brother), and adults who are indifferent to the existence of their children (Gordie's mother and father prefer to maintain a shrine to their dead son at the expense of the one still living). As Biddle has argued: "On the surface, the sterility of Castle Rock is a result of the prolonged drought and extraordinary heat of the summer. But at a deeper level, it is the aridity of a community that cannot love" (86). The journey these four boys undertake leads them out of Castle Rock and through the town's symbolic center—Milo's junkyard—a befouled and hostile place that embodies the values of the society that produced it. In the Castle Rock wasteland, it is people like Ace and his gang, "consumers" in the most appalling sense of the word, who survive: Feeding off the weaknesses, the genuine emotions, or the fears of others, they move like profane engines of destruction, cruising the back roads of the town in lumbering automobiles, searching for mailboxes to pulverize or working men to scare off the roads, using and breaking, and then discarding all that gets in their path. The destructive images of the machine age represent a subtle subtext for this film and are always employed as a threat to the boys' welfare: Most notably, the train itself—thundering along without any effort to apply brakes or slow down when it is obvious that children are directly ahead in its path—always comes from the direction of Castle Rock, as if it were sent by the town in pursuit of wayward boys trying to escape. The hulking black engine of destruction, already responsible for killing one child, embodies the machinelike personalities of the Castle Rock adults, who are always prepared to inflict damage with poundings from their fists. The train can also be viewed as a metaphor for the town environment itself, a hard, mechanical place that presses down upon its children with an almost preternatural intensity to forge them into its own image and likeness.

In King's novella *The Body,* Gordie looks back on the importance of the journey to view Brower's body as a rite of passage:

> There's a high ritual to all fundamental events, the rites of passage, the magic corridor where the change happens. Buying the condoms. Standing before the minister. Raising your hand and taking the oath. Or, if you please, walking down the railroad tracks. . . . It seemed right to do it this way, because the rite of passage *is* a magic corridor and so we always provide an aisle—it's what you walk down when you get married, what they carry you down when you get buried. Our corridor was those twin rails, and we walked between them. . . . Events surrounding our hike had turned it into what we had suspected it was all along: serious business. (415)

For Chris and Gordie, Ray Brower's mutilated corpse comes to symbolize the dead world of Castle Rock. Its homes and community are emblematic of the type of social environment that often destroys King's protagonists, indeed that eventually swallows Vern and Teddy. At the end of the film, Vern and Teddy are left symbolically trapped between the restrictive social "corridor of those twin rails": They become subsumed into the world of Castle Rock, as Teddy will be transformed into a version of Ace, spending time in jail and doing odd jobs, while Vern marries directly out of high school and becomes another parent with too many children to raise properly.

The story of Chris and Gordie, however, remains "serious business"; it is a story of wonder and devotion pitted against the machine of society's false values. For both of them, "the rite of passage is a magic corridor where the change happens." In their efforts to avoid inclusion in the mechanistic world that ends up ensnaring Teddy and Vern, Chris and Gordie construct an alternative society of two based on the radical values of individual courage and interpersonal loyalty and respect. As Chris informs Gordie during a dark moment when the latter expresses his anxiety about "being weird" and unloved by his father: "Kids lose everything unless someone looks out for them—and if your parents are too fucked up to do it, then maybe I should." These two boys end up looking out for one another. With Gordie's academic help and encouragement, Chris makes his way through college to become a lawyer, while Gordie continues to build on the confidence that is initially instilled in him by Denny and Chris that he should not be ashamed of being a writer and that he possesses a rare and magical gift. "It's like God gave you something, man, all those stories that you can make up. And He said, 'This is what we got for you, kid. Try not to lose it.'" While his father (Marshall Bell) dismisses Gordie's literary attributes because they are neither practical nor athletic, Chris understands intuitively that his friend possesses a rare and valuable talent—a means for both coping and escaping the oppression of Castle Rock.

As we will examine in greater detail in the following chapter, the role the writer maintains in Stephen King's world is uniquely special: nothing less than that of shaman. The creative writer works from a power source that both insulates him from the sterility of American cultural hegemony at the same time as it provides a conduit to the imagination and its magical link back to childhood. In this film Gordie Lachance is, like many of the other writers who populate Stephen King's movies, a portrait of the author in terms of both the powers he possesses as a result of being a writer and in his ability to utilize these powers to shape and influence events. Gordie exits this film as an adult man at work on his word processor, writing the ending to the tale we have just witnessed. His own son waits patiently for him to finish work, and it is clear after he has that the two maintain a close and playful relationship. The film concludes as the camera follows Gordie out of his study and into the front yard of his house, where he begins wrestling with his son before he takes him swimming. This final scene is meant to stand in direct contrast to all the abominable child-parent relationships that characterize the rest of *Stand by Me*.

Throughout Stephen King's fiction, older adults who possess the gift of prophecy, a highly developed sense of moral integrity, and an instinctive understanding of how the world operates often aid vulnerable children. In *The Shining, The Stand,* and *The Talisman,* these adults are all African Americans, and, by virtue of their race and class, outcasts from mainstream American life. As such, they are in the position to instruct and guide King's younger, highly impressionable white protagonists through the wastelands of each respective novel and toward a vision of greater self-perception and moral growth. Neither the black outcast nor the white adolescent outsider occupies a secure place in American society. Their relationship challenges the core limitations of this society, and therefore must remain secretive and illicit. Based initially on a common danger or sense of exclusion and psychic correspondences, this bond belies a loneliness that demands love; its very vitality highlights the disavowal of oppressive social conventions in favor of a broader-based spirit of acceptance. In her essay "Reading King Darkly: Issues of Race in Stephen King's Novels," Samantha Figliola argues persuasively that King "returns to the romantic pairing of white youths with 'savage' mentors again and again, drawn to its ideological possibilities. . . . As surrogate parents, King's black characters educate their 'children' to seek alternatives to the many evil institutions that surround them: War, environmental destruction, psychological abuse, racism, and patriarchal domination" (147).

The film *Silver Bullet* (1985), based on the Stephen King novelette *Cycle of the Werewolf* (1983), restates the theme of the adult outsider bonding with the vulnerable child. In Stephen King's films and fictions, this is one of the few positive relationships that is allowed to exist between child and adult; the latter must occupy some position that is divorced from traditional notions of an adult as either a parent or an authority surrogate. Although Uncle Red (Gary Busey) is not African American, he is viewed as uniquely different from the other adults in Tarker's Mills, an outsider to their bourgeois values and work ethics. A "chronic drunk" working on his third divorce, even his own sister, Nan (Robin Groves), barely tolerates his presence in their suburban home. She is especially fearful that Red's negative self-image will cause her handicapped son, Marty (Corey Haim), to follow his uncle's example of self-pity and produce another adult who has likewise "given up" on life.

At first, Marty Coslow appears isolated and quietly tormented by a society that cannot comprehend his physical disability (in one scene we watch him wistfully observing other boys playing baseball while confined to his wheelchair behind the barrier of a chain-link fence), a sister who is often inconvenienced because she is expected to help care for her brother, and parents who appear, like those in *Stand by Me,* in possession of no real insight into the needs and talents of their handicapped son. As a consequence, Marty turns to his only ally, Uncle Red (his name is changed from Al to Red in the film adaptation), who appears to be the only one capable of recognizing that "There's more to Marty than him just not being able to walk." Uncle Red neither pities Marty nor treats him condescendingly; he merely responds to the child with genuine and spontaneous affection. He even builds Marty a motorized wheelchair, named "Silver Bullet," that is so dangerously powerful both know that Marty's parents will object to his riding in it. Ironically, it is because of this souped-up vehicle that Marty is able to avoid being killed by the werewolf on two separate occasions.

Perhaps Marty and Red form such a close bond because the latter identifies with Marty's isolation, as Red is an eccentric, alcoholic, single, middle-age man who does not fit comfortably into the adult community of Tarker's Mills. However, none of these past experiences has hardened Uncle Red. The audience senses that his spirit of mischief and his love of play (he and Marty play poker for baseball cards to delay Marty's bedtime, and Red supplies the boy with illegal fireworks) are in no small part responsible for his marriage failures and the lack of respect he garners from his disapproving sister. Red has remained a man-child—certainly more in need of a baby-sitter than his adolescent niece and nephew. Indeed, Red drives a Triumph sports car convertible, symbol of his arrested development, while in contrast, Marty's parents are the owners of a large dark blue station wagon. Like Chris and Gordie in *Stand by Me,* Marty and his uncle are "losers" in the judgment of everyone else except themselves. Together they form a bond that is strengthened by the differences that separate them from the rest of society. Marty and Red endure because they take care of one another.

In the novelette *Cycle of the Werewolf,* King constructs a narrative that conforms closely to the mythic tradition of the werewolf: Once a month on nights of a full moon the human transforms into a beast and ravages the human community to which he belongs. In the film version of this narrative directed by Daniel Attias, Stephen King's screenplay features a werewolf that is unregulated by the cycle of the moon; instead, *Silver Bullet*'s werewolf, the Reverend Lowe (Everett McGill), is shown capable of transforming himself into a beast almost at will. In addition to this unique variation on the werewolf tradition, which represents King's only real tinkering with lycanthropic folklore, *Silver Bullet* is narrated from the point of view of Marty's sister, Jane Coslow (Megan Follows), who is absent from the *Cycle* novelette. She occupies an expansive role that deepens and enriches the cinematic adaptation of this text. As Michael Collings points out, her relationship with Marty is at least as rich as the one that Uncle Red and his nephew share together: "Rather than merely being given to occasional sniping remarks about his being crippled, Jane is allowed a full range of reactions, from frustration to anger to childish petulance to deep love and trust" (140).

Although the werewolf has been preying on the town of Tarker's Mills from the beginning of the film, no one knows that a werewolf is perpetrating the murders. When the reverend/beast kills Marty's best friend, however, the two plot lines converge, and Marty and the monster spend the rest of the picture actively pursuing the destruction of one another. By creating a dual narrative that eventually confluences into a single plot line, King's screenplay provides a more detailed and coherent story line for *Silver Bullet* than is present in the more fragmented—because it is divided into a cycle of episodes that correspond to Lowe's monthly transformations—*Cycle of the Werewolf.*

Late one night while igniting fireworks supplied by Uncle Red in a deserted rural area, Marty confronts the werewolf. In defending himself, the boy manages to hit the creature in its eye with one of the rockets, and this allows him to escape. The next day his sister Jane discovers that the Reverend Lowe is wearing an eye patch, and this commences a brother-sister bond that deepens in the face of imminent danger and their shared secret knowledge. Jane and Marty solicit help from Uncle Red, the only adult in Tarker's Mill whom they trust enough to help them destroy the werewolf. Although he initially scoffs at the very concept of a real werewolf, Red respects his niece and nephew sufficiently to follow their instructions and construct a silver bullet out of Jane's silver crucifix and Marty's religious medal and chain. This bullet—coupled with the faith that Red demonstrates toward these two lost children—eventually allows them all to survive when the werewolf singles out their group for a Halloween attack during a full moon. Uncle Red still possesses enough of the child in himself that his true loyalties and sympathies remain with children. Moreover, because of these childlike attributes, Red is imaginatively open to the possibility of a werewolf's existence. His childlike spirit and faith in his niece and nephew are rewarded at the film's climax when the werewolf is slain by the silver bullet Marty fires from Red's gun.

Children in Stephen King's celluloid and fictional worlds occupy a tenuous place. They are caught between states of being: Not quite adults, yet forced to experience the complex emotions that push them toward a maturation that remains as terrifying as it is desirable. Along the way, his children-heroes must confront other children as well as adults who shape irrevocably this journey toward adulthood. In many of the films we have considered in this chapter, King's childhood protagonists must struggle to protect their innocence in spite of various moments of mayhem and violence. At the end of both *Carrie* and *Firestarter,* for example, Sue Snell and Charlie McGee are left alone, reeling in an effort to comprehend exactly what they have suffered and lost. But movies such as *Silver Bullet* and *Hearts in Atlantis* (2001), on the other hand, show young protagonists balancing and organizing the trauma that typically accompanies the movement into adulthood in King's world. They do so through the inclusion of "strange" adult friends who nurture children and establish sympathetic bonds with them. Uncle Red and Ted Brautigan (Anthony Hopkins) in *Atlantis* counterbalance the negative or absent parenting that these child protagonists receive as well as supply them with alternative examples for managing their own emergence into adulthood.

Like *Silver Bullet*'s Uncle Red, *Atlantis*'s Brautigan is a man whose life is in harmony with the children who are drawn to him. He takes the time both to listen and to instruct eleven-year-old Bobby Garfield (Anton Yelchin) and to provide him with the paternal guidance he has been missing since the death of his father six years earlier. His attitude prompts Liz Garfield (Hope Davis), Bobby's mother, to question: "Why would a man his age want to spend so much time with a kid?" This question is an indictment of Mrs. Garfield's parenting at the same time as it highlights her unfounded concern that Ted may be a pedophile preying on her young son. Early in their relationship she worries that Brautigan may be touching her son inappropriately, and later, when she grossly misinterprets Brautigan's efforts to fix Carol Gerber's (Mika Boorem) dislocated shoulder, the film ironically subverts this issue by revealing that Ted deliberately avoids trying to touch other people. He is in possession of the gift of prophecy, very similar to Johnny Smith in *The Dead Zone* and John Coffey in *The Green*

Mile, and his powers are momentarily passed on to those who come into direct contact with him. When Ted touches someone, he creates a "kind of window into other people's minds. I know certain things. See certain things. Some people think of it as a gift. I've always seen it as a burden." Ted can sense, for example, that the "low men" are closing in on him, and that Bobby will kiss Carol and it will be "the kiss by which all the others will be judged—and found wanting." In the film version of *Atlantis,* Bobby comes to realize that the "low men" who drive flashy cars and announce their presence by putting up posters for lost pets on telephone booths and poles are actually FBI agents who are pursuing psychics such as Brautigan to help in their battle against communism. But in King's novel, the "low men" are more ambiguous creatures, inhuman aliens who wish to apprehend Ted and whisk him away to the mysterious realm that animates King's ongoing Dark Tower series.

King's 1999 narrative is actually a collection divided into four novellas and one short story, all interconnected. The film's director, Scott Hicks, and its screenwriter, William Goldman, elected to concentrate the film on only the first (longest) and last (shortest) sections of King's book. As in *Stand by Me, Atlantis* is a tale in which an adult male narrator is looking back on his own childhood. The death of a close boyhood friend serves as the impetus that stimulates this adult's recollection of his "last summer of innocence," literally taking him back via a protracted flashback to the house and neighborhood where he grew up. His memory is set in the early 1960s, in the time just prior to the explosive events of Vietnam and Watergate. Bobby and his country share an undiluted innocence that is on the verge of vanishing, and the film's subtle criticism of J. Edgar Hoover and the FBI's nefarious and illegal methods of pursuit and seizure of Brautigan anticipate this fact.

King's narrative, however, follows Bobby and his friends as they age into jaded adults who are scarred by the tumultuous events of the war and the fallout of their own betrayed childhoods. Because the film does not explore their development into adults, it depicts a far more optimistic and nostalgic experience than King's novel. The novel, in fact, grows ever more sobering as Bobby's estrangement from his mother deepens and eventually results in his drug use, general alienation from society and school, and eventual incarceration. In the second half of the collection, King's book shifts its emphasis from Bobby Garfield to Carol Gerber. She comes to occupy a core position as the central female around whom all the various males in the book revolve. The Vietnam war radicalizes Carol during her years as an undergraduate college student, pushing her toward extreme acts of violent resistance in reaction against American participation in the conflict. Like Bobby, Carol's early adulthood is filled with disillusionment and despair. Driven insane by her sense of political impotence, Carol dies at the hands of the police who set fire to the house she inhabits in Los Angeles in a scene that is nearly a direct parallel to Patty Hearst's involvement with the radical Symbonese Liberation Army in the early 1970s. In the penultimate section of King's book, a character named Dieffenbaker looks back on himself and the generation that thought it would change the world; he pronounces a judgment that serves as a representative statement for Carol and Bobby, and perhaps even King himself. It is a reminder of the uncomfortable and yet unanswered issue of why it is that the adult so rarely evolves into what the child gave promise of becoming: "I loathe and despise my generation. We had an opportunity to change everything. We actually did. Instead we settled for designer jeans, two tickets to Mariah Carey at Radio City Music Hall, frequent-flier miles, James Cameron's *Titanic,* and retirement portfolios" (498).

None of this finds its way into Hicks's film; perhaps that is a major reason why the movie has been criticized for simplifying the complex range of vision that informs King's narrative text. The adult Bobby Garfield (David Morse) is portrayed as an overly sentimental but nonetheless well-adjusted father and husband whose adolescent contact with Ted Brautigan continues to inform his adulthood, transforming him into the kind of grown-up who resembles Uncle Red or even Ted himself. As we witness in his tender interaction with Carol's daughter at the end of *Atlantis,* Bobby is essentially unburdened by his personal losses, a man who is still capable of being reinvigorated through his bond with childhood and children.

At the conclusion of this film, Bobby acknowledges that Ted has had a profound effect on his development into manhood: "What Ted did was open my eyes and let the future in." Bobby's single mother, as Brautigan opines, is too distracted by her perceived financial woes, her efforts "to better herself," her misguided resentment and anger toward her dead husband, and her own vanity as she clings to her fading beauty. Thus, she fails to pay sufficient attention to the emotional needs of her young son. Although she often complains about the family's lack of money (she gives Bobby a library card for his birthday instead of the new bike he yearns to own), the audience and her son watch her indulge her desire for expensive dresses and fashionable accessories. In the course of this summer, Bobby learns that his mother lies—to both him and herself—and that she operates with a reckless selfishness and a fatal inability to recognize the true natures of the men around her. At the end of the film, when she betrays Brautigan to the "low men," Bobby correctly accuses her of "betraying us both [Ted and Bobby]."

Although it is clear that Brautigan has exerted a positive influence on Bobby and his two friends, he is the one who informs Carol that childhood is a magical but ephemeral period of time, like Atlantis itself, that must necessarily end in "our hearts breaking into two." To some extent, his interpretation is verified in the film, as Bobby and Carol stop writing to each other and then fall completely out of contact; the adult Bobby doesn't even know that his former girlfriend has been dead for two years. When Carol and Bobby meet for the final time as children, they are framed together on Carol's front lawn interacting within a layered curtain of white sheets that Carol has been hanging on clotheslines to dry. The clean sheets in the summer sunshine form a kind of translucent cocoon that encloses both children, symbolizing the last moment of their collective innocence. "That summer was the last of my childhood," the adult Bobby confirms, for even as they share their final brief kiss amid the clean laundry, Bobby is being pulled from Carol's embrace and away from the purity of this place in time by his mother's need to move them to Boston and into an uncertain future.

Stephen King has often revisited the highly Freudian remark that writing for him is like archeology—the digging of something up from deep beneath the surface—uncovering that which has been lost or buried. The "site" or ground that perhaps has been most productive for the majority of King's literary and cinemagraphic excavations exists somewhere between the ages of five and twelve, childhood. King identifies this period with an innocent magic that is forever in danger of being exploited or squashed or forgotten. But it is also a time of great power, for as King's notes in *Danse Macabre,* children "may not see things with the clarity of an adult, [but they] see events more intensely" (107) because their experiences are often more visceral, they are of a more tactile nature, and they are apprehended instinctually as much as cerebrally. Sometimes the children in Stephen King's films are placed in situations where they must experience a severe fall from grace; their innocence, as we have seen in the examples of Carrie White and Charlie McGee, shattered by the abuses and machinations of others. The destruction of childhood in King's world is often more than a simple restating of the fall-from-grace theme: It enlarges into a specific critique of the adult world—its values and priorities. And in nearly every

King film dealing with the coming-of-age theme, there are children who have turned themselves into hateful things because they have so thoroughly abandoned whatever is wonderful about childhood.

Transience is a necessary condition of childhood—why else do we mourn its loss?—but for as long as it lasts, childhood remains in King's art a state that is innocent at the same time as it is full of endurance and guile. In spite of its precarious status, childhood sustains its lure as a romantic ideal in Hollywood's adaptations of King's fictional world. His portraits of children are about the end of childhood and about its persistence, about undergoing loss and yet learning from it, about defying the adult world and reconciling oneself to it, about returning to the past and finding a way to make it a viable part of the present. As many commentators on King's fiction have already noted, a substantial portion of his canon explores the issue of exactly what elements of childhood an individual can carry with him into adulthood. Always in King's universe, as in Wordsworth's before him, "the child is father to the man." Thus, in order to enter into and navigate through adulthood with imagination and courage and morality intact, it is imperative that the adult not lose sight of the child he once was. King is committed to the belief that the adult must remember his own Wordsworthian "spots in time," those moments from an individual's past that provide meaning for the rest of his life.

Many of King's most memorable adult characters—Gordie Lachance in *Stand by Me,* John Coffey in *The Green Mile,* John Smith in *The Dead Zone,* the Losers in *IT,* Uncle Red in *Silver Bullet,* Bobby Garfield in *Hearts in Atlantis,* even Andy Dufresne in *The Shawshank Redemption*—retain an intuitive bond with childhood. In adhering to childlike loyalties and a simple faith in the imaginative life, it is possible for King's adults to avoid the corruption embodied in his critical portraits of social and cultural institutions. His children-heroes often represent the resilient good in humankind, employing the horrific circumstances of their personal lives to grow into better people.

In nearly every one of the major films that have been produced from King's novels and screenplays, the presence of goodness—the white force, blind faith, small-group solidarity, the authority of a writer's or a young boy's expansive imagination, simple love—exists in Manichean opposition to the powers of evil. As King expressed in a 1981 interview, "I really do believe in the White force. Children are part of that force, which is why I write about them the way I do. There are a lot of horror writers who deal with this struggle, but they tend to concentrate on the Black. But the other force is there, too" (Underwood and Miller, *Bare Bones* 21). This force of goodness essentially breaks the stranglehold of evil regardless of how its corruption is manifested in human or institutionalized or supernatural form. This unselfish principle is always expressed as a highly romantic, antirational essence—something very much akin to the experience of childhood. "Hope," says Andy Dufrense in *The Shawshank Redemption,* "is always a good thing," but in King's world it is also a subversive thing born in the individual adult's conscious refusal to relinquish his connection to childhood and resign himself to the conforming strictures of the social mainstream. Confronting worldly evil with independence intact, King's boy-men summon an inner strength that is greater than the forces of destruction—both human and supernatural—that surround them and seek their complicity. "I'm interested in the mythic power that childhood holds over our imagination," King remarked in an interview with me in *Stephen King: The Second Decade,* "the raising of children into decent adults—and that means adults who have not lost touch with the essential qualities of childhood" (7).

Interestingly, this child-adult conduit is almost exclusively gendered masculine in King's world, certainly reflective of the writer's own personal experience, as his male heroes are those who sustain an intimate relationship with their own childhood histories. As we will consider in the next chapter, King's female protagonists are more often pictured in flight from their pasts. Victims of sexual violence, domestic upheaval, and patriarchal abuse, King seems to imply in many of his novels and the films made from them that there is something within the female psyche that "both acquiesces to masculine dominance and violence and responds to that violence with an equally compelling power" (Lant and Thompson 5). In the end, however, the female survivors in King's films relate more to their children and to other women than to an idealized memory of their own childhood pasts. Many of his adult women have been so traumatized by events from childhood that they seek to repress its awful history, and this stands in sharp contrast to the male protagonists who must rely so heavily on positive recollections of boyhood play and male bonding in order to survive.

CHAPTER 3

MATERNAL ARCHETYPES:
CUJO, MISERY, DOLORES CLAIBORNE

Since the 1970s, feminist scholars have observed that the roles Stephen King has traditionally allotted women in his fiction and specifically female sexuality itself are patronizingly restricted and frequently negative. His women characters, especially those populating his earliest fiction, tend to fall into the category of either diabolical sorceress or passive victim. Critic Chelsea Quinn Yarbro was first to lament that "it is disheartening when a writer with so much talent and strength of vision is not able to develop a believable woman character between the ages of seventeen and sixty" (65). Mary Pharr, in a seminal essay that broadens and deepens Yarbro's position, noted that "despite his best efforts, King's women are reflective of American stereotypes. . . . His most convincing female characters are precisely those who are least threatening to men" ("Partners" 21). And in her discussion of the novel *IT* (1986), Karen Thoens reduced the monster in the text to an essentially feminine archetype: "It could be repulsive female sexuality. But mostly It is actually She. . . . It is your mother. It, nameless terror. It is bloody, filthy, horrible. The boy-men heroes have returned to Derry to face IT again, HER, the bitch, the force that is really responsible for their lost youth" (137).

Sharply aware of such criticism and generally concurring with it, Stephen King has labored to create more human and less stereotypical female personalities, at least since the publication of *Misery* (1987). In the novel *Dolores Claiborne* (1993), for example, the author completely eschewed his traditional third-person narrative form to provide Dolores with an autobiographical voice and consciousness. This departure from omniscient point of view to a first-person monologue signals the weight of

King's investment in legitimizing Dolores' perspective and the domestic issues her narrative explores. Perhaps the truism that middle-age males begin to explore their "feminine" side is another explanation for King's evolving interest in developing better women characters. Also, in focusing on women's issues, King's more recent writing has become more circumscribed, centering on one or two individuals almost exclusively, especially when compared to his early works, such as *'Salem's Lot* or *The Stand,* which feature a large and diverse cast of characters.

The majority of women who populate Stephen King's fiction are often judged by the same rules that determine the fitness of romance-novel heroines. Kay Mussell has described a "domestic test" such heroines must pass to prove their worthiness. This test conforms to "the three traditional and interrelated roles of female socialization: wife, mother, and house maker" (89). To pass the test, individuals must possess "the innate traits of good women—sexual control, modesty, intuition, selflessness, caring—[and] use those qualities actively to benefit others" (90). (These are, incidentally, some of the same qualities that constitute King's definition of masculine heroism, as will be discussed in a later chapter.) More often than not, the "good women" personality traits, when applied to King's females, are found in mothers and pregnant women, who possess highly impressive levels of inner strength and intuitive knowledge. And like King's male hero counterparts, the heroines of his books and films are situated at crisis points in their lives where they must either rise above their oppression or capitulate to it entirely.

King's mother-heroines distinguish themselves from the negative association between evil and feminine sexuality found elsewhere in his canon, particularly his early novels and stories. King frequently portrays feminine sexuality—when it is not moored in a loving, heterosexual relationship—as dangerous because it serves only itself or, more precisely, the evil that is just beneath the surface of its lascivious hunger. In much of his work, female sexuality, when not grounded in such a relationship, functions as a mask that hides an unsavory agenda. It is a force of manipulation that really seeks control and perversion under the guise of sexual seduction. Like the many examples of masculine evil in his fiction—the steady maintenance of dark secrets that connect Jack Torrance to Louis Creed, the obsessive power politics of Greg Stillson, or the spectral guest list animating the Overlook Hotel—King's characterizations of feminine evil are delineated by an absence of compassion and the urge to isolate and destroy. His mother figures, on the other hand, tend to represent a more nurturing collection of personalities.

Yet as many commentators have noted, there is certainly an ample array of negative mother figures throughout King's canon. The novel *IT,* for example, presents a nearly exhaustive club of mothers who either obsess neurotically about their sons or have abandoned them altogether. In either case, whether from excessive nurturing or from not enough, these women tend to thwart healthy masculine development in their offspring. Linda Anderson makes the point that the various mothers in *IT* not only fail to protect their children but are actually aligned with the monster that preys upon them: "It [the monster] is an objectification of the book's many monstrous mothers, who are powerful but un-nurturing" (120). In *Gerald's Game* (1992), Sally Mahout senses prophetically that there is an unnatural bond between her husband and daughter, saying "sometimes you behave as if she were your girlfriend instead of your daughter!" (144), but she does nothing to impede the progression toward father-daughter incest that occurs in this novel. In fact, the argument could be made that her deliberate physical withdrawal the day of the eclipse presents the opportunity for her husband to molest their daughter and perhaps represents her tacit surrender to the inevitability of the act. Similarly, the mothers in *Carrie* and *Hearts in Atlantis* have lost touch with the unifying bond that King feels should exist between mothers and their children. Interestingly, when a mother-child separation does occur in King's art, it is always the adult's fault—the result of some fundamental warping of the woman's personality due to mental illness, alcoholism, religious zealotry, or emotional indifference. As Gail Burns and Melinda Kanner insist, King's "mothers and maternal figures alike are very often the agents of destruction . . . at the mercy of their hormones, a force of nature that he links with the supernatural and which results in death rather than life" (159–160).

But not always. On several notable occasions, King's women show themselves to be as strong as the supernatural agents they encounter and stronger than the men with whom they associate. The moral centers of narratives such as *The Shining* (1977), *The Stand* (1978), *Cujo* (1981), *Dolores Claiborne,* and *Bag of Bones* (1998) revolve around the special relationship that exists between a mother and her child. King's "simple" American wives and mothers may not always emerge as paragons of radical feminist consciousness, but neither are they wholly simpering or passive. In a final analysis, the women characters, at least in the aforementioned texts, act in a manner that is more courageous than their husbands or mates. And in the last decade or so, Hollywood has provided a medium for portraying—and perhaps even advancing—this evolution of King's female characters.

Film critic Tony Williams posits that "the family is a crucial component in King's vision. His world depicts its dysfunctional and abusive nature" (238). This point is certainly aptly illustrated in Lewis Teague's film adaptation of *Cujo* (1983). Although the film centers its most impressive energies on the attack of a rabid St. Bernard and Donna Trenton's (Dee Wallace) efforts to defend herself and her son against the dog, several events before this attack anticipate and even parallel the masculine ferocity of Cujo's assault. Unhappily married to Vic Trenton (Daniel Hugh Kelly), who spends most of his life as a workaholic advertising executive, Donna feels abandoned by her husband and consequently embarks in an extramarital affair with Steve Kemp (Christopher Stone), a neighbor who does carpentry work for the Trentons. She eventually elects to end this extramarital relationship, but when her husband learns of her infidelity, he is uncertain about how to react. When he leaves town on an important business trip, Donna and her son, Tad (Danny Pintauro), drive the family's ailing Ford Pinto to Joe Camber's (Ed Lauter) home to get the car repaired. There, in the secluded Maine countryside, Donna and Tad encounter the Cambers' rabid dog, Cujo, which spends the remainder of the film trying to maul Donna and her son.

The St. Bernard's slow disintegration from trusted family pet to vicious fiend parallels the disintegration of the families featured in this film. At night young Tad Trenton is visited by a vague presence he is certain inhabits his closet. As the film unfolds, Tad's nocturnal monster reassembles in daylight—taking shape in Tad's mother's sexual infidelity, Steve Kemp's aggressive outbursts toward her, the consequent threat of Tad's parents' divorce, the void of his father's absence, and finally coalesces into the fury of Cujo's madness. As Cujo's rabid condition progresses, the individual features of the dog's face gradually disappear into an oozing mass of pus, blood, and foam. By the end of the film, the dog's head literally embodies the blackness inside of Tad's closet. Cujo emerges, as Robin Wood argues convincingly, as a great symbol of masculine aggression toward women and the domestic world itself. Teague is careful to depict this fury in Steve's misogynistic assault on Donna and the Trenton home when she elects to end their affair, in Vic Trenton's outrage when he discovers his wife's infidelity, and in Joe Camber's threatening attitude toward his own wife and son. The first two of Cujo's deadly attacks occur in a kitchen—the initial one against Gary Pervier (Mills Watson) and the second a few scenes later against his owner, Joe Camber, when Camber discovers

Gary's body. These two attacks sandwich the sequence where Steve Kemp assails Donna in her own kitchen. Kemp's aggression forces Donna to spill eggs, milk, and sugar on the floor, effectively illustrating the chaos and disruption he has brought to the Trentons' domestic sphere. Immediately after this altercation, both Tad and Donna's husband enter the kitchen. While cleaning up the mess, Donna is forced to acknowledge her affair to Vic, and this sets in motion the three-day encounter Donna will have with Cujo that will finally conclude with the shooting of the dog, which occurs in yet another kitchen.

Cujo's advanced illness also turns a sweet-tempered pet into a formidable foe. He demonstrates the degree of his raging madness when he attacks the car with his head or howls in pain on hearing the telephone ring, and yet, at the same time, he remains rational enough to stalk Donna with a patient and determined cunning. When Sheriff Bannerman's (Sandy Ward) police cruiser approaches the Cambers' driveway, Cujo knows enough to hide so that his attack will be a surprise. Perhaps what is most impressive about the rabid Cujo is what links him to the traditional gothic monster: The dog is at once both irrational and cunning, producing random violent outbursts that are effectively planned and executed. This subtle blending of masculine violence and omnipresent survival skills effectively links Cujo with the film's human males. Both Donna's husband and her lover barely control—and often fail to control—their rage to punish Donna for decisions she makes. Just as Cujo views her as an object to be dominated, the human men in her life demand her compliance to their wills. They remain both uninterested and unaffected by what she wants out of life, refusing to engage her in dialogue whenever she changes her mind about the status of her relationships with them. Cujo at least has the excuse of rabies; Vic and Steve suffer only from the disease of rabid egotism.

When Teague was asked to direct *Cujo*, his initial reaction was unfavorable: "I wanted to do something more ambitious. But when I read the book, I got very excited about the dynamics of the family—they were completely plagued by their fears. Cujo was only part of the story" (Horsting 42). Since the movie's central theme is the essential inability of men and women to coexist harmoniously, Cujo's attack on Donna and Tad Trenton—a brutal three-day ordeal that is rendered in graphic detailing that often resembles a rape—represents a climax to the sexual tensions associated with all the film's impaired male-female interactions. Similarly, the film's secondary emphasis on the Camber relationship should be seen as an exaggerated dark mirror to the Trentons' marriage. When the severely oppressed Charity Camber (Kaiulani Lee) prepares to take her son on a rare trip to visit her sister, she has to cajole her abusive and alcoholic husband into accepting the lottery money she has recently won in exchange for his permission to make the trip. Once it is granted, the audience watches her pack a photo album so discreetly that we get the distinct impression she has no intention of returning. Indeed, when her son reports that Cujo is showing signs of being rabid, Mrs. Camber insists that Joe Camber not be informed, as this may jeopardize their escape. That Charity Camber consciously allows a rabid two-hundred-pound dog to roam free is an indication of how desperate her life and marriage have become. Donna Trenton is far better off than Charity Cambers, both financially and in the degree of personal freedom she exercises in her marriage. Yet, as Douglas Winter points out in "The Night Journeys of Stephen King," *Cujo's* "storyline evolves about two marriages," and both of these "marriages are in jeopardy" (245). King's novel parallels these two relationships more thoroughly than does Teague's film, but the latter still manages effectively to convey the sense of marital desperation that both wives experience and, even more important, to suggest that both Donna and Charity are fully capable of establishing control over their lives.

The film opens in a bucolic setting as the camera follows a rabbit running across an open meadow on a lovely summer afternoon accompanied by the innocuous strings of violin music. This setting abruptly darkens when the camera swivels to reveal the rabbit framed through the muscled legs of Cujo, shot from a close-to-the-ground angle that serves to emphasize the dog's formidable mass and weight as well as the rabbit's vulnerability. The dog immediately begins to chase the rabbit (half threateningly, half in play). But the movie's introductory atmosphere of sweetness and light completely disappears when the rabbit leads the dog into a dark burrow where his head is then entrapped. Cujo's panicked barking awakens a group of bats inhabiting the burrow, and one bites the dog mercilessly on the nose, thereby inflicting the rabies virus. After this opening sequence, the camera cuts immediately to Tad Trenton's well-lighted, spacious, and neatly furnished bedroom. As the child prepares for bed, turning out the lights in his room and huddling apprehensively under the covers, a dark closet in the corner of the room comes to life. As in the opening of the film, where Cujo's lighthearted romp with the rabbit in pastoral nature ends abruptly in the dark mouth of a bat's bite, the suburban security of Tad's bedroom is ultimately threatened by the open maw of his closet. In both sequences, child and dog—who will soon meet one another in their own danse macabre—conclude their respective opening scenes in screams of fear and pain. The sweet appearances of nature's innocent calm and the domestic protection purchased through affluence are displaced by an unknown terror.

Michael Collings further notes the film's propensity for contrasting imagery in the scene in which Donna and Tad are trapped inside their car with the windows raised. "We see the characters through their car windows; yet those same windows simultaneously reflect an alternate world of pastoral-seeming trees. What is in fact an epitome of terror is screened by an illusion of peaceful, pastoral nature" (85). This is an excellent observation, but *every* sense of a "peaceful, pastoral nature" in this film is a screened illusion. The pastoral nature surrounding the Camber house stands indifferent to the plight of Donna and Tad; it is devoid of any human presence. We also know that Cujo contracted rabies in these woods, and that he now returns to them as a place to hide from his human foe and as a place from which to launch his surprise assaults. In short, all of nature appears pitted against the Trentons and thus in league with the rabid Cujo—from the hot sun that bakes them during relentless summer afternoons to the woods that are reflected darkly in their car windows.

All through the first half of the film Teague performs a similar job of setting up a series of ironic contrasts between appearances and actuality, light and dark. And these contrasts underscore the unstable nature of reality, as families are revealed riddled with duplicity and violence, the friendly affect of a good-natured carpenter is a guise for coveting his neighbor's wife, and monsters are not so easily contained in reality as they are in language. Tad's father keeps reminding the boy "Nothing will hurt Tad here. . . . There's no such thing as real monsters. Only in stories." His reassuring—albeit ultimately empty—words echo the sophomoric pronouncements issued from the Sharp professor Vic has invented to as an advertising ploy to sell cereal. And just as the advertising slogan—"Nothing wrong here"—turns into a public relations disaster when people begin to get sick from the breakfast food, Vic's confident sense of masculine control over his wife, his career, his cant assurances to his son, his language, and the world around him creates a false level of complacency that the film systematically exploits and undermines.

Donna Trenton's perceptions, on the other hand, are always more trenchant than her husband's. Perhaps because of the insight into her own heart of darkness that she has obtained as a result of her illicit affair, Donna possesses an intimate understanding of human frailty and the various disguises of false innocence. When she first spots Cujo cresting a hill on the Camber property, her instinctive reaction is to grab her son and run in terror. While the Camber family assures her that the dog is harmless and "loves kids," Donna's maternal instincts never permit her to indulge the superficial security of her husband; instead, her attention is drawn compulsively to the nasty red bite festering on Cujo's snout.

Although Donna must struggle in the absence of a supportive husband and from within the shadow of an abusive illicit lover, her unselfish commitment to her son never wavers. She surely bears a portion of responsibility for the erosion of her marriage; she has been neither a faithful nor a forthright wife. But most of the film shows her trying to recover her domestic balance by doing the right thing and ending her extramarital affair. And as a mother, her greatest personal virtues emerge unqualified and triumphant. In spite of the intensity of Cujo's assault upon her son and car, she never panics. Instead, she comforts her hysterical child while maintaining her own composure in the face of Cujo's increasing monstrosity. From the onset of the dog's attack Donna reveals her resourcefulness—rolling up the car's window to thwart Cujo's surprise assault and then blowing the horn to frighten the dog when he climbs atop the car's hood. Three days later, wounded and exhausted, she emerges from her battered Ford Pinto as nothing less than an Amazon warrior, first equaling Cujo's ferocity in defending herself with a baseball bat and later shooting the dog when it bursts through the kitchen window. She literally wills her son back to life by performing CPR on the Cambers' kitchen table. It is also impressive that she performs all these feats while wearing a pair of high-heeled sling-back shoes. When Donna opens the door of the Pinto for the last time, it is no longer as a passive victim of Cujo's rage and insanity. All through this movie Donna has been victimized by male rage, which she meekly accepts as punishment for straying beyond the perimeters of her marriage. By the picture's conclusion, however, Donna has paid whatever dues she needs to pay, and she is no longer the same woman who began this film; her ordeals have toughened her. She emerges instead as a proactive defender of (her son's) life. When Cujo confronts this version of Donna, brandishing the baseball bat and challenging the beast to "come on," the dog is at first stunned to the point where he actually backs away in fear.

Donna Trenton is motivated not so much by self-preservation as by a mother's awareness that her son is dying of dehydration; "I'm losing my baby" becomes her clarion call to action. It is absolutely imperative to note that in this film, Cujo ends up killing three healthy adult males, and that Vic Trenton arrives on the scene too late to help his wife in her battle against the rabid dog. In King's 1981 novel, a less hopeful and more deterministic narrative than Teague's adaptation, Donna fails to save her son; Tad dies of dehydration while she remains helpless to act until it is too late. In the film, it is significant that she saves the child and the manner in which she does so. For in the screenplay, written by Don Carlos Dunaway and Lauren Currier, Donna defies the stereotypical Hollywood formula of the besieged female as an object of terror, the victim who is forever at the mercy of the genre's seductive monsters and psychopathic villains.

In most horror films and psychological thrillers, the heroine usually finds herself entrapped—often bound and gagged, or at least held captive in some imposed configuration or environment—where she remains passively confined, forced to await rescue from a heroic male. The way Donna is dressed on the afternoon her siege begins, in a flowing skirt and high-heeled shoes, signals her initial vulnerability as well as her nexus to traditional femininity. Trapped inside the Pinto, which becomes for Carol Senf "a symbol of her entire life as a dependent, Donna slowly begins to take control of her life" ("Donna Trenton" 97). At first, she expects to be rescued—by Joe Camber, by her husband, by the mailman when he delivers mail to the house—but she gradually comes to realize that none of these males will be forthcoming. If she is to be rescued, Donna will have to effect her own salvation; she and her son survive not because of the timely intrusion of a male but as a result of a lone mother's bravery and self-reliance. Senf concludes that Donna is "a new kind of heroine," not only in Stephen King's world but also for the larger culture, as she learns to accept responsibility for her own life while "abandoning the notion that the heroine is someone who needs to be rescued" ("Donna Trenton" 97, 91). Additionally, Donna's emergence as a heroine appropriates the terms and intensity of male fury; what has been done to her, she now does to Cujo. Like the battered Pinto that nonetheless manages to survive Cujo's relentless assault, Donna wins her family's reunion through her ability to endure, protect, and defend. It is important to point out that during her battle royal against Cujo, one of Donna's high heels breaks off. This becomes a symbol for the internal change in feminine status that occurs to her character: In the course of her ordeal, Donna progresses from an embodiment of the archetypical gothic maiden—a trapped and passive victim of forces beyond her control—to an emerging heroine who appropriates the phallic imagery of masculine power (a baseball bat and a pistol) and uses it to defend herself and her child. By the end of *Cujo,* Donna comes to resemble more the bandaged and muscular, zealously driven mother-warrior, Sarah Connor (Linda Hamilton) in *Terminator 2: Judgment Day,* than the cringing and weepy suburban housewife who left home to get her car fixed.

Indeed, Donna Trenton emerges as a version of Carol Clover's conception of the Final Girl, the sole female survivor in many modern horror films who "becomes her own savior" (60). Gendered female, the Final Girl combines the functions of suffering victim and avenging hero. Like Donna, she appropriates the phallic symbols of the male killer, and in the course of her struggle to stay alive she finds the strength to "stop screaming, face the killer, reach for a weapon, and address the monster on his own terms" (48). Clover does not include a specific analysis of Donna Trenton as a prototypical Final Girl, an odd oversight given the fact that *Cujo* merely features a canine stalker instead of a human one. Released in 1983 at the height of a generation of horror films that provoke Clover's interest, Teague's film includes a female heroine that conforms almost exactly to the definition of a Final Girl, even to the point where the audience "cheers the survivor on as she assaults the killer" (23).

Trying to generalize about Stephen King's career as a writer is a daunting task. Nevertheless, for the sake of this analysis, King's extensive canon can be divided roughly in half, since the books prior to *Misery* constitute the first part of his career, while those that follow tend to reflect a markedly different set of priorities for the writer and, in turn, those who have adapted King's work into film and televised miniseries. King's inaugural fifteen years of publications produced novels such as *The Shining, The Stand, Firestarter,* and *IT.* These are fictions that present a macrocosmic view of postmodern America, providing the reader with a journey to the center of a post-Watergate heart of darkness. These texts are further linked because they are rendered from a tremendous narratological range and vision; King's epic propensities are never stronger evinced than in *The Stand, The Talisman,* and *IT,* books that weave a vast historical, mythological, and social matrix into extended journey quests.

In contrast to this macrocosmic examination of America frequently considered from the off-ramps of its interstate highway system, *Misery* and the novels that follow it show evidence of King's ability to produce highly circumscribed, tightly wrought fictions bearing few of his epic tendencies toward narrative and thematic expansiveness. If *The Shining* and *The Stand* can be likened to an epic saga played out on a big screen to accommodate their involvement with exotic and dangerous voyages to strange places and complex societal reconfigurations, then books such as *Misery* and *Gerald's Game* are more like classical Greek drama presented on a circumscribed stage, employing a consistent scenic backdrop and a small cast of characters, and performed in front of an intimate theater audience.

Furthermore, King's writing in the 1990s, in addition to being generally more compact, also tends to include a more realistic treatment of women. The novels *Gerald's Game, Dolores Claiborne,* and *Rose Madder* (1995)—a trio that should be considered together because the narratives share similar themes and were written and published consecutively—differ markedly from King's previous fiction. Feminist in orientation, the novels present most of the action from a woman's point of view. If the first half of King's literary canon can be generalized as a potent rendition of Everyman wandering amid the expansive wastelands of a postapocalyptic America, the second half of this body of work has tended to focus on representations of the American Everywoman and her disgruntled home life.

In their introduction to the unfortunately titled collection of essays *Imagining the Worst: Stephen King and the Representation of Women,* editors Kathleen Margaret Lant and Theresa Thompson write that the writer's female characters "often provoke hostility as well as admiration. When analyzing King's depiction of women, it is tempting to relegate him to the category of unregenerate misogynist or conversely to elevate him to the status of newly sensitive male" (4). This patronizing and unfairly negative evaluation notwithstanding, Lant and Thompson are correct in noting that the more women-centered novels published in the 1990s are a clear departure from King's earlier portraits of women. These later books likewise represented a substantial risk in potentially alienating King's popular readership. After his first two decades of writing, his loyal audience had come to expect tales of supernatural horror and epic fantasy rather than reality-based stories depicting the horror of domestic dysfunction. The publication of *Misery* must be viewed as a harbinger of change in King's career, as the novel signaled a new focus on "mainstream" subject matter—domestic and gender issues. At least in terms of market sales figures, this emphasis change helps to explain the minor erosion of King's established reputation as a mega-seller, since books that follow *Misery* generally remained on the *New York Times* Bestseller List only half as long as those published prior to it (Carvajal 1, 8). Yet, ironically, during this period his audience base did not enlarge to the point where his more female-centered work was included (as it legitimately should be) on the syllabi of women's studies curricula.

Misery thus holds a pivotal position in Stephen King's canon; the novel marks a transition that begins to emphasize a new significance for women characters. In *Misery,* the reader encounters one of King's first attempts to create a fiercely independent woman who is neither madonna nor whore. Unlike *Cujo*'s Donna Trenton, who moves from passive victim to active heroine only when her son's life is endangered, Annie Wilkes is one of the few women in Stephen King's fiction who wields real power all of the time, even if she ultimately fails to exercise it reasonably. Although the novel is not a feminist text, as it remains mired in the destructive, potentially castrating nature of women, its female character is a prototype— at least in terms of her strength, intelligence, and angry resolve—for King's feminist protagonists who follow her in a series of heroine-centered books published during the 1990s. Moreover, if Annie Wilkes can be seen as a marker on King's road to producing women who demand to be taken more seriously, then the efforts of Paul Sheldon, the novel's protagonist, to write a serious narrative should be viewed as a kind of autobiographical reference point for King's own authorial rebellion to expand beyond the horror genre in which he himself had been typecast.

Rob Reiner's 1990 film adaptation of *Misery* parallels King's novel quite closely, although the film presents a "lighter" version of the plot. For example, in the novel Paul is severely addicted to Novril, a pain medication, while the film shows him much less dependent on it (on at least two occasions he feigns his need for a dose to cover his escape attempts). Further, throughout the book Sheldon appears in a more perilous situation than in the movie; it is not so much escape that he contemplates as suicide. His despair is a large element of the novel, whereas in the movie Paul Sheldon (James Caan) is always thinking of ways to save himself and solicit rescue. Perhaps an explanation for this is in the dual portrayals of Annie herself: The cinematic Annie Wilkes (Kathy Bates) is less sadistic and violent than King's version. In the film, she hobbles Paul by breaking his ankles; in the book, she amputates his foot and then cauterizes the wound with a blowtorch. While Reiner's direction and Goldman's screenplay sought to soften King's portrait of Annie, their efforts are also a reflection of Hollywood's desire to tone down her character—the movie institution's belief that all women must be reigned in to a point, even the unstable ones. Finally, in Reiner's film there is the addition of Sheriff "Buster" McCain (Richard Farnsworth) and his wife, Virginia (Frances Sternhagen), who are both missing from King's text. Their presence serves once more to lighten the darkness of Paul's entrapment by providing a measure of comic relief for the audience, as the older married couple poses an amusing counterpoint to the intensely serious relationship that is forged between Annie and Paul. When we encounter a long scene featuring Paul inside his bedroom or witness a specifically terrifying moment between Annie and Paul, the sheriff and his wife often appear in the next sequence to provide a comic and less oppressive view of reality. Their inclusion in the film contrasts sharply with the relentless claustrophobic perspective afforded the reader of King's novel, where Annie is not only Paul's jailer, she is also his sole connection to the rest of the world.

Paul Sheldon is a highly successful romance novelist whose fortune and fame is the result of a series of novels featuring a plucky heroine named Misery Chastain. Although these books have proven highly successful, Paul views himself as a "serious" writer capable of producing better work. His most recent manuscript, which he has just finished writing when the film commences, is a complete departure from the romance genre. Before Paul can deliver the book to his publisher, however, his car slides off the road during a blinding snowstorm. Rescued from certain death by Annie Wilkes, an unemployed professional nurse (an occupation that is normally nurturing and healing) who is also Sheldon's "number one fan" as well as a psychopathic killer, Sheldon spends the winter recovering in her secluded Colorado farmhouse. He learns quickly that under Wilkes's care his life is still very much in jeopardy; his broken legs (the result of the car accident) make him captive to her capricious whims and wishes. Although he is proud of his new novel, Annie declares it obscene, and she insists that Paul burn the only copy of the manuscript. This is the first in a series of fascinating albeit paradoxical behaviors that highlight Annie's mental illness: She judges Paul's writing objectionable when it employs language or moments that deviate from the strict standards of the romance genre, yet she cannot recognize her own obscenity in committing against her guest various acts of increasing cruelty and humiliation when he has displeased her; she is a professional nurse whose duties have included murdering former patients, especially infants, when she deems it appropriate; she is a hard-edged survivalist who passionately identifies with an extremely vulnerable and feminine romance heroine.

Through a combination of drugs, threats, and violent acts against him (including the breaking of his ankles), Annie forces Paul to spend his recuperation writing one last Misery Chastain novel. King's novel contains whole sections of this work in progress—which make for a mesmerizing metatextual parallel to Paul's own plight—but Reiner's film unfortunately only alludes to selected passages and plot lines that Annie reads aloud. Sheldon is initially reluctant to write this new book, but he learns that his survival is linked to his writing: As long as he can keep Annie interested in the evolving narrative, she will keep him alive. At the conclusion of the film, Sheldon tricks her by pretending to burn his story's conclusion before she learns how the book is ultimately resolved, an ironic payback for her destruction of his other novel. The now partially recuperated writer is able to overpower Annie physically because she is so distracted by the burning pages. But Sheldon's real strength proves ultimately to be less physical than psychological: His abilities as a storyteller buy him time to heal his broken body and devise a plan to free himself from Annie's tyranny.

Annie emerges in this film as a kind of country vampire: She sucks out Paul's inspiration and creativity in order to fashion a self-enclosed world. Just as her rural farmhouse, complete with its empty telephone shell and other warped attempts to disguise her abnormality, mirrors her paranoid mental condition, she means to have her favorite author create a fictional realm exactly to her specifications. She remains a demanding editor who "expects nothing less than [Paul's] masterpiece." Whenever the writer fails to satisfy her insistence on narratological plausibility, he is severely chastised; on the other hand, Misery's newest entanglements fill Annie with profound delight. In short, as long as Paul satisfies Annie's demands as a reader, she exercises restraint over her sadistic tendencies. She is the reader-response critic pushed to its ultimate extreme.

The film's plot reflects the spirit of its historical time by inverting the gothic male villain/besieged maiden prototype: The story's female character is no longer a passive victim but rather the agenda-setter. Annie Wilkes may be viewed as an unfortunate victim of her own mental illness, as she exhibits nearly textbook symptoms of a manic-depressive personality. Yet she is also a victimizer. Like the masculine rogues and rakes that precede her in the tradition of the eighteenth- and nineteenth-century gothic romance, Annie is a version of the gothic villain-monster, and her aggressive impulses are frequently identified with masculine images of rape, as when she forces her captive to swallow pain medications that she inserts forcibly into his mouth or on the two occasions when she injects him with a powerful sedative to ensure his compliance to her will. Conversely, Paul is placed into the role of the traditional romance heroine: Kidnapped and held against his volition, bound to his bed, trying desperately to use language that will placate his tormentor and save his life, profoundly aware of his utter dependency on Annie for food and medications, and terrified as he anticipates the next torment devised by his sadistic captor.

Annie's role as gothic sociopath is strengthened by the manner in which the camera observes her in various scenes. Often in the film Annie is framed in front of the door to Paul's bedroom; she appears "boxed in," barely able to contain her fury at the same time as she stands as the impediment to Paul's escape and the outside world. Or just as often the audience views her face against a black background, the camera focusing on her in an upward diagonal angle, essentially duplicating the perspective from Paul's prone or wheelchair-bound point of view. In these scenes, the camera moves upward and ever closer to reveal the distortions of her face. For example, after Annie has read the part in Paul's new novel where Misery dies, she enters Paul's bedroom unseen, presumably in the middle of the night, while a thunderstorm rages outside. Like Paul, we feel her presence before we actually see her. As Annie rants against Paul's "murdering" Misery, moving toward his bed, half of her face disappears into the dark shadows that fill the bedroom. The scene highlights her role as a horror monster, the terror she invokes all the more intense because her body and head fragment into the shadows of the bedroom even as her rage is being unleashed and fills up the room. The camera, therefore, helps contribute to the intrusive and violating presence associated with Annie's character. Moreover, throughout the film the camera's angle and perspective is almost exclusively Paul's, cementing the audience's identification with his victimization while distancing us from Annie herself. This is another element that distinguishes this film from a woman-centered or feminist orientation; if it took such a view, we would be getting at least some of the angles from Annie's point of view.

Aware that her authority is in constant jeopardy—from the police and from Paul himself as he regains his strength to rebel against her (Annie tells Paul: "You'll never know what it's like for someone like me to love someone like you.")—Annie's every action reflects her need for domination. And to this perversely independent end, she is willing to sacrifice everything: The farm and its animals, the officious local sheriff who comes in search of Sheldon, whatever is left of her nursing ethics, Paul himself, and, eventually, even her own life. The audience is led to identify wholly with Sheldon's desperate plight throughout, but both the viewers and Paul learn to respect Annie for her cunning intelligence and resolute commitment to having her will carried out. And certainly, at least some women who watch this film must feel some degree of poetic justice in *Misery*'s gender role reversal: Watching a kidnapped, helpless male forced to obey the imperious and capricious commands of a strong-willed female captor.

In the end, however, Annie is more dominatrix than feminist, and perhaps this explains why her reaction to Misery Chastain remains so puzzling. Paul's plight links him unequivocally to his intrepid heroine in this film, but any effort to explore Annie's personality must likewise address her intense identification with this fictional character. For Misery— the lovely, highly feminized romantic heroine—is, at least superficially, an oppositional personality to Annie Wilkes. Annie may be attracted to the literary character precisely because of their differences, as Misery is capable of helping her to "forget about the world." The romance genre, appealing to an almost exclusively female audience, requires its authors to adhere to several rigidly encoded rules. Among them are that: The sex be titillating, but not graphic; the identities of the heroine and hero be clearly and morally demarcated; whatever perils befall the main characters, a happy ending still ensues in the heterosexual celebration of heroine and hero united. While Annie lives alone and inhabits a world where she often feels compelled to run away during bouts of depression, Misery lives in a world where at least things make sense, even when she is pursued by unscrupulous villains or confronted with overly dramatic situations and challenges. With her many male suitors and feminine wiles, Misery emerges as Annie's feminine alter ego—the woman Annie fantasizes herself to be at points with Paul, as in the scene where they share a candlelit dinner together or when she blows him a kiss as she exits his bedroom to play Liberace records. But another way to interpret Annie's obsession with Misery is that the character is also an extremely resourceful female personality who, while often placed in difficult situations, always manages to find a way out. Both Annie and Misery are like the characters in the chapter plays (or cliffhanger films) that Annie refers to from her childhood: They are both survivors. Just as Misery always finds a way to circumvent disaster or death, while Nurse Wilkes may be linked to the mysterious deaths of her hospital patients, she is never actually convicted of their murders.

Annie Wilkes begins the film in a highly stylized maternal role: Dressed in loosely flowing, earth-toned housedresses, gently stroking Paul's writing ego, nursing him back to health by tending to his bedside needs, even feeding and shaving him until his broken arm heals. Close to the conclusion of the film, after Annie has tortured and humiliated Paul during the course of his winter incarceration, she still insists on viewing herself in distinctly maternal terms. She chastises Paul as a wayward child who has failed to appreciate the sacrifices made by his parent: "I don't think I'll ever understand you. I cook your meals. I tend to you practically twenty-four hours a day. And you continue to fight me. When are we going to develop a sense of trust?" Although these lines strike the audience as ridiculous, given the fact that Annie herself has consistently undermined any "sense of trust" in this relationship, she is completely unconscious of their inherent irony. She loves Paul and wants only that he should love her back. Thus, even on those occasions when she must resort to physical violence against him, Annie justifies each act as serving the greater purpose of guiding Paul in the direction of her love.

When the two are first brought together, Annie is highly solicitous of Paul, genuflecting at the altar of his fame and talent. Her mood darkens, however, when she reads his new manuscript and objects to its level of profanity. In a very real way, Paul's writing is the only thing Annie and he ever share in common, and it is therefore appropriate that her mood swings are frequently tied to his writing. When he frustrates her by failing to perform this task to her liking—as with the untitled new manuscript or when he tries to "cheat" the reader by resurrecting Misery in an unrealistic fashion—Annie punishes him severely. Paul does not view himself as Annie does; the new novel is an attempt to prove to himself that he is a "real" writer instead of just a hack. Although his literary agent (Lauren Bacall) reminds him that "Misery put braces on [his] daughter's teeth and is putting her through college," Paul is embarrassed by what he has become, for he feels his talents have been prostituted in the writing of eight Misery novels. Typecast into a genre that has made him wealthy and famous, he feels a captive to its form and to his audience. As the film unfolds, Annie's initial sense of awe degenerates into a less-than-respectful attitude toward her favorite writer. Conversely, in writing for his life, Paul is forced into a position where for the first time he can begin to appreciate the skills he does possess. While Annie gradually demystifies his godliness, Paul gains a healthy insight and level of respect for the writer in himself— even the writer of romances—which he has doubted as a result of his popular acclaim. Like Rocket Man who cheats his audience in Annie's recollected chapter play, Paul believed he had been cheating his fans as well as himself. But his ordeal with Annie brings him to a deeper—more humble—awareness of his craft. Misery's character not only educates his daughter, she also educates Paul.

Although he will probably never walk normally again, having been crippled permanently by both the accident and Annie's efforts to hobble him, Paul emerges from his experience a more complete human being than when he began it. Before his enforced recuperation at Annie's farmhouse, Paul appears to have had much in common with Harry in Ernest Hemingway's short story "The Snows of Kilamanjaro." Like Harry, Paul has not been true to his literary craft; he has not lived up to his potential as a writer or as a human being. He sold out his talents as an artist for the commercial success of the *Misery* series just as Harry has abandoned his own writing after marrying a woman with money. But it is significant that Paul Sheldon survives while Harry dies a slow and painful death from gangrene.

The film documents Sheldon's subtle transformations as a writer and a human being. Nearly his last words in the movie are a self-acknowledgment of the bizarre debt he owes to Annie: "In some way, Annie Wilkes, that whole experience, helped me." His agent may be baffled by such a pronouncement, but "that whole experience" has taught Sheldon a deeper respect for the literary craft he had formerly taken for granted in viewing it solely as a meal ticket. He has also become a better "reader" through the act of writing *Misery's Return*. Paul learns to "read" Annie's moods, to provide the appropriate reaction to a given situation, and her many brutal lessons in humility teach him to moderate his temper and language. The discipline he has cultivated as a writer enables him to restrain himself from lashing out at Annie or making any attempt to overpower her physically (thus avoiding further punishments) until he is in a position to do so successfully. In contrast to Annie's volatility, Paul's self-control keeps him focused on survival and life. Annie loses final control over an environment that began to change the afternoon she presented Sheldon with a typewriter and the challenge to resurrect Misery. It is only slightly ironic that this same typewriter should become one of the weapons (the other an iron doorstop replica of the pig Annie has named "Misery") that bring about Annie's death when Paul hits her with it. The old Royal machine with its missing "N" key not only buys him time in his life-and-death struggle with Annie, it also aids him in regaining his physical strength, as on several occasions the audience sees him use it secretly as a conditioning tool by lifting it up and down. The typewriter functions as the symbolic instrument for both his mental and physical rejuvenation. It is therefore no mere coincidence that eighteen months after escaping Annie Wilkes the novel Paul Sheldon publishes is entitled *The Higher Education of J. Philip Stone*. Although the film tells us nothing about the contents of this new book, the words "higher education" in its title are suggestive of a unique learning experience that transcends conventional schooling and expectations.

Like many of the child savants discussed in the preceding chapter, King's writer-protagonists are similarly endowed with tremendous imaginative capacities. Indeed, King's writers often share much in common with his children; certainly both are far removed from the realm of adulthood by virtue of their relative independence and romantic optimism. Ben Mears in *'Salem's Lot* (1975), Gordie Lachance in *Stand by Me*, Bill Denbrough in *IT*, Paul Sheldon in *Misery*, Thad Beaumont in *The Dark Half* (1989), and Mike Noonan in *Bag of Bones* all share the writer's job to reassert order in the midst of madness and destruction. While these individuals may not possess the supernatural powers often identified with King's children, their powers are nonetheless considerable. In the interview published in *Stephen King: The Second Decade*, King reminded me of the omnipresence of writers throughout his own fictional canon and the important roles they frequently play: "I've written so much myself that writing has become a vital part of my life. It's the biggest figure in my landscape, the analogue of the statue of the Bourka Bee goddess in *Misery*. Wherever you go in my little part of landscape, the writer is always there, looking back at the reader. . . . [Writers] do have powers. [They] are the only recognized mediums of our society" (11).

Without his craft, Paul Sheldon could not have survived his sentence as a prisoner in Annie Wilkes's haunted farmhouse; similarly, novelist Ben Mears is one of the few inhabitants of 'Salem's Lot with the childlike conduit to his imagination still open enough to believe in the reality of vampires—and thereby in his ability to destroy them.

The vast majority of writers in Stephen King's universe are male. The only notable exception is Jessie Burlingame in the novel *Gerald's Game*, a book that begins in King's typical third-person narration but concludes in a long first-person letter that Jessie writes to her friend Ruth Neary. This is a significant signal to readers, since Jessie's new role as a writer—telling her own story in her own voice and through her own words—is indicative of an emerging unified selfhood and the continuing process of her rehabilitation. As a writer, Jessie is linked to the many other authors who populate the fictional and cinemagraphic landscapes of Stephen King—all of whom are invariably invested with impressive powers of self-understanding, imagination, and even magic—and all of whom are invariably male. In "The Rape of Constant Reader: Stephen King's Construction of the Female Reader and Violation of the Female Body in *Misery*," feminist critic Kathleen Margaret Lant has noted this gendered exclusivity and interprets it in explicitly sexual terms: "In *Misery*, creativity is solely a masculine prerogative, for the artist is male, and both the reader and the character/antagonist—made one in Paul Sheldon's vicious and dangerous fan Annie Wilkes—are female. The artist's power, moreover, is conveyed in terms of his sexuality; as a sexually potent male, Paul Sheldon is creative" (93).

Lant's provocative insight may well be applied to other King novels and films where the masculine hero is likewise a writer. But what of those narratives, however few, where a woman is in control, occupying the role of the central protagonist? Since women are typically not creative artists in King's world, what powers belong to them, and where do these powers come from?

Misery and *Dolores Claiborne* might be viewed as domestic bookends: Both films are intense explorations of gendered psychological relationships. If *Misery* is a portrait of a cannibalizing matriarchy, then *Dolores Claiborne* "balances" the misogyny implicit in *Misery,* revisiting its themes of gender antagonism and domestic abuse, but this time considering both topics from a point of view more sympathetic to women. Dolores Claiborne is, finally, the most feminist of King's heroines; she concentrates on saving herself and saving her child instead of waiting to be saved by some outside agency.

Kathy Bates is superbly cast in both roles as Annie Wilkes and Dolores Claiborne. She has emerged as arguably the ultimate female lead in films made from Stephen King's fiction. It was therefore not surprising that Bates was one of the selected actors included on the exclusive guest list for the 1999 party held at Manhattan's Tavern on the Green that King hosted to commemorate twenty-five years as a novelist and freelance writer. Bates won the Best Actress Oscar for her role in *Misery* but was passed over by the Academy for her equally demanding characterization of Dolores Claiborne. This is an unfortunate oversight for many reasons, not the least being that the two characters share great similarities. They are, for a start, both stubborn and cantankerous individualists. Annie's fierce resolve, however, is fueled by her aggressive sociopathology, while Dolores remains a much more humane mix; her hard edges reveal themselves to be necessary defenses against a threatening and gender-biased world. The violence that Dolores commits is out of an effort to protect her daughter, Selena (Ellen Muth/Jennifer Jason Leigh), who is a victim of sexual abuse by her father, Joe St. George (David Strathairn). While Annie's behavior is always capriciously stimulated by her psychological instability, Claiborne emerges as a long-suffering and unselfish woman who does her best to keep her family together and pursues violent action only as a last resort and as a final way to liberate both herself and her daughter from her husband's tyranny. Both Annie and Dolores are victims of a cruel fate, but whereas Annie remains forever its victim, Dolores acts to change the destinies of herself and her daughter. The two characters certainly emerge as two of the strongest women portrayed in the films of Stephen King. Claiborne's identity, however, is always inseparable from her role as mother, while Wilkes lacks this defining principle. In fact, I do not believe it is too far an interpretative reach to suggest that King views Annie's single-woman lifestyle as a source for her psychopathology. As a woman without children, her maternal instincts, as we have already seen, manifest themselves in distorted forms. She resembles most the dark mothers in *IT:* Compulsion replaces nurturance, the need for her will to be obeyed replaces respect for the individuals under her care. In short, Annie

Wilkes is an unmoored being, bereft of the social and familial bonds critical to making life meaningful for the majority of King's adult females. As Mary Pharr reminds us in the beginning of this chapter, motherhood is often a stabilizing force in King's universe, while single women appear susceptible to all the corrupting forces that define his portraits of both female and male self-absorption.

Dolores Claiborne begins with its protagonist charged with the murder of her employer, Vera Donovan (Judy Parfitt). When the film opens, the audience sees only the moment of Vera's death, where it appears that Dolores is about to hit her with a rolling pin. Later on, we learn through a revealing flashback that the invalid Vera wishes to commit suicide and has deliberately thrown herself down a flight a stairs. When Dolores finds her crumpled at the base of the stairs, Vera begs her maid (and, as we learn later, her best friend) to finish the job.

After she is arraigned for murder at Little Tall Island's Town Hall, Dolores is reunited with her daughter, Selena St. George, who is now a magazine reporter living in New York City. The detective in charge of the investigation, John Mackey (Christopher Plummer), summons Selena back to her Maine hometown with a newspaper clipping describing Vera's death and Claiborne's arraignment. Foiled in his efforts to convict Dolores in the murder of her husband years earlier, Mackey takes the Donovan case personally, insisting that this time he will not "underestimate" Dolores. Mother and daughter have not seen one another for fifteen years. Much of the rest of the film is an exploration of their estrangement. Selena's memories of her childhood are partial at best. She recalls her mother's acts of violence against her father but has completely repressed any understanding of why her mother behaved in such a manner. Selena also believes that her mother caused her father's "accidental" death when he fell into the shaft of an abandoned well. As Selena reveals her incomplete and flawed understanding of the past, Dolores sets about trying to fill in her daughter's memory gaps. Dolores and the audience learn together that Selena has, with the help of powerful prescription medications, alcohol, and physical distance from Maine, repressed her recollection of Joe St. George's incestual molestation during her adolescence. Dolores forces her to revisit this experience, and although she tries to deny its veracity, Selena comes to a startling epiphany on a ferry taking her away from the island when she revisits a scene of her own molestation. Instead of continuing her flight from both her past and her mother, Selena returns to attend the murder investigation's preliminary hearing and argues convincingly against the report submitted by Detective Mackey. The ending of the film thereby reverses its central plot: Daughter must act to protect her mother who is now the one being victimized by an obsessively aggressive male.

King's novel is a first-person narrative rendered exclusively from Dolores Claiborne's point of view (purportedly it is the written transcript of the title character's confession recited into a tape recorder). Dolores begins the novel by saying she remains uncertain as to how to go about telling it, "back to front or front to back" (4). She compromises by beginning in the middle and working both ways, moving freely back and forth in time. Like the novel, Taylor Hackford's film begins with Dolores being arraigned for Vera Donovan's murder, but unlike the King text, which maintains Dolores's monologue throughout, Selena's character in the film emerges as an active participant in the story's exposition as well as in her mother's legal defense. In King's book, Dolores is the mother of two other children in addition to Selena, and has yet to explain her complete history to any of her offspring. The novel ends at the point where Dolores is preparing a Christmas celebration for her son, Joe Junior, and his family, who will be joined by Selena. Thus, Hackford's direction and Tony Gilroy's screenplay essentially *begin* at the point where King's narrative *concludes*—with Selena's reunion with her mother. In this way, the novel and film emerge as uniquely separate entities, two widely varying renditions of the exact same history.

The movie elects to reveal Claiborne's past in a series of startling flashbacks that intrude abruptly on present-tense action at various points. Each time one of these flashbacks occurs, the film's color scheme "fills out," abruptly intensifying in a way that poses a distinct contrast to the gray, dismal monochrome that characterizes the rest of the film. This stylistic technique is meant, in part, to symbolize and highlight a present that is drained and exhausted—and the charcoal-gray atmosphere corresponds precisely with a sense of Maine caught in-between seasons (late fall/early winter, or late winter/early spring). The gray environment symbolizes the oppression that Dolores faces from the men around her: Joe, Mackey, the bank president (Bob Gunton), the little boys on the bicycles, and the teenage males throwing Molotov cocktails from their truck. Although Selena is dressed primarily in black—clothes, sunglasses, and gloves—her face is a pasty, ashen white, devoid of makeup. Moreover, her drink of choice, Black and White scotch whiskey, in addition to being her father's favorite, also underscores further the monochrome life that Selena is currently living—devoid of color, happiness, joy. In a world stripped of color and rendered a uniform gray, suspended between seasons and time fragments, past and present, the revelatory flashbacks—all of which, incidentally, are initiated by Dolores except for the final one, which occurs to Selena on her way off the island—are intense color portraits meant to suggest the nearly overwhelming significance of the past. Indeed, Dolores and Selena are like two characters trapped in a Faulkner novel: The events that occurred years ago exert such an overwhelming presence on their contemporary lives that neither woman is free of their influence.

In one memorable scene, Dolores uses an ax to shatter a broken window in the house where many of these events had taken place. The window, already cracked by vandals, can be seen as a symbol of the present for both Selena and Dolores, and when the latter breaks through it, shards of glass fall away in slow motion to reveal a different moment in time—a telephone conversation between Selena and the editor at the magazine that employs her. Once Selena and her mother move back into their old island house, linear time is similarly subverted: The intrusive nature of the past breaks through and shatters their unsettled present. The latter, in turn, is like a window offering a continual view of past events that cannot be forgotten. Selena and her mother are often pictured looking out from the St. George house—standing on the porch, in the driveway, gazing out a doorway or window—and *toward* the yard where Joe was killed in what was officially declared an "accident by misadventure." It is as if the site of his death creates an inexorable pull on both mother and daughter, but especially Dolores. While Selena continues to labor hard at repressing her incest memories, when Dolores returns to the St. George house she is forced to re-confront the murder she perpetrated years ago—a crime that she has apparently managed, at least until her return to its scene with her adult daughter, to repress quite successfully.

Thus, the sheer dominance of the past explains why Selena must struggle to block her recollection of it and why for fifteen years both women have been reluctant to communicate with one another. (Dolores fails to recognize her daughter when they are reintroduced at the island's Town Hall in the beginning of the film, while Selena is reluctant to embrace her.) The contrasting use of the camera's color filters to define the film's shifting sense of time and place thereby underscores the fact that Dolores and Selena remain suspended in a gray and murky present because the tumultuous events of their shared past have yet to be mutually confronted and resolved.

The published articles reverently collected in Dolores's scrapbook suggest that her daughter is particularly adept at authoring professional portraits about men and women who mirror in some way her own personal situation. Richard Nixon and Jean Harris, the subjects of two of her most impressive exposés, are both similar to Selena insofar as they, too, were involved, however indirectly, with murders, cover-ups, lies, and secreted behavior. Selena's hands become a barometer for measuring her own level of repression and sense of self-abjection. On board the ferry we learn that her father has instructed the adolescent Selena in the technique of masturbating him with her hand. As an adult woman, Selena is often shown wearing tight black leather gloves. Moreover, she is the only character in the film who wears gloves, and her covered hands are meant to contrast with Dolores Claiborne's overexposed and work-worn fingers and palms. Certainly Selena's fashionable gloves distinguish her as an affluent and urbane female while helping to insulate her from the cold Maine climate, but they also operate metaphorically, as a psychological manifestation of her efforts to insulate herself from the memory of what her father once forced her to do with her hands. In addition, when she is pictured without her gloves, Selena's fingers hold cigarette after cigarette, and she is frequently shown applying hand cream and washing her hands. Like Lady Macbeth, this is a woman obsessed with her guilty hands—and with the acts she has been forced to perform with them.

At the time of its utterance, Dolores fails to appreciate the full significance of her comment on hands as a measurement of personal identity: "Scary. I guess if you want to know somebody's life, just look at their hands." But it is not just Selena's hands that speak to the nature of her inner being; the other main characters in this film also reveal much about their personalities through their hands. Dolores's hands are callused, arthritic, cracked, and weathered. She has endured years of physical toil as a domestic laborer, and a memorable scene in the film occurs when Vera reminds Dolores to always use six clothespins when hanging bed linens in the bitter winter wind. Although her hands, like Dolores herself, have not led a pampered life, she has used them to take care of others. Her hands are constantly employed as a means for helping—and this is displayed in scenes as minor as her cleaning up the debris in Little Tall Island's Town Hall where she is being held as a murder suspect, to helping Selena unpack her clothes and settle in, to straightening the welcome mat on Vera's doorstep. As much as Dolores relies on her hands as a means for distinguishing her character as a domestic worker and nurturing agent in this film, it is interesting that after Joe falls into the well and begs for Dolores to help him, she merely stands and watches with her hands by her side, choosing to ignore both his pleas and his curses.

Vera Donovan, on the other hand, is accustomed to having things done for her by others, and in the few scenes where her hands are central, her nails appear manicured and her fingers adorned with expensive rings. Unlike Dolores, Vera has performed very little manual labor with her hands; among the few physical actions that the audience sees her perform with them is needlepoint and ringing a bell for a maid to service her. At one point Vera implicates herself in the "accidental" automobile death of her husband, but it remains doubtful that she herself performed the actual tampering with his brakes, as her hands indicate she is incapable of such technical work. Actually, the only time Vera literally relies on her hands is at the end of her life, where she is left with the use of only one hand, which she employs to help her commit suicide.

Joe St. George's hands reflect deeply his blue-collar background; he uses them to make a living fixing boats. When Joe's hands are shown in close-ups, they often appear embedded with black dirt, and they are always capable of instantaneously inflicting hurt on others. Indeed, he is an abusive man who constantly works his hands to pound things, from the top of the television set to his own wife. By exerting this physical power, he gains attention and authority to live in the world at the cost of the women who are with him. A major activity that Joe engages with his hands is the feeding of his addictions: So many of his scenes begin with close-ups of his hands holding an alcoholic drink or a cigarette. And, of course, he uses his hands to teach Selena how to satisfy him sexually with her own hand. Ironically, the only successful action Joe performs with his hands is the infliction of pain and suffering on others and statisfying his own addictive behavior. In the end, these tainted hands, which he has misused throughout the picture, prove incapable of saving him as he clings to a rotted plank across the top of an open well and tries desperately to grab at Dolores's legs.

In the course of the film, each character's hands transform in some way, and each of these transformations signals something about the character's relative behavior and life experience. Vera's manicured and pampered hands become gnarled and useless as a consequence of old age and her debilitating illness. Joe's strong and forceful hands are reduced eventually to a helpless thrashing among shattered wood splinters as he falls to his doom. Dolores's once-young and supple hands bear the results of twenty-two years of performing domestic work for Vera Donovan. And Selena's hands change from being overly cared for and concealed by gloves that hide at the same time as they protect to being accepted for what they are. In light of this particular discussion, it is important to note that after Selena so eloquently comes to her mother's defense at the police inquest hearing, she reaches out her hand to Dolores, and the latter, in turn, accepts it. In the film's final scene, again on board a ferry, Selena's hands are free of both the leather gloves and a cigarette, perhaps signaling the advent of her psychological recovery.

That Selena is shown with her hands tightly encased in black leather gloves, holding a cigarette, shot of liquor, or in need of constant hand cream application is a signifier to the deep subconscious guilt associations she simultaneously manifests and denies. Throughout the film, she struggles to avoid acknowledging the reason she is addicted to drugs and alcohol, and why her personal life consists of "a lot of nobodies." When she decides on board the ferry to return to the island to help her mother, it is after she has reexperienced a sexual episode with her father. Immediately after "witnessing" this hitherto repressed violation, she enters the ship's head only to see the back of her own head reflected through a mirror. This surreal image might be interpreted in many ways. As a child hides behind her hair out of shame and guilt, the self-reflection Selena encounters may be a form of self-reproach, a kind of mocking self-portrait that reveals her own self-protective refusal to acknowledge what has been done to her. On the bathroom wall directly behind her is a white plaque that bears the ominous message in bold black letters: "REPORT ALL INJURIES." Ironically, Selena has failed to report—either to the authorities or to herself—the most grievous "injury" of her life. But at this junction she is on the verge of acknowledging it. And because of the epiphany she has just made herself experience, her reversed mirrored image may also signal that Selena finally sees what she has not been willing to look at before. In an earlier scene in another bathroom—this one in her mother's house on the island—Selena avoids the truth Dolores tries to impart by taking prescription pills to block out memory, so that "in fifteen minutes everything will be just fine." But on board the ferry, after paying witness to her own violation, Selena is no longer able to repress and retreat.

Turning her back on her mother is equated with turning her back on the memory of her own violation as a child. To move forward, she must turn herself around and come "full circle" to face the truth of her past and rescue the mother who once saved her from her father. Thus, Selena follows a course of action that parallels her mother's earlier choice to find a more permanent solution to the problems generated by Joe St. George instead of emptying her savings account and fleeing in a state of panic. In electing to return to the island to help Dolores defend herself, Selena stops running away from her own past centered in dark, dreary Maine, where, as she notes sardonically at the end of the film, "even when it's warm here, it's cold," at the same time that she abandons her effort to escape into the lie of a dream assignment in a sunlit Arizona devoid of memories.

The movement of a solar eclipse across the landscape of this film becomes a defining moment in the lives of its women characters; the eclipse's passage parallels the plot's emphasis on evolving female empowerment. As noted already, the atmosphere of *Dolores Claiborne* is intentionally constructed to highlight the secreted domestic abuse issues that drive the film—from the frequent portraits of dense clouds that suggest the layers of dark memories that must be penetrated (the only time the sky is clear is on the day of the eclipse), to the many occasions when major moments in the film occur in transitory or "suspended" conditions: The indeterminable season of the year, two critical ferry rides across the water that separates the island from the mainland where on each occasion important truths about the past are revealed, the time during the solar eclipse itself. While the actual physical eclipse is important, its metaphorical significance is even more so. Joe St. George has interposed himself between daughter and mother, essentially "eclipsing" the latter. On the afternoon of the eclipse, Joe is murdered by his wife who lures him into an abandoned well where he falls to his death. Hackford's camera work is extremely evocative all through this scene, as the murder occurs precisely at the time of the sun's total eclipse. At one point, Dolores's full vertical figure is cast in-between the hole in the ground and the corresponding hole in the sky, and she appears to assume similar mythic proportions to the eclipse itself. Indeed, she reveals the extent of her supremacy in the voiceover that accompanies her flashback to the "accident," that killing Joe "was easier than I thought."

The fully exposed well in the earth, certainly a vaginal image, is linked to Dolores (full of sorrow) Claiborne (clay-born: earth mother) while the "death" of the sun, the latter associated with masculine archetypes in Greek and Roman mythologies, underscores the symbolic destruction of the father patriarch. Indeed, while Joe's actual fall into the pit signals the "eclipsing" of his husband-father phallic dominance, the entire scene prior to that moment emphasizes the steady erosion of his potency and power. Just before the total eclipse occurs, Joe, thoroughly intoxicated on Black and White scotch, struggles to "erect" his white reflector box, and ultimately fails to do so as the cardboard device keeps collapsing in on itself. His loss of potency becomes even more exaggerated when he is confronted with Dolores's knowledge that he has been sexually molesting their daughter. Joe abruptly pulls back from his physical assault on his wife in a posture that indicates both his humiliation and shock, as he claims sheepishly that Selena's "a little liar" and a "tease" in need of a whipping from his patriarchal belt. Dolores is relentless in her verbal emasculation, however, employing highly sexualized language designed to throw her husband off balance while simultaneously infuriating him: "How come you look like the devil just reached in and grabbed them little raisins you call balls?" And Dolores establishes full dominance over the sequence when she reveals that Joe apparently is impotent with her—"if you can get that limp noodle of yours to stand up"—even as he is prone to brag about his masculine bravado: "I wonder if [your pals at the barbershop] are going to think you're such a stud when they find out the only ass you can get your hands on belongs to your thirteen-year-old daughter." In controlling completely the linguistical tone and tempo of this scene, Dolores succeeds in enflaming her husband (thus making him chase her into the open field), rouses herself for the murderous act she is about to commit, and likewise prepares the audience for the dramatic shift in power that culminates in Joe's literal fall.

Joe's death is punishment for the moral violations he has committed against the women in his home. As a solar eclipse creates an unnatural ambiance for those who observe it, the incestual acts that Joe St. George perpetrates on his daughter and the casual violence that characterizes his marriage to Dolores wreck havoc on the order of his family and the psychosexual development of Selena. Abusing the entitlements traditionally conferred on father over child and husband over wife, St. George becomes one of King's secret-driven monsters. The cameo that Joe gives to Selena is nothing more than an attempt to buy her silence and establish collusion in their illicit behavior. The cameo belonged to Joe's mother, and to her mother before her. Joe has appropriated it from an exclusively female line of descent—a mother→daughter inheritance. He has breached its natural line of gendered succession just as he comes to impose himself unnaturally between Dolores and Selena.

The eclipse, like the misused cameo, should be read as another metaphor for the condition of being female in a patriarchal culture: Cut off, blocked, obscured. If male abuse, by objectification and oppression, is what continues to eclipse women, then King and Hackford argue in *Dolores Claiborne* that women must face the truth, like facing the partially blocked sun, even at the risk of hurting their eyes. Turning her back on the problem, as Selena has tried to do throughout her young adulthood, only complicates the situation and compounds the guilt felt by the victim. It may seem easier for Selena and Dolores to ignore gender oppression to get along in the world, but the consequences of this ignorance are long lasting and profound. The eclipse in a woman's life, this film also suggests, occurs in that period when a man is sexually prominent in it: From Selena's adolescence to the end of Dolores's wifehood. A female is free only when she acts on the recognition that "sometimes being a bitch is all a woman has to hold on to"—and escapes from beneath the sexual shadow cast by a man—be that man her father or her husband. Silence is equivalent to darkness, and this film insists that true survival, physical as well as psychological, depends not upon silence, but in confronting the past and understanding its secrets and becoming an active agent as a result. This is why Selena's reflected image in the ferry's bathroom mirror is reversed. Until this moment in the picture, she has been reluctant to confront the truth of her own past; she has "turned her back" on her mother, herself, and her father's culpability.

In contrast to the singular and self-serving actions that characterize male behavior in *Dolores Claiborne*—stealing money from Dolores's bank account; secretive drinking of alcohol; sexist language and behavior; Selena's molestations—which essentially climax in masturbatory actions, women are defined in this film by virtue of their relationships with other women. When women work together, the film implies, they can overcome even the trauma of domestic abuse. Dolores and, to a less direct extent, Selena find the courage to emerge from their eclipsed lives through the guidance and proactive example offered by another abused woman. Vera (Latin for "truth") Donovan shapes Dolores's decision to murder her husband instead of merely running away by providing her own dramatic illustration of how to deal with a negligent husband: "It's a depressingly masculine world we live in, Dolores. Husbands die everyday. Why one is probably dying right now, while you're sitting here. They die and leave their wives their money. Sometimes they're driving home from their mistresses' apartments and their brakes suddenly fail. An accident, Dolores, can be an unhappy woman's best friend." Selena's ultimate assessment that Vera and Dolores loved one another proves to be indisputable, for the two women, despite their different social classes and financial status, parallel one another in personality and life experiences. Each woman is all that is left in the other's life, forming an often contentious, but always brutally honest and effective support system. Vera wills her entire estate—$1.6 million—to Dolores largely because the latter has not only served as her steady caregiver, but also as her only friend. Most important, Dolores chooses to care for Vera even after the latter becomes a disconsolate and self-absorbed invalid because Vera gave her the courage and the hard-edged example of how to deal effectively with an intolerable marriage. The two women share and maintain similar dark insights into the murderous actions that were necessary to liberate them both from patriarchal and financial oppression. In some fashion, Vera and Dolores are married to one another—the natural consequence of two "widowed" women who have "remarried," this time into a more mature relationship based on mutual respect and friendship instead of sex. Vera's death, and the charge of murder wrongfully leveled against Dolores, occasions Selena's return back to the island and the need for the two estranged women to once again inhabit the house where the film's real crimes took place. It is as if Vera has posthumously come to Dolores's rescue a final time, forcing mother and daughter to confront each another and the issue that has divided them for so many years. The end of the film transfers the female bond that Dolores shared with Vera to her daughter, while Selena herself comes finally to appreciate the secret sacrifices that women must often make for one another—and specifically the one her mother has made for her.

Dolores Claiborne is a particularly appealing film in the daring way in which it poses a plethora of untraditional notions about women and interpersonal female dynamics. American culture—and Hollywood mirrors and extends this propensity—is obsessed with the rite of passage to masculinity. Treatments of father-son conflict resolutions, explorations of male bonding, and masculine initiation rituals abound in the Hollywood film canon and can be seen crossing genre boundaries. Moreover, they tend to eclipse mother-son interactions and especially portraits of mother-daughter relationships. Mother-daughter relationships are nearly the exclusive province of the romantic melodrama, while it is in the horror film that we find the most frequent—and the most damning—portraits of mother-son associations. *Claiborne* is a persuasive counterpoint to these tendencies in that it focuses upon truly positive images of women, and particularly their ability to establish and maintain genuine female friendships. Just as important, the female bonds in Dolores Claiborne are unsentimentally portrayed—indeed, they are earned through honest suffering and conflict resolution that is true to life. The film's protagonists are neither glamorous nor romantic; Dolores and Vera are tough and cranky crones. Yet they are nonetheless heroines. They are realistic females smart enough to commit murder and get away with it, while still attaining the audience's sympathy and identification.

In an essay entitled "*Gerald's Game* and *Dolores Claiborne:* Stephen King and the Evolution of an Authentic Female Narrative Voice," Carol Senf has argued: "Certainly, King's novels are conservative in that they celebrate fairly traditional values, including life and health and love. They are also radical in that they condemn both men and political institutions who

use the power of patriarchy against women and children, and they celebrate women who manage to carve out positions for themselves" (95).
These sentiments are fundamentally accurate, although there is not a great
deal of evidence to support the fact that King's work "celebrates women
who manage to carve out positions for themselves," unless these positions
first embody the conservative nature of "fairly traditional values." *Dolores
Claiborne* provides us with a unique collection of the most independent
women in Hollywood's adaptations of Stephen King. But this film is more
the exception than the rule. Female characters in other King narratives
who do live alone, outside the authority of husbands and the insulation of
domestic obligations, are particularly susceptible to the extreme perver-
sions and psychological aberrations already noted in Annie Wilkes.

Moreover, the main way in which women in King-inspired movies
come to possess integral, powerful lives is initially through violent efforts,
even if their behavior eventually produces positive results. Violence and
murder are more than acts of passion for the females in *Carrie, Firestarter,
Cujo,* and *Dolores Claiborne;* they are the only options in their quest toward survival and self-destiny. Dolores, Vera, and perhaps even Selena's
character at the end of *Claiborne,* achieve true independence only after
they have completely detached themselves from the various male bonds
that have held them captive and move on to create alternative social
realms devoid of men. The notion set forth by Vera Donovan that "sometimes being a bitch is the only thing a woman has to hold on to" is the negative model by which many female characters in Stephen King's films and
novels (e.g., *Gerald's Game* and *Rose Madder*) come to assert their independence in a male-dominated world. Perhaps this helps to explain why
all but one of the flashbacks that occur in *Dolores Claiborne* is initiated by
Dolores herself. She may have long ago reconciled herself to the necessity
of the murder that she was compelled to commit, yet moving back into her
former home summons back the restive ghosts of her violent marriage and
the murder she has since kept secret for many years. Unlike Selena, Dolores may not require the help of drug and liquor stores to help her cope
with her personal history, but the intensity and the frequency of her flashbacks make it apparent that Dolores is still haunted by selected images
from her past.

The strong maternal figures in *Cujo* and *Claiborne* (and, as we will
consider in the next chapter, *The Shining* and *Pet Sematary*) support the
premise that women may seek alternatives to relationships with abusive
men, but a selfless devotion to their children remains a consistent priority
that guides every one of their choices. At least at this point in its treatment

of Stephen King, Hollywood mirrors his novelistic conceptions of mother-hood as the primary avenue available to women to demonstrate levels of determination and power equal to or greater than a man's. Just as the Madonna has always been at the opposite extreme from the whore in the reductive view of patriarchal culture, King's perception of women reflects this bias. His women characters can be seen to inhabit a continuum that features at one extreme the realm of wanton sexuality and, at the other, the responsibilities of motherhood. All his female characters have a place somewhere along this moral spectrum: from the ethical vacuum of a Chris Hargenson (*Carrie*) at one end, to the quietly heroic stature of Dolores Claiborne at the other. Just as King's male fiction writers discover their connection to salvation in exercising their creative imaginations, and his heroic male protagonists learn to recognize and temper the indulgence of egotism, it is in the maternal-child relationship that his women characters tend to reveal their most positive assets. As Selena St. George acknowl-edges at the end of *Dolores Claiborne,* she may never be able to forgive completely Dolores's decision to kill her father, but she now understands enough to know that the action was motivated by a mother's selfless love.

CHAPTER 4

PATERNAL ARCHETYPES:
THE SHINING, PET SEMATARY, APT PUPIL

Stephen King's fiction is filled with many examples of negative fathers. Without warning or apparent provocation, King's own biological father, Donald, abandoned the family one night when Stephen was two years old and was never seen or heard from again by his family. The absence of a positive father in his life may have shaped King's attitude toward creating fictional fathers, as King's patriarchs are, generally speaking, benignly indifferent at best, abusive and self-destructive at worst. Most are representative of adulthood's worst inclinations—selfish, secretive, and manipulative. Several of the cinemagraphic fathers from films made of King's narratives likewise underscore a fundamental thesis that can be traced throughout King's oeuvre: The most treacherous formulations of sin, and certainly their most pervasive designs, are male-generated and sustained. King's portrayal of evil most often appears to require an active, illicit bond between a male (often in the role of a father or father surrogate) and a younger, formerly innocent individual (often in the role of biological or surrogate progeny) who is initiated into sin. And this is a pattern that is repeated in work as diverse as *Dolores Claiborne* and *Pet*

Sematary: An unspoken collusion between fathers and (surrogate) children that upholds some kind of dark, secret covenant.

The Shining does not fit this pattern exactly, unless we choose to see Jack Torrance (Jack Nicholson) as a man who is often relegated to childlike status and initiated into evil by the adult ghosts that populate the Overlook Hotel. King's novel makes a better case for such an interpretation than does the film, as Jack's father occupies a more central role in his son's corruption. But such a viewing is not so easily argued in Stanley Kubrick's movie, as it presupposes that Jack is more innocent than he is before his arrival at the hotel. The situation Jack encounters in the film merely continues, at the same time that it deepens, Torrance's already precarious relationship with his wife and small son. He is aided in his descent into madness by a coven of ghosts interested in destroying the winter caretaker and his family, but their real goal appears to be the death of the young child, particularly if it occurs at the hands of his own father, whose enormous paranormal capabilities—his so-called *shining*—make him an attractive addition to the supernatural energies already at work in the hotel. In the end, the haunted spirits manipulate the father to the point where he becomes merely a mad extension of the hotel itself and dies by freezing to death inside a hedge maze in the pursuit of his son. The wife and child manage to escape, while the father is left as a permanent ghost-guest on the hotel's register.

Of all the films that have been adapted from Stephen King's fiction, Kubrick's version of *The Shining* remains the picture that has received the most interpretative analysis from critics over the years. Certainly one explanation for this attention is attributable to Kubrick's reputation and his inimitable contribution to the history of filmmaking. Kubrick scholars often point to the fact that *The Shining* is reflective of many of the director's central concerns throughout his canon—from gender issues and familial dynamics, to explorations of masculine violence, to psychological allegories of the individual man and his relationship to larger cultural forms and institutions. But the *amount* of critical attention this particular film has drawn is truly staggering; in the years since its release, *The Shining* has been the subject of over a hundred scholarly articles and book chapters. Why has this film garnered such elaborate critical appraisal, especially in light of the fact that so many other cinemagraphic adaptations of King have received so little?

To begin, Kubrick's *Shining* rewards multiple viewings. As this chapter will demonstrate, individual scenes in Kubrick's cinema must be "read" carefully, in a process that is akin to experiencing a poem or viewing a complex oil painting. In fact, *The Shining,* arguably more than any other Kubrick film or other movie adapted from King's fiction, demands a careful and detailed analysis of its many multileveled and subtle scenes. Only in struggling to verbalize meaning from these scenes is it possible to appreciate fully the film's interwoven matrix of images and metaphors. One of King's own complaints about Kubrick's effort is that it is finally too artistic to operate effectively as a horror film. I think King is probably right here, but whatever Kubrick sacrifices in visceral or psychological terror, he more than rewards in visual evocative brilliance.

Kubrick's rendition has inspired a myriad of critical interpretations. Many of these have stressed the social and economic implications inherent in the film's portrait of the Torrance family's demise. Fredric Jameson reads the film as a Marxist allegory of the abuses of American capitalism. The movie's central protagonist, Jack Torrance, is overwhelmed by history—his own personal his-story, but also by America's past, as represented in the ghosts that animate the Overlook Hotel. Hired by "faceless organization men" (95) to service the upper-class playground for the rich and famous, Torrance is "painfully out of place" (94) in this rarefied atmosphere of the American ruling class. He is victimized by "History, by the American past as it has left its sedimented traces in the [hotel's] corridors and dismembered suites" (90). Other critics, such as Patricia Ferreira, and Flo Leibowitz and Lynn Jeffres, have narrowed Jameson's broad social-historical analysis and given it a more specific feminist orientation, arguing that Jack Torrance actually identifies with the patriarchal abuses of the Overlook's male hierarchy. His efforts to kill his wife and child merely illustrate Torrance's ultimate capitulation to the misogynist system that he willingly serves. On the other hand, Frank Manchel complicates this position by insisting that Jack is just as much a victim to the manipulative agents at the hotel as Wendy (Shelley Duvall) and Danny (Danny Lloyd) because of the burdening pressures of success that define the American male's masculinity. The Overlook plays upon this essential insecurity in Torrance's personality by flaunting its lavish levels of materialism and social status; these become constant reminders to Jack of what he simultaneously has failed to accomplish himself and may be left with only this final opportunity to attain.

Other viewers have considered the film less as a social allegory than a psychological portrait of a mind collapsing in on itself. Thomas Allen Nelson argues for just such a reading in his analysis of Kubrick's use of a complex series of maze images that are really metaphors defining Torrance's mental entrapment and estrangement: "In *The Shining,* the maze concept encompasses the film thematically and aesthetically; it not only helps explain Jack's madness (that is, the subconscious as a labyrinth in which the conscious self gets lost) but inspires the Overlook's floor plan and décor, as well as the events which occur there" (206). The Native American rug patterns on the Overlook's floors and walls, the hotel's excruciatingly long corridors exaggerated by the use of a wide-angle lens camera, the maze of words that Jack types into various convoluted forms on sheets of paper, and even Danny's line of snow prints that eventually trap his father deep within the hedge maze outside the hotel—all of these images of enclosure are metaphors for the encroaching perimeters of Jack's mind. In fact, one scene that few critics of *The Shining* have noted actually shows Jack looking down into a small-scale model of the outdoor maze. As he stares down into its green-patterned labyrinth, minuscule figures of Wendy and Danny appear walking in its center. The image is startling not only because of its surreal juxtapositions, but also because the maze itself—which can be divided perfectly into two identical halves, or hemispheres—resembles nothing so much as the interior of the human brain. Kubrick implies through this brief allusion that Danny and Wendy (and, of course, Jack himself) are lost inside the darkest recesses of Jack's mind—just as all three of the Torrances are trapped within the abandoned corridors of the hotel and the sculpted rows of shrubbery in the maze. Ironically, Wendy and Danny escape their entrapment by literally emerging from these various mazes, Danny from the frozen maze and Wendy from her futile search to locate the boy on an upstairs floor of the hotel.

The movie's consistent patterns of imagery—from its utilization of a variety of mazes and maze-like designs to its abundant reliance on mirrors and reflected surfaces—creates a hauntingly "atmospheric text" that rewards careful and repeated viewings. Throughout the film, Jack Torrance's descent into personal psychosis is accompanied and underscored by Kubrick's reliance on reflective imagery (as well as the accumulated mazes that Nelson enumerates). Early in the picture when Wendy brings Jack his breakfast in their hotel suite, Jack is filmed through a vanity mirror. The doubling implications are further strengthened in the scene when he reveals to Wendy that he possesses a "ridiculous" sense of déjà vu that he associates with the Overlook. Later in the film, as Jack's psychosis deepens, this same bedroom mirror is once again employed. The camera films Torrance's entire body through the reflective glass as he sits upright on the bed just before summoning Danny to sit on his lap. In both instances, the mirror "frames" Jack Torrance exclusively; both Wendy and Danny remain outside the mirror's perimeters. Moreover, the verbal discourse is likewise restricted, as in each scene the subject always centers on the hotel and

Jack's attitude toward it. In comparing these two moments in the film, it is interesting to note that Jack's body and verbal language are shown to regress—from the initial déjà vu banter he shares with Wendy to the more ominous desire to remain at the hotel "forever and ever and ever" while talking somberly to Danny. This phrase does not even belong to Jack Torrance; he appropriates it from Grady's twin daughters (another image of mirroring) and thus telegraphs to both the audience and to Danny his evolving connection to the spirits haunting the hotel.

Every major scene in the film in which Torrance is shown interacting with the specters at the Overlook is cast with a mirror either off to the side or directly in front or behind the central characters. And inevitably, the mirror is pulled directly into the mis-en-scène, becoming a framing device that Kubrick utilizes to penetrate more deeply into the mystery of the hotel itself or to complicate further Jack's relationship with the place. For example, when Jack enters room 237 to investigate Wendy's insistence that there is someone in the hotel threatening Danny, he encounters a beautiful, naked female who emerges from the bathtub and seductively welcomes him into her embrace. The naked woman is a shock to both Jack and the audience. We have been prepared for something horrific eventually to appear from room 237 since the discussion early in the film in which Dick Hallorann (Scatman Crothers) warns Danny to "stay out," but a sexual seduction is not exactly what the audience expects. After emerging from the bathtub and walking gracefully to the center of the room, the ghost-woman embraces Torrance in an assertive if not aggressive manner, her eyes moving languidly from his crotch up his torso to stare into his face. As the two engage in a passionate kiss, the camera slowly moves around the couple and over Torrance's shoulder to reveal their reflected forms in a large bathroom mirror to their side. The audience's horror at what appears in that reflection is experienced first by Torrance himself: The beautiful woman has somehow transformed into a hideous crone. In this surreal place where ghosts quaff champagne and a sea of blood rides the elevator to the lobby, it appears perfectly appropriate that the inverted and artificial image projected by a mirror is more real than the object itself.

What is important about most of the mirror scenes in this film is that they reveal the reality hiding beneath the various masks that the hotel employs to disguise its true identity. The polymorphic female in room 237 is presented in a manner that is similar to the reflected REDRUM/MURDER written by Danny in lipstick that Wendy views later in the film: Mirrors are a visual aid for revealing the demonic inversions lurking beneath the deceptive surfaces of the Overlook. The hotel begins its seduction of Jack Torrance from the moment he steps through its front door and into Mr. Ullman's (Barry Nelson) office. He is overwhelmed by the hotel's physical magnificence, the affluence and prestige that have been associated with it, and its impressive historical legacy. The beautiful woman in room 237 is merely a feminized extension of the same fantasy projection Torrance manifests throughout the film as his identification with the hotel deepens to the point where he is willing to surrender both himself and his family to it. But just as the hotel continually deceives Torrance with promises that it has no intention of keeping, the erotic ghost-woman in room 237 is merely a mask for a monstrous reality that is finally revealed in the mirrored projection that Torrance recognizes only after he has been seduced by its false front. Jack is duped and manipulated by the hotel each time he interacts with it. This is why at the end of this scene the crone chases him out of the bedroom with her humiliating laughter. Like the three vampire women in Stoker's *Dracula,* the crone's derisive laughter underscores the scorn that evil ultimately holds for those it seduces. Kubrick seems to be suggesting here that evil is an active principle that is never content with merely asserting its control over individuals—it also insists on their humiliation to complete its design.

Unlike King's novel—which really focuses on Danny Torrance, his supernatural abilities, and the Overlook's efforts to subsume the boy's powers into it—Kubrick's film is almost exclusively centered on Jack Torrance. In part, the movie is about the destruction of his marriage to Wendy, but even that relationship is secondary to the bond that Torrance establishes with the hotel. Perhaps this helps to explain why all of Jack's encounters with the corporealized revenants—the woman in room 237, Delbert Grady (Philip Stone), and Lloyd (Joe Turkel) in the bar scenes—are experienced in isolation, in the physical absence of either Wendy or Danny. Both the mirrors in front of Grady and Torrance in the red bathroom scene as well as the long bar mirror that hangs behind Lloyd in the Overlook's Gold Room are meant to suggest the sequestration of Jack's identity apart from the world of the living and likewise his submersion into the identities of the ghosts reflected back at him through these mirrored surfaces.

The Shining is about fear in well-lighted places. Its deepest moments of terror come not from the shadows or claustrophobic crypts of the traditional horror film, but from within highly reflective surfaces and brightly illuminated bathroom interiors. Kubrick himself reminds us of this just after the release of *The Shining,* when he commented on the ability of horror stories to "show us the dark side without having to confront it directly" (Kroll 99). Bathrooms and bathtubs have always held a baleful fascination for filmmakers (Walker, Taylor, and Ruchti 304). One needs to look no further than Hitchcock's *Psycho* (1960) for evidence of their significance to horror art. (Incidentally, as an indication of this film's impact on the popular consciousness, sales of glass shower stalls skyrocketed immediately following the release of *Psycho.*) In Kubrick's later work, *Full Metal Jacket* (1987), a psychologically distressed Marine commits suicide while seated on a toilet, while the opening scene in *Eyes Wide Shut* (1999), a movie that closely resembles *The Shining* in its shared theme of marital discord, takes place in the interior of a bathroom. In *The Shining,* the use of four individual lavatory sequences—Danny's initial telepathic vision of the hotel's elevator doors depositing a river of blood, Jack and the ghost-woman in room 237, Wendy trapped inside her apartment's bathroom as Jack endeavors to break down the door separating them, and the conversation that occurs between Torrance and Delbert Grady in the Gold Ballroom's red lavatory—alerts the audience to the way that Kubrick's film is a comment on a surreal domesticity and the manner in which the supernatural possesses the ability to invade and displace the commonplace. The bathroom represents the most "gothic" space in most homes; water pipes and sewage lines form a direct conduit to the underworld. Further, activities are performed within the room's space that are both idiosyncratic and not meant to be shared in public. Perhaps this is why most bathrooms have only a single door for both entrance and exit. Bathrooms stand in contrast to the parlor or kitchen, sites of social intercourse, often with multiple means for egress and ingress. The most important moments in *The Shining* occur inside bathrooms where the hotel "speaks" to and through characters in various visual and verbal communications. Where these "interactions" happen implies that a location usually as private and unthreatening as a bathtub or lavatory can no longer be trusted; that the Overlook is capable of intruding on these sites means that none of the characters is safe anywhere. Ironically, a shared bathroom also implies a certain level of intimacy. The only people with whom we ever share a bathroom are those we trust implicitly, because of the private nature of our exposed bodies and the nature of excretion. In each of these scenes, the Overlook reveals something of itself—albeit its darkest inclinations—with the occupant while the latter exposes his or her vulnerability.

Inside the red bathroom, Kubrick's camera initially commences shooting from opposite ends of the lavatory. Torrance and Grady are centered in this room, a row of mirrors on one wall opposite a row of white urinals attached on the other. As the scene unfolds, the camera distance narrows, getting ever closer to the two principle figures. The camera inches closer in a series of alternating angle shots, switching randomly back and forth between Torrance and Grady to create a kind of "dialogue" between the two men. The camera eventually stabilizes in a closely centered, medium shot of Grady and Torrance standing face-to-face. The two males are continually juxtaposed, guest and servant. As the audience listens carefully to their dialogue, it becomes clear that the camera's series of alternating positions is meant to reinforce the fact that Grady and Torrance are mirror images of each other. This scene is shot very differently from the rest of the film, in which the camera is constantly moving and searching up and down the length of serpentine corridors. The uniquely static and circumscribed nature of the shots inside this crimson lavatory signal the importance of the scene; it should be read as a turning point in the movie.

The two men enter the bathroom as a result of Grady accidentally bumping into Torrance in a crowd on the floor of the Gold Ballroom. The manservant spills a tray of cocktails on Torrance. As Torrance points out sarcastically, Grady's drinks mix with the one Torrance is holding, and his amber bourbon is tainted by the milky Advocaat being transported on Grady's tray. Just as the two drinks blend together, forcing valet and guest into the men's room in an effort to clean Torrance's jacket, the identities of the two men also merge together once they are alone in the red lavatory.

In the first part of this scene, Torrance stares deeply into the mirror over one of the sinks at Grady's reflected image, the latter working obsequiously to remove a stain from Torrance's jacket with a white towel and some cold water. When Grady informs him of his name, which Torrance immediately recognizes as that of the former infamous caretaker, Torrance signals his own uneasiness in the valet's presence: His voice cracks, "You a married man are you, Mr. Grady?" and the fingers of Jack's left hand begin to twitch nervously. That the camera views Torrance intensely focused on Grady's bent-over mirrored reflection deepens the association that Kubrick's earlier alternating cameras serve to underscore: Jack is losing his own point of view and the two men are merging into one another. After Torrance learns Grady's name, he continues to address the servant's mirrored image, reminding Grady of the violent murders he perpetrated on his own wife and daughters years ago while serving in Torrance's current job as caretaker of the Overlook. Grady professes to be unaware of this event and "begs to differ" that it is Torrance who has "always been the caretaker." The confusing dialogue is deliberately ambiguous in an effort to force the audience to see that the identities of these two men, one dead and the other moving closer to the edge of death, are blurring into one another. To underscore this fact, Jack empathetically takes the white towel from Grady, symbolically stripping him of his role as servant and opening the possibility for Grady to assume a new identity. Ironically, Torrance not only recognizes Grady's true identity as the former caretaker of the Overlook who "chopped [his wife and daughters] into little bits," he is also unconsciously revealing *his own* future link to Grady—the soiled towel passes from Grady's hands into Jack's—completing the cycle of murderous caretakers serving the will of the hotel.

The dialogue in the bathroom scene commences with Torrance patronizing Grady—referring to him as "Jeeves"—and easily accepting his role as "the important one" whose jacket must be cleaned by the offending valet. By the conclusion of this sequence, however, the two men have switched roles; in fact, it is really Torrance who assumes the position of "servant," taking instruction from Delbert Grady. From him, Torrance learns that his son, Danny, is in possession of "a very great talent" and that he is attempting to "use it against your will" by summoning, in the racist language of the hotel's patriarchy, "a nigger cook." Entranced by this information—it is highly significant that Jack repeats the phrase "a nigger cook" in the form of a question, as though he is being introduced to racist diction at the same time as he learns about Hallorann—Torrance listens carefully to Grady's counsel and is noticeably embarrassed by his own "interfering" wife and "willful boy." Danny's effort to summon "a nigger cook" forges a parallel with Grady's daughter, who once "stole a pack of matches and tried to burn [the Overlook] down." Both children engage in subversive activity, against both their fathers and the patriarchal hotel, and require an immediate and definitive response. Torrance is forced to acknowledge that his own child and wife, like Grady's, may require "a good talking to—perhaps a bit more." All this time that the two men dialogue, Grady is framed by one of the wall mirrors above the sink. To a very real degree, Jack is talking to himself, or at least an extension of himself, his dark alter ego. The former caretaker actually supplies Torrance with a definition of "male duty": That women and children, when they misbehave, as they inevitably will, must be severely "corrected." It is really the first time in the film that Torrance begins to consider the violent course of action that he will follow for the remainder of the movie. And Delbert Grady plants the initial seeds for such a premise inside a room appropriately painted blood red, a color so intensely bright that it almost hurts the eyes.

When the two men first enter the bathroom, Grady's face is obscured as he attends to the Advocaat stains on Torrance's jacket. But as the scene unfolds and the power dynamic switches between the two men (notably at the point where Jack takes the towel and Grady insists that Torrance has "always been the caretaker"), the manservant's face and upper body are revealed to the camera in a frontal close-up, his torso framed inside one of the bathroom mirrors hanging on the wall behind him. At this moment, the camera also shifts its angle of exposition. In most movies, when the camera angles up into the face or torso of a character, he or she assumes a position of dominance. The opposite is also true: A character's status is diminished whenever the camera's gaze looks down on him or her. By the end of the red bathroom scene, as he provides Torrance with instruction about his son and marital situation, Grady is filmed in an upward-angled medium close-up, signaling his position of dominance. In contrast, Torrance concludes the sequence filmed at an angle of descent, that is, with the camera looking down at him, indicating that he has lost the narrative advantage to Grady visually as well as linguistically.

The action that occurs in the red bathroom brilliantly reverses the roles Grady and Torrance occupy before entering the lavatory. It concludes with the two men establishing a violent paternalistic collusion with one another, revealing that the valet is no mere servant and that Torrance is no longer a man who is in control of his own destiny. In fact, by the end of the sequence Jack's face has become wildly distorted, he is merely listening and no longer talking, his unshaven grimaces make him appear insane and frightfully lost, and his head appears completely engulfed in a sea of red paint. He ends the scene with a primitive smirk of dawning and grateful recognition: That Grady has informed him of several great truths and that Torrance now needs to act accordingly.

Kubrick's reliance on mirrors as visual aids for underscoring the thematic meaning of this film portrays visually the internal transformations and oppositions that are occurring to Jack Torrance psychologically. Through extended use of these devices, Kubrick dramatizes the hotel's methodical assault on Torrance's identity, its ability to stimulate the myriad of self-doubts and anxieties that have always been part of his nature by creating opportunities to warp Torrance's perspective on himself and the other members of his family. Furthermore, the fact that Jack looks into a mirror whenever he "speaks" to the hotel means, to some extent, that Kubrick implicates him directly into the hotel's "consciousness," because Jack is, in effect, talking to himself. The first time Jack is sitting at the bar in the Overlook's ballroom facing the mirror at the back of the bar, he places his hands over his eyes and face. When he removes them, Jack begins to speak, apparently to himself. Kubrick constructs the scene so that the audience assumes Jack is merely addressing his own reflection in the mirror. When the camera shifts to Jack's point of view, however, we discover that he is actually speaking to a man, Lloyd the bartender, who stands directly in front of the mirror behind the bar, framed as if he were in a portrait.

As in the scene filmed inside the red bathroom, is Jack speaking to a hallucinogenic ghost, to a projected (mirror) version of himself, or some combination of both? Since the film never really answers this definitively, the audience is left to ponder the mysterious nature of Jack's psychological dualism. It is significant that he greets Lloyd by name, as if the two are close personal acquaintances, and that Jack appears not at all surprised to find "the best goddamn bartender" patiently awaiting his drink order. Lighted softly from below, both Lloyd and Jack take on similar demonic appearances that underscore Jack's frustrating confession of alcoholism and his own version of the day he broke his son's arm. Once more Kubrick employs a mirror to reveal the hidden truth of Jack's shadowed past and the bond he comes to share with the evil embodied in the hotel. As with Grady in the red bathroom, the bartender and Jack share a desperate masculine alliance. Although Lloyd says very little in either of his two scenes with Jack, when he does speak it is significant. He confirms not only Torrance's positive status at the Overlook—his drinks are free, "orders from the house"—but also continues the process of creating a wedge between Jack and Wendy by reminding Jack of the sexist cliché, "women, can't live with them, can't live without them." In short, Lloyd's role is similar to Grady's: He is both a mirror of Torrance's own darkest inclinations toward child abuse and gender antagonism and a visible representative of the hotel's efforts to advance Jack further along in his estrangement from wife, son, and all things human.

The various mirrored surfaces with which we watch Jack Torrance interact are markers or signifiers that visually identify and dramatize his loss of identity and eventual supernatural possession by the evil spirits at the Overlook. That this vampirelike possession may take place too quickly and with insufficient transitions for the audience is a criticism that King himself has leveled on several different occasions: "The book is about Jack Torrance's gradual descent into madness through the malign influences of the Overlook. . . . If the guy is nuts to begin with, then the entire tragedy of his downfall is wasted. For that reason, the film has no center and no heart, despite its brilliantly unnerving camera angles and dazzling use of the Steadicam" (Underwood and Miller, *Bare Bones* 29).

This is just one of several objections that King has raised when asked to comment on Kubrick's film. His dissatisfaction has fermented over the years, and, as will be discussed in chapter 7, eventually resulted in the 1997 remake of *The Shining* using the original King screenplay that was rejected by Kubrick in favor of one authored by the director himself and Diane

Johnson. Michael Collings offers some trenchant advice when he cautions "that perhaps the best approach to Kubrick's *The Shining* is to divorce it from connections with Stephen King—not because Kubrick failed to do justice to King's narrative, but simply because it has ceased to be King's" (62).

Kubrick's film remains a devastating portrait of evil as something negative, weakening, a principle of death. Nicholson plays Jack Torrance as a man who is ever more isolated (his self-image reflected inside the various hotel mirrors help subtly to reinforce this) and mastered by a self-destructive impulse that attempts to annihilate both him and those individuals who are closest to him. In the course of the film, Jack appears alone in scene after scene. Significantly, Jack elects to remain inside the hotel's corridors and rooms—especially within the Gold Ballroom, which appears to be the center of the Overlook's "brain"—while Wendy and Danny are free to explore its outdoor surroundings. Until the final chase through the snow-encrusted hedge maze, Jack is never seen outside the hotel's interior. In maintaining this limited perspective, Kubrick restates the purpose of the scenes where Jack is shown trapped inside mirrors: Torrance is physically and mentally a prisoner inside the hotel. His desire to isolate both himself and his family is further illustrated in his deliberate dismantling of the snow cat and the radio. Wendy, in contrast, is frequently paired with Danny, as is Hallorann. But Jack's mental anguish and spiritual possession is underscored by his estrangement from his wife and child as much as it is by his association with the various "mirror ghosts" he meets in residence at the hotel. When Torrance does share a scene with Wendy or Danny, the effect is always one of undisguised violent intent or stilted awkwardness, as when Danny sits on his lap and asks nervously, "Dad, you would never hurt Mommy or me, would you?"

Late in the film, Wendy Torrance stumbles upon the typed manuscript of her husband's new literary opus, a work that is certain to be entitled "All work and no play makes Jack a dull boy." The phrase is written on successive pages in various permutations: As poetry, dramatic dialogue, and conventional prose. Whatever the genre form it takes, however, Jack has typed only this single sentence. While most interpreters of *The Shining* have tended to ignore the significance of what this phrase means, even when they mention the bizarre "manuscript" itself, the typed statement itself reflects the twisted sense of humor present in Jack's very serious mental breakdown and quite a bit more. Jack has literally typed the phrase thousands of times, signaling to both Wendy and the audience that his mind now belongs, or at least is in intellectual harmony with, the voice of the Overlook. Even more disturbing, the grammatically incorrect phrase (together "work" and "play" form a compound subject requiring a plural conjugation of the verb "make") is written in third-person narrative voice, affirming that Jack Torrance the professional author and former English teacher did not compose this sentence—the *hotel* did. And as such, Jack's "manuscript" represents the first time in the movie that the hotel actually "speaks" to Wendy. Correspondingly, it employs a deliberate diction— both condescending and judgmental—that is appropriate to the jet-set guests who reside permanently at the hotel.

Play and *work,* at least as they are defined at the Overlook, are always variable and slippery concepts; in keeping with the surreal spirit of the place, these words are devoid of clear definitions. *Play* might range from the humiliating interaction Jack experiences in room 237 to his delirious exclamation, "Heeeeere's Johnny," as he forces his deranged face between the splintered wood of the bathroom door he has just hacked to pieces with an ax. And the concept of *work* is similarly ambiguous, since the most important *work* of the Overlook's caretaker is the *play* of murdering his family. After the Torrances have taken up residency at the hotel and the first snowfall is imminent, Wendy and Danny play outside in the hedge maze while Jack is pictured alone inside the hotel bouncing a ball against the wall. The scene actually begins with a shot of Jack's typewriter containing a blank sheet of paper, indicating that he has not yet been able to commence his writing work and is, instead, playing catch with himself— or, more specifically, with the hotel. Jack throws the ball at a wall of the Overlook, and the hotel throws it back. In this game of call and response, the Overlook is literally making Jack jump for the ball, which foreshadows what will happen later when the hotel's expectations of play will become even more extreme. In any event, this bizarre game of catch, accompanied with mysterious sound effects and jarring notes of music, ends when the Overlook takes the ball and refuses to throw it back to Jack. Later, the same ball will roll down an empty hallway toward Danny in an attempt to lure the child into beginning yet another game of catch with the hotel's invisible residents. The play idiom thereby poses a haunting echo to Grady's dead twin daughters who twice invite Danny to "come *play* with us," using this single expression exclusively.

To return to the diction of Jack's typed "manuscript," the hotel's patronizing voice is most pronounced in its judgment of Jack himself as "a dull boy." Just as Grady employs derisive language prior to releasing Jack from the locked pantry and the ghost woman in room 237 mocks him with her laughter, the hotel once more seeks to goad Torrance into violent action by condemning him to the worst possible status in the lexicon of spoiled party brats: That he is *dull*. At the same time, the phrase serves to remind the audience and Torrance himself that his five months of sobriety represent hard *work* that has come at the great expense of *play*. The omniscient voice of the Overlook apparently wishes Jack to inculcate the meaning of the idiom at the same time as it challenges him to react to it (thus the onerous purpose of retyping its exact phrasing so many times). The only way to escape his currently unfavorable social standing is for Jack to entertain his decadent hosts by following their own carnival regime of misrule in subverting all conventional notions of *work* and *play*.

If we assume that Jack's "new writing project" in Kubrick's film, which is never defined, is the same as it is in King's novel—that is, a drama—then the possible meanings for the word *play* continue to expand. "All work and no play" subtly ridicules the dedicated work ethic with which Torrance began the writing of his new theatrical drama, which has now been displaced in the typing of this monotonous phrase (work at the hotel = no play written by Jack). Moreover, the various literary genres that are visualized on paper in the typed "All work and no play makes Jack a dull boy" manuscript represent yet another example of the hotel mocking Jack and his occupation as a writer. Pictured are the standard forms of language arrangements that a writer employs in defining himself as a poet, dramatist, novelist, or essayist. In misusing and subverting them to reproduce the same mindless concept over and over, however, the Overlook is *playing* with the very *work* of Jack's livelihood and potential future.

The endlessly repeated idiom ultimately suggests again another type of mirroring sequence. As Wendy shuffles her way through page after page of the same nonsensical language restated in recognizable arrangements, it is as if she were viewing the successive phrases from within a hall of mirrors. The typed forms of repeated words also mirror one of the central images in the film: The hedge maze. Shaped in simple and identifiable patterns that become infinitely more complex when multiplied and viewed as a whole, Jack's literary "manuscript" and the maze present parallel structures that initially are easily penetrated, only to grow, as we have seen, increasingly more convoluted. Just as Jack loses himself geographically at the end of the film as he moves more deeply within the hedge maze, his intellectual abandonment is reflected in the linguistic maze created from the infinite pursuit of this single idiom.

The use of mirrored sequences in this film is further buttressed by the manner in which Kubrick measures and regulates time. In a film in which linear time is warped by both the design of the hotel (where past becomes present) and in the deathless winter that rages on outside, Kubrick is at liberty to impose his own sense of time over the film's universe. Stretching over nearly two and a half hours, this film maintains a certain languidness that roughly corresponds to a distant era in American history. Very little dramatic action actually occurs in the first two-thirds of *The Shining*—as we view the Torrances exercising, preparing meals, watching television, riding Big Wheels; like the characters in the film *2001: A Space Odyssey* (1968), they are essentially adrift in the massive space they inhabit.

Contrary to the tight and episodic qualities that distinguish a work such as *The Dead Zone*, Kubrick's film possesses an open-ended, dream-like atmosphere, even as chronological time can be seen to "shorten" in the imposed sequential series of blackouts with white letters typed on the screen: "The Interview," "Closing Day," "One Month Later," "Monday," "8 AM," "4 PM." These nonspecific demarcations suggest the fluid nature of historical reality as it operates within the Overlook, where it is always time for a party. The manner in which the hotel's guests are dressed (as well as the music they listen to) indicates that the Overlook itself prefers the 1920s rather than any other era. Just as Danny's "shining" is capable of tra-versing conventional notions of time and space (e.g., his vision of the ele-vator of blood in his bathroom mirror), the Overlook likewise possesses the ability to suspend time and free itself from the constraints of a linear chronology. (Perhaps this connection is the reason the hotel simultane-ously fears Danny and desires to possess his supernatural talent?)

On the other hand, Kubrick's imposed chronological segments im-pose a definite pattern, from the vague open-ended implications of the ini-tial "The Interview," which could conceivably occur at any time on any day, toward a series of ever-more narrowing moments—"One Month Later," for example, eventually constricts into "Monday" and then "4 PM." The film's sense of time occupying a narrowing continuum parallels the re-strictive rendering that is occurring to the Torrance family psychologically. A palpable sense of doom closes in on this family as the weather worsens and they gradually become more estranged from the world and from each other. Like Kubrick's employment of mirrors and mazes, his manipulation of time in *The Shining* reinforces the film's alternating atmosphere of ex-tension and compression.

Many of Kubrick's films have as their subtext the collapse of language and the inability to communicate. Sometimes this linguistical depreciation occurs as a result of the dislocation between machine and man, as in *2001;* sometimes it undermines the deterioration between bureaucratic systems of authority and the individual, as in *Dr. Strangelove* (1963), *Clockwork Orange* (1971), and *Full Metal Jacket;* but most often the deleterious consequences of language failure in Kubrick occur between individual human beings—particularly those in marital relationships—as evinced in *Eyes Wide Shut* and *The Shining*. Throughout his career, Stanley Kubrick directed technically brilliant masterpieces of postmodern alienation and despair. His genius is most evident in scenes such as the one that begins *The Shining:* A long overhead tracking shot of stunning Rocky Mountain scenery that is coldly intimidating and capable of reducing its human presence to minuscule dots literally on the edge of disappearing into nature's enormity. Lest we forget, Kubrick's last film, *A. I.* (2001), may have received some romantic tweaking in Steven Spielberg's revisions and final editing, but Kubrick's own artistic vision nevertheless concluded in the end of the world, with the absolute obliteration of the human race.

Underscoring this misanthropic view of existence, a recurring definition of madness and monstrosity in Kubrick's oeuvre is found in the self's total absorption with itself to the exclusion of meaningful connections with other people. Consider, for example, the fate that both HAL in *2001* and Alex in *A Clockwork Orange* share in common. Although HAL is a computer, the machine no longer serves the humans who created it. As a monster, it views human beings as nothing more than servants to its will, objects to be tossed into space once they are no longer useful to it. Alex the Droog is another version of HAL, insofar as he is a being without conscience or humanity. His gratuitous love of violence is a degenerate symptom of his cynicism toward society and interpersonal communication. It is interesting that in Kubrick's *The Shining* there is no attempt to portray a divided Jack Torrance as he exists in King's novel, who struggles right to the end with the two opposing forces—his family and the hotel—that literally tear him apart. Kubrick's version of Torrance is much closer to the tyrannical HAL and Alex than he is to King's more conflicted, more sympathetically human characterization. In Kubrick's film, Jack's loyalties are never really in doubt.

In the destruction of the Torrance father-son bond, Kubrick exploits one of humankind's deepest fears: that we are unwanted by our parents, repulsive to our children. If a father can turn so irrevocably inward that he rejects his family completely, then there is nothing inviolable in the universe, nothing is secure, and there is no basis for hope. At the end of *The Shining,* Jack is transformed into a monster—hand wrapped in bandages, lurching with a limp, the once-articulate language skills of a writer reduced to an anguished howl indistinguishable from the winds of winter and the roar of the snow cat's engine. In his terrible isolation, uncontrolled fury, and impending doom, Jack becomes an appropriate extension of the hotel itself. The Overlook's irrational propensities are mirrored in Jack's inability (unwillingness?) to follow Danny out of the hedge maze. Instead of merely turning around and retracing his own snow prints (as Danny does) once he realizes he has been tricked, Jack sets off haphazardly into virginal snow, moving deeper into the maze, deeper into the night storm, and deeper into the madness of his own mind. He loses his bearings, both geographically and spiritually, and freezing in the snow symbolizes the degree of his self-enclosure. Torrance becomes a creature of the night, wandering in the darkness and without moral direction, as well as a creature of the winter—much like the Wendigo monster in *Pet Sematary*—embodying its cruel and violent indifference toward human life. Indeed, one of the last scenes in this film is another mirror of sorts. It features a frozen Jack Torrance finally at rest alongside a snow-covered wall of the hedge maze, his frosted glare as much a mirror to the winter landscape surrounding him as it is a way of measuring the distance from the self he has forever lost.

The fathers in both the film versions of *The Shining* and *Pet Sematary* undergo elaborate initiations into evil, and neither Torrance nor Louis Creed (Dale Midkiff), nor the families who must bear witness to the consequences of these male-centered rites of passage, survive the experience unchanged. In *The Shining,* Jack Torrance serves the patriarchal design that operates the Overlook. In doing so, he is often relegated to childlike status. Not only do the hotel's ghostly ambassadors instruct him on how to behave and to maintain the secrets that are disclosed to him, Torrance is also chastised (e.g., before Grady releases him from the dry food pantry) when he fails to obey and perform the tasks according to the hotel's specifications. All through Kubrick's *The Shining* Torrance seeks to appease the unseen yet nonetheless omnipresent patriarchal authority at the Overlook; the hotel's very name implies such a relationship. In *Pet Sematary,* Louis Creed is initiated into the diabolical realm of the Micmac burial ground by Jud Crandall (Fred Gwynne), an old neighbor who likewise serves as Creed's surrogate father. Unlike the patriarchy at the Overlook, however, Jud is well-intentioned; he introduces Louis to the vampiric mystery of the Micmac cemetery because he sincerely wants to help him deal with the problem of his dead cat. But in once again transgressing the "barrier that was not meant to be crossed," Jud is also serving evil's design. He becomes, albeit unwittingly, as much manipulated by the powers located at the Micmac gravesite as the specters Torrance must confront in residence at the Overlook. As he acknowledges to Louis on the evening of Gage

Creed's (Miko Hughes) funeral: "I'm responsible for more pain in your heart than you should have tonight. For all I know, I may even be responsible for the death of your son." Moreover, because Louis comes to love and respect Jud, he trusts him, and this leaves Creed vulnerable to the old and always restless power that Victor Pascow's (Brad Greenquist) ghost warns him looms just beyond the deadfall barrier. It is noteworthy that in the scene immediately following Pascow's nocturnal visitation and second warning to Creed, the doctor throws Pascow's medical file into the wastebasket in his office, effectively symbolizing his unwillingness to heed the spectral warning that has been delivered to him. By the end of the film, Jud has passed down the cemetery's awful secret to his neighbor whom he comes to love as a son, and Creed's blank eyes signaling the collapse of his sanity indicate that he is now trapped in the same cycle that has ensnared many of the other males in this small town.

In *The Shining,* Jack Torrance relinquishes his body as well as his mind to powers that ultimately betray him. He is victimized, as we have seen, by supernatural energies that are larger than himself, but with whom he strikes a Faustian bargain of sorts: He will sacrifice his family in return for immortality at the Overlook. Like Torrance, Louis Creed forges an infernal bond with a supernatural agency to secure what he needs. While Torrance desperately seeks the hotel's affirmation because of his own masculine insecurities, Creed is searching for something even grander in scope and scale. He attempts to usurp the role of God when he learns the ultimate secret associated with his occupation as a physician—control over life and death. Once he is in position to access this power, he cannot help but use it. At the Overlook, Jack Torrance's loss of mental balance costs him his only son; in *Pet Sematary,* it is the death of his only son that pushes Dr. Creed into Torrance's world of personal madness. And in each film, a supernatural phenomenon is at work exploiting the remarkably similar weaknesses that these men share in common.

Like *The Shining, Pet Sematary* is a film about the destruction of a family exploited by supernatural forces that exist outside the perimeters of the family itself. In both films, it is the particular susceptibility of the fathers who are at the head these respective families that make their collapse possible.

King's screenplay for *Pet Sematary* is a faithful rendition of the original 1983 novel, and its priorities are identical in its focus on Creed's slow seduction into evil and descent into madness. Creed reveals himself initially to be a good husband and father who has recently begun work as an infirmary physician at a local Maine university. When he discovers magical powers of regeneration available in the Indian burial ground deep in the woods behind his house, he cannot resist exploring their properties. But as in any great tragedy, Louis Creed's destruction is not merely personal, nor is it experienced in isolation. He is manipulated by an unseen force that manifests itself through a distinct shaping of events—from Jud Crandall's introduction of the burial site as a misguided favor to Louis, to the death of Creed's son on the highway in front of his house, to the return of Gage as a perverse host for the malefic energy that resides in the burial site. When Gage follows Church, the Creed cat, and is killed on the same high-way in front of their home, the cyclic pattern of the film is established as the grieving father inters his son's corpse in the Indian burial ground. Recognizing that the resurrected Gage bears little resemblance to his beloved son, Louis must dispatch the child monster, but not before the latter has murdered both Jud Crandall and Rachel (Denise Crosby), Louis's wife and Gage's mother. The film ends in Louis's insane attempt to experiment yet a third time with the Micmac site, burying Rachel there and embracing her when she returns stumbling into their kitchen, one oozing eye dislocated from its socket and a sharp knife cradled ominously in her hand.

Louis makes up his mind almost immediately after the death of his child to test the powers of resurrection of the Micmac burial ground. After putting his wife and daughter on a plane and promising to join them in three days (the biblical allusion to Christ rising from the dead after three days is an ironic parallel), Creed reassures himself that he will simply "put Gage back to sleep" should the child come back the monster that Jud has prophesied. Always the rational scientist even in his most irrational moments, Louis believes he can experiment with powers greater than himself without retribution. His grief as a suffering father overwhelms his logic as a man of science, and he foolishly trusts that he can control a force that has already proven to be greater than himself. He is burdened with a promise he makes throughout the movie to both his wife and daughter that he is capable of making "everything all right." His hubris does not permit him to recognize that "sometimes dead is better" and that he is being manipulated by an evil that not only preys upon his grief, but is likewise responsible for causing it in the first place.

Critics of *The Shining* seldom note that after Jack Torrance experiences the ghost woman residing in room 237, he deliberately lies to Wendy, who is afraid that "there's someone else in the hotel." Torrance refuses to disclose what he has encountered in room 237 primarily because he wishes to protect the ghosts at work in the hotel and to keep their presence a secret from his wife. But he also goes so far as to implicate his son in a lie by trying to convince Wendy that Danny has imagined the ghost woman's presence. A whole system of secrets and lies underscores Jack's relationship with his wife, epitomized in his inability to cope honestly with his alcoholism, his own lack of self-knowledge and unrealistic writing ambitions, and the degree to which he represses his escalating antagonism toward his family.

Like the hierarchy in place at the Overlook Hotel, the world of mystery and superstition residing deep inside the woods that is known only to town locals and the occasional folklorist in *Pet Sematary* is an exclusively male domain. When Jud introduces Louis to the secret powers that long ago belonged to Native American warriors and fishermen, he does so when Louis's wife and family are out of town during a long Thanksgiving holiday, and with the pledge that Louis will not reveal the source that produced his cat's regeneration. "Women are supposed to be the ones good at keeping secrets," Jud proposes to Louis after they have buried Church, "but any woman who knows anything at all will tell you she's never seen into a man's heart. The soil of a man's heart is stonier, like the soil up there in the old Micmac burying ground." Jud's childhood memories of local use of the burial ground center exclusively around male experimentation; the town's women, in contrast, view the transformational results of the Micmac cemetery as "abominations" and choose deliberately not to avail themselves of its properties. Like Jack Torrance, Louis Creed is given ample opportunity to reject the lure of this dangerous place, to extricate himself from an intimate bond with it, and to find the strength to resist it in the love of his family. But evil confronts both Creed and Torrance with an intoxicating admixture of power and corruption that proves too alluring for them to resist. Torrance succumbs to it because of his low self-esteem; Louis Creed gives himself over to the dark power at the Micmac site for opposite reasons, because of his high regard for himself, his faith—his "creed"—in his rational abilities as a doctor to control even the most irrational events. Initially, he cannot bear the pain he anticipates his daughter will undergo in the loss of her beloved cat. Later, he himself is unable to bear the death of his son. As a man of science trained in cause-and-effect relationships, he trusts that he will be able to harness the powers of the Micmac burial ground and employ them for his own purposes, to relieve his personal pain. Although he has been provided with plenty of evidence that experimenting with the Wendigo results in lethal consequences, his grief as a father who is unable to accept the loss of his only son plus his professional hubris push him forward.

As different as the personal circumstances that tempt Torrance and Creed are, what they share in common is the degree of rationalization that allows each man to justify even his most outrageous action and, even more important, the total failure on the part of both men to include their wives as potential solutions to their respective problems. As these men become more deeply involved in the secret world of supernatural evil, they grow ever more estranged from their wives, pulled into a sphere where, ironically, their last remaining asset—love of family—is forfeited. Early in *Pet Sematary,* Louis Creed decides to have Church neutered. He makes this decision without consulting either his wife or daughter, basing it exclusively upon the advice of Jud, who counsels him that this may help prolong the cat's life. Louis does not merely *neuter* the animal so much as he *feminizes* it. By castrating Church, "cutting his nuts off" in Missy Dandridge's (Susan Blommaert) "colorful phrase," the cat is stripped of its masculinity and becomes essentially feminine. According to Jud, this act will make the cat safer by forcing it to become more tractable, keeping it under Louis's male gaze, close to home, away from the dangers of the road. In this same way, Louis excludes Rachel and Ellie (Blaze Berdahl) from knowledge that he decides will be dangerous for them to possess—his nocturnal visitation from Victor Pascow's ghost, the location and history of the Micmac burial ground beyond the pet cemetery, the resurrected Church, and finally his decision to disinter and relocate Gage Creed's corpse. The film explores to some extent the feminine intuition that both Rachel and particularly Ellie possess in their evolving contact with Pascow's ghost and their dawning awareness of Louis Creed's predicament. But Louis secretly fears his wife at the same time that he wishes, like Jack Torrance, to maintain his power over her in the keeping of masculine secrets. Although he appears to bear the trappings of a New Age father husband, Louis Creed is as patriarchal a control freak as any male in King's cinematic universe. The women in his life—from his neutered cat to his wife and daughter—are to be neither trusted nor liberated. Creed's need to control his family extends to include his attitude toward the supernatural powers residing in the burial ground above his house. What is missing in this man is clearly the humility necessary to cope with issues beyond the individual's ability to control, such as death.

In her essay "In Words Not Their Own: Dangerous Women in Stephen King," Karen A. Hohne posits that women in King's novels are "never allowed to speak themselves, to make themselves with words" (328). In contrast, Hohne insists, the "language of power" belongs exclusively to his male characters, thereby marginalizing women even further. While Hohne's thesis seems right to me, at least up until the onset of King's feminist work, such as *Gerald's Game* and *Dolores Claiborne,* it is likewise true that his male protagonists incorporate the *silence* of secrets—that is, the deliberate omission of language—to exclude women from narrative action and empowerment. Perhaps it is this very preclusion of women that makes the keeping of these secrets so dangerous and ultimately self-destructive for the men who maintain them.

In *Pet Sematary,* director Mary Lambert emphasizes Creed's growing isolation. Paralleling Torrance's demise at the Overlook, the more involved Louis becomes with the cryptic agency governing the Micmac woods, the less connected he remains to the world of the human—his friends, his career, and his family. In turn, their bonds with other males—in Torrance's case, Lloyd and Grady, for Dr. Creed, his neighbor Jud—strengthen and increase in relative importance. Like Mary Shelley's *Frankenstein,* these two films are sobering reminders that in the realm of horror art, men are often severely punished and surrender their potential for personal salvation when they engage in secretive acts that require them to lie or to mislead the most important women in their lives. It is no accident that both Torrance and Creed share remarkably similar fates. Having strayed from the civilizing influences represented by women and family, both men are reduced to their basest, most selfish level—relinquishing their most human traits, they are transformed into extensions of nature at its most misanthropic.

In her analysis of *The Shining,* Cynthia A. Freeland notes that Kubrick portrays nature as "ominous, not simply as an indifferent force that will suck things up and leave no sign behind. It is a dark force of evil that can be reflected in but is not confined to human nature" (224). This is precisely the view of the natural world that animates Lambert's *Pet Sematary;* in fact, Freeland's description applies equally well to both these films. The Micmac burial site is itself a barren and hostile place. Louis visits it on two separate occasions, once on a clear, cold day late in November at the onset of winter, and the second time in the darkness of night. Each time he makes the trek into the woods we are aware of a force residing there that is aligned with the particularly "stony soil" of a hostile New England environment and nature's general antipathy to human welfare. The barren topography of space that exists above the deadfall barrier stands in stark contrast to the richly bucolic pet cemetery tended by the children of the town. As Louis moves beyond this green and grassy enclave, the vast forest and the immense slabs of gray granite at the Micmac site exercises such a dominating presence that it tends to dwarf any human who stumbles into it. It is a place of terrifying loneliness, where nature appears to be antagonistic to a human presence, where the air appears clear and frigid cold, and where lightning, darkness, and eerie moonlight join forces with whatever preternatural being stirs the earth to infernal life. Indeed, the transmogrified monsters that rise from the "sour ground" of the Micmac site bear little in common with the personalities of the deceased. Although the original bodies may be reanimated, they are now inhabited by a violent and primitive supernatural energy that exists to foment chaos in the mortal world. Like the ghosts who come to possess Jack Torrance, this energy is likewise vampiric: It utilizes the physical body of its host as a means for manifesting its evil design. As the resurrected Gage Creed aptly demonstrates in his unholy alliance with the reborn Church, the perverse spirit occupying his corpse is capable of assuming different shapes and identities; its only real consistency is that it employs its former personality as a means for seducing and attacking susceptible mortals.

The natural world of *Pet Sematary* underscores the fact that the human world is confronted by forces it neither wholly comprehends nor is in a position to engage sympathetically. Even more than *The Shining, Pet Sematary* is a deeply pessimistic film that highlights the limitations of being human, the malefic design of fate and its consistent pressure to push us toward tragic consequences. Not only are Jud and Louis punished severely for their lapses in judgment, they are also victimized by a supernatural force that remains in active opposition to their best intentions and personal needs. From the opening scene, the film is punctuated continually by the sound of Orinco tanker trucks laboring down the highway in front of Louis Creed's house at excessive rates of speed. When Church returns from the dead, his dark presence haunts the Creed house and almost appears to form an unholy collusion with these omnipresent trucks: Both are reminders of a malevolent fate that is larger than the individual human beings who must suffer the full extent of its influence. The theme of *Pet Sematary* is the helplessness of humanity in the face of powers that are both larger than the individual human and committed to his obliteration. This theme is a quintessential element of many horror films—that human beings are destined to struggle against forces of evil that are too great to be overcome. Sometimes these powers can be endured, but in this film they prove totally overwhelming. Just as Rachel Creed's rental car is inexplicably swept off the road in her last desperate effort to save her husband, the events that occur in this film all appear to be shaped by an unseen and inhuman hand. Once Louis and Jud pass beyond the barrier and trespass into the realm of the Indian dead, their lives are no longer within their control.

Two of the most effective scenic props in *Pet Sematary* are the actual sites of the film's cemeteries. Arranged in a series of concentric spirals containing individual cairns, their gravestones do more than simply reflect Jud Crandall's lighthearted comment to Ellie early in the film that this is the manner in which the "dead speak." Lambert is careful to have the two cemeteries mirror one another; the Pet Sematary belonging to the town's children is a benign and miniature version of the rocky plateau where the Micmac burial site is situated. Jud informs Louis that the circular shape of the children's animal graves likewise radiate outward—the oldest occupying the center circles, those more recent on the periphery. This utilization of spiral and circular patterns at both graveyards establishes the dominant thematic metaphor for the entire film, as the most important action as well as the major characters themselves keep circling back to the Micmac burial ground, and they in turn to Dr. Creed himself. Moreover, while the film deftly avoids the provocative issue of the white man's intrusion and violation of once-sacred Indian ground, images of the spiral and circle have mystical significance in Native American lore: They are often employed by artists and shamans to suggest levels of supernatural power, deviousness, and the torturous.

In King's 1975 novel, *'Salem's Lot,* a book that in many ways is the thematic prototype for *The Shining* and *Pet Sematary,* the main character, Ben Mears, develops an obsession with the Marsten House because he views it as a "monument to evil, a supernatural beacon . . . [a place where] the evil that men do lives after them" (128). Many of the novels and films that follow *'Salem's Lot* echo its core sentiment: The evil perpetrated in a particular place transcends time and calls other men to it. So in *Pet Sematary,* the spiral is likewise symbolic of a continuous fact of life—that the wrongdoings and fateful consequences of one man can and soon enough will be the evil of the next man. The male inhabitants of this small Maine town constitute a line of participants spiraling up through historical time to the Micmac site, passing its dark secret on to the next generation. Jud and Louis are the town's most recent embodiment of the biblical decree that the sins of the father will be visited upon the son.

The two cemeteries in *Pet Sematary* are not the only examples of circular and spiral imagery in this film. The ghost of Victor Pascow—clad in the jogging suit he was wearing on the day he died, the clotted blood from his head trauma still in place—joins the Orinco trucks as a cyclical entity that reappears at various critical points throughout the movie. Unfortunately, his prophetic efforts to counterbalance the ancient energies at work destroying Louis Creed's world are fruitless. Pascow is a representative of whatever good still operates in the universe, but in this film his powers prove vastly inferior to those aligned with darkness and evil. His well-intentioned effort to guide the Creeds in circumventing tragedy amounts to a feeble gesture when compared to the supernatural agency at work in pushing this family toward the abyss. Nonetheless, his warnings are a plea for self-restraint and personal accountability. As a cryptic spirit literally poised between the mortal realm and the afterlife, Pascow understands intimately the transgressive urge to cross barriers, the human temptation to make oneself into a god. But he also warns against the danger inherent in such choices. There are certain conditions man must simply learn to accept, certain secrets he has no business protecting, and certain barriers that he crosses at the expense of his happiness and sanity. As such, Pascow's somber message spirals out from beyond the woods surrounding the pet cemetery and even the perimeters of this film itself to become one of the most important voices heard in cinemagraphic adaptations of Stephen King. Among the most recurrent themes found in many of these films is this: That one's humanity—or one's soul—is dreadfully easy to lose, and what we abandon ourselves to possess, we necessarily become. The romantic poet William Blake may have found perfect serenity residing in "the lineaments of gratified desire." But for Louis Creed, such delusionary self-absorption leads to the internment of his dead wife in the Micmac cemetery under the totally unfounded justification that he "waited too long" to transplant his son and that "this time will be different."

The 1998 film *Apt Pupil* is best viewed as yet another example of the male urge to violate Pascow's "barriers not meant to be crossed" admonition. If *The Shining* and *Pet Sematary* display similar attitudes toward the natural world at its most misanthropic, *Apt Pupil* is a study in the inherent cruelty of *human* nature and its propensity for acts of perverse cruelty. Set in an innocuous American suburb, Todd Bowden (Brad Renfro), a precocious adolescent fascinated with the grisly details of Nazi involvement in World War II, recognizes an aging war criminal, Kurt Dussander (Ian McKellen), hiding in his neighborhood. Instead of alerting the authorities to his remarkable discovery, Todd begins an elaborate drama of blackmail: He will not turn the Nazi over to the police if the latter will describe in detail what took place in the concentration camps he formerly commanded. Thus, what begins as a kind of personalized history lesson slowly escalates into the desire to re-create the past. Both Todd and Dussander are drawn into the violence that distinguished the Nazi regime, and they begin to perform their own acts of cruelty, eventually culminating in Dussander's attack on an itinerate man whom Todd must finish killing and then bury in the Nazi's basement. Suffering a heart attack as a result of this strenuous action, Dussander is rushed to a local hospital, where he is recognized by a fellow patient. The Nazi takes his own life before he can be brought into custody, leaving Todd to practice the sophistry he has now honed into an art by convincingly denying any knowledge of Dussander's criminal past.

The screenplay for the film version of *Apt Pupil* is much more concentrated than King's novella. Although both film and book are fascinating studies into the attractiveness of evil, the film manages to avoid the overreliance on coincidence that characterizes the last third of the book. Indeed, most fortuitous is the decision to forgo King's conclusion, where Todd, on the verge of being arrested for his collusion with Dussander, takes a rifle to a hill overlooking an interstate highway and begins randomly shooting passing automobiles. Instead, the Todd of the film is a confident and highly skilled adult—rather than King's panic-stricken adolescent—manipulator, willing to sacrifice anyone in order to protect himself and the secret knowledge he possesses. The difference between these two Todds may indicate the difference between absorbing history and being absorbed by history.

Like *The Shining* and *Pet Sematary*, *Apt Pupil* is a cinematic work that centers on the dangers inherent in the keeping of male secrets. As young Todd Bowden opens himself to the history of violence and abuse that Kurt Dussander perpetrated as a commander of a Nazi concentration camp, his prurient interest in the secret history Dussander possesses becomes addictive. The innocuous curiosity that initiates this relationship—an "apt pupil" who wishes to expand his knowledge beyond the classroom and into the actual detailing of what took place inside the death camps—evolves into an active and mutually exploitative relationship that neither participant can finally control.

The film's opening credits occur behind the backdrop of a series of black-and-white photographs of Nazi officers gleaned from history books and newspapers. The audience watches a young boy examine thoughtfully these various faces, most of them not much older than his own. At one point, the camera superimposes Todd's face alongside black-and-white headshots of several Nazi officers (one of them proves to be a youthful portrait of Kurt Dussander). For a brief moment the photographs on the page become transparent, and Todd's face, through the magic of film, appears aligned with them. The effect, albeit momentary, creates for the audience a merging between Todd's head and those of the men he is studying—as if the boy had suddenly transgressed across the borders of time and place, imposing himself into the history associated with these men. In other words, from the onset of this film past and present virtually intersect, melding into an indistinguishable juxtaposition. As this echoes exactly the narrative design of *Apt Pupil*—that is, that a historical act of evil exerts a dynamic influence on the present—this film shares much in common with *The Shining* and *Pet Sematary*. All three cinematic texts revolve around a similar premise: That a sin severe enough never really dies; it resembles more a dormant virus that eventually reawakens all the more virulent as a result of its prolonged sleep.

As Todd practices ever more devious and intricate methods of extracting a personal history from the former Nazi officer, their interaction brings Dussander back into intimate contact with his past. Reliving his misconduct during the war affects his new life in California. His blood lust is reawakened; he tries to kill a cat in his oven and eventually commits a murder in his kitchen. Moreover, the boy's incessant probing threatens to explode beyond both their control when he forces the old man to wear again the uniform of a Nazi officer. Dressed in the uniform, Dussander's response to a series of maneuvers issued by his young tormenter creates a moment where the film appears to borrow from "The Sorcerer's Apprentice," and the dark magic that is summoned momentarily releases a monster no longer capable of obeying its master. During this sequence Todd commands Dussander, who is framed in a doorway separating the bright yellow kitchen from the dark wood interior of rest of the house, to march in alternating directions. As the pace of the sequence accelerates through quick camera cuts between Todd and Dussander, the boy loses control over the Nazi, as the old man is responding to something instinctively within himself that is more akin to the muscle memory of the past. Just before the boy makes a desperate effort to stop what he has started, Dussander issues a Nazi salute on his own, almost in defiance of his adolescent commander. Appropriately, the scene ends with the old man's exhausted warning: "Be careful boy, you play with fire." Indeed, the question of who is the exploiter and who is the victim in this film bears careful watching. Initially, it is young Todd who uses his identification as a threat that helps him to extort the war criminal; midway through the film, however, the power dynamic shifts, and the Nazi begins to reclaim authority from his aggressive protégé.

Just as Dussander's recollections spark an active and violent reawakening in the old man of his repressed Nazi identity, Todd's deepening relationship with him also causes the child to metamorphose. In one particularly interesting scene early in the film, Todd showers with his gym class in a high school boys' locker room. The audience watches Todd slowly relax in the warm water while the film drains of color, darkening to an ashen gray, as several naked old men abruptly displace Todd's adolescent classmates. Awakening from his daydream (or perhaps entering into one; the film is not clear on this), the boy finds himself transported in time, back to a concentration camp shower, face-to-face with several inmates. The men in the shower stare at Todd not only with looks that indicate their own curiosity regarding his presence, but also with a certain level of accusation— as if Todd, like their German jailers, has also violated their privacy. And, of course, in a very real way this exactly what he has done. In part, this scene is meant to suggest the level to which Todd's extracurricular research has affected his subconscious. As psychological studies of exposure to aggressive acts indicate, the more an individual is exposed to violence, the deeper his response to it. As he learns the specific details of the Holocaust, "everything they are afraid to show us in school," Todd loses the ability to view the event as an objective historical moment locked in time. Dussander's daily detailings bring the atrocities of the Holocaust to dramatic life; steady contact with it pushes Todd into a more intimate and a more active participation in the events that transpired fifty years ago.

It is also significant that young Bowden's daydream centers on sharing a shower with the miserable camp prisoners, for he has ironically become a victim of their history, experiencing vicariously the intimate torments and violations Nazi prisoners were forced to undergo. The film goes on to explore the increasingly distracting and subversive degrees to which Todd's history lessons are influencing him. His grades plummet, and he is forced to forge his father's signature on school documents. As he confesses to Dussander, "The shit you tell me keeps me up at night." Todd's changing dreamscape resembles the successive stages of embryonic development in a monstrous chrysalis, signaling the fact that he is losing control over himself. Yet Todd keeps returning to hear more. Later in the movie, parked in a car with his girlfriend Becky Trask (Heather McComb), Todd is unable to perform sexually. In his apology to her, he acknowledges, "This has never happened to me before." Indeed, Todd undergoes a metamorphosis in his identity—from precocious suburban youth to *enfant terrible*—which he neither understands nor is capable of abating. Dussander's warning, "Boy, be careful. You play with fire," is this film's equivalent of Victor Pascow's admonition in *Pet Sematary*.

Like *The Shining* and *Pet Sematary, Apt Pupil* details the corrosive and pernicious passage of male initiations into evil. All of these films, to a greater or lesser extent, document falls from innocence, if not grace. As Torrance and Creed find themselves transformed by their contact with older men who introduce them to their own hearts of darkness, Dussander fuels a flame that has always burned inside Todd. It should be emphasized that the spirit of a nascent Nazi exists in Todd (whose name means "death" in German) even before he makes contact with Dussander. The fact that he is capable of manipulating the old man with such devious ruthlessness suggests that his link to the Nazi is more than academic. But through the tutelage of his father surrogate—Dussander even poses as Todd's paternal grandfather to deceive the school guidance counselor, while his biological father is virtually nonexistent in the film—Todd's puerile fascination is transformed into an active specialization.

What is perhaps most disturbing about *Apt Pupil*'s revelations into the nature of what took place during the Holocaust are the implicating questions that the film asks us to contemplate. At what point, for example, does the audience separate itself from Todd by acknowledging that he has pursued his history lesson too far? To what extent do we share a similar fascination with the secret knowledge that Dussander possesses? Exactly how far removed are any of us—given the right amount of pressure and historical circumstances—from performing our own ghastly acts of mass violence and subjugation? While most students of the Holocaust, especially the most apt, pay lip service to the infamous phrase "Never again," this disquieting film suggests that humans have encoded within their nature the potential for reenacting another Holocaust—as postmodern history continues to document—at any moment in time.

By the end of *Apt Pupil,* this precocious adolescent has honed his talents from extortion and forgery to murder, from ardent student of history to a violent extension of the Nazi legacy. Furthermore, Todd's descent is cultural as well as personal. What begins this film as a distinctly American boy adroit at baseball and in possession of a prurient interest in the macabre exits as a jaded "German adult" who will bear forever the Nazis' stain on history and his own degree of collusion with it. Todd's deepening involvement with the Holocaust poses a parallel to the German populace during World War II. As the power and ruthlessness of the Nazi machine gained momentum, it took on a life of its own, and many individual Germans were, like Todd himself, swept away in its potency. What began as an exciting fascination with power and Arian chauvinism, transformed itself and all those associated with it into something much larger than the individual will proved capable of resisting.

The final scenes of *Apt Pupil* reveal the full range of the survival prowess that Dussander still possesses and that his American pupil has now acquired. The ex-Nazi thwarts the authorities that pursue him one last time even after he is recognized and placed in their custody. In his hospital bed recovering from a stroke, Dussander commits suicide to avoid extradition and trial in Israel. Concurrent with this subversive event is Todd's blackmail threat against another authority figure, his former guidance counselor, Edward French (David Schwimmer). In fact, at one point the camera cuts to a series of quick, individual head shots of Todd, Dussander, French, and Weiskopf (Jan Triska), the Israeli agent pursuing Dussander, linking them all together in a drama of power, manipulation, and escape. In response to French's efforts to explore further the connection between Todd and Dussander, the adolescent calmly warns him that he will invent a charge of homosexual assault and use it to destroy French's professional career. "You have no idea what I can do," Todd threatens, indicating that he has learned his lessons well from Dussander, "I'm better at this than you are."

Todd exits the film successfully shooting a basket with his basketball. This act is more important than it appears, as all through the film Todd has been unable to make a basket. Steady contact with Dussander produces increasing levels of frustration and brutality in the boy and these elements are reflected most immediately in his lack of basketball expertise (at one point he even viciously dispatches a wounded pigeon by crushing it with a basketball). Todd's shot lacks a deft touch; he shoots with too much force and not enough finesse. By the end of the film, however, after he has successfully intimidated French (who drives away from Todd's house as frightened as he is confused), Todd's stroke is accurate and smooth. Indeed, the movie's closing camera shot juxtaposes Dussander's dead face inside the center of Todd's basketball hoop. This final association is a subtle reminder that many of Dussander's coercive survival skills have now passed on to his apt pupil.

The Shining, Pet Sematary, and *Apt Pupil* are films that trace the inextricable diminution of their male protagonists into varying states of madness. This descent evokes the emotions of pity and terror from the film audience because all of the main characters in these movies possess the potential for greatness. We witness a combination of events—selfish and ultimately lethal personal choices aligned with the cruel machinations of a deterministic fate—that end up destroying these men in spite of their many attributes as husbands, fathers, sons, and essentially decent, albeit flawed, human beings. The protection of secrets is a theme that pervades each of the films discussed in this chapter—and the secrets that are maintained result in the moral erosion of those who insist on keeping them. While it is true that these characters derive a certain perverse power from the concealed knowledge they possess, their secret knowledge is also a forbidden knowledge. No secret in any of these films ever goes unpunished. Invariably the secret takes on a life of its own; the men in possession of it become possessed by it. The human, and perhaps particularly masculine, urge to exploit the mysteries of a supernatural burial ground or to conjure the specters of Nazism for personal gratification paves the way for the corruption of the individual.

In *Danse Macabre*, Stephen King asserts that "if the horror story is our rehearsal for death, then its strict moralities make it also a reaffirmation of life and good will and simple imagination—just one more pipeline to the infinite" (380). A filmgoer would be hard-pressed to find "a reaffirmation of life" in the movies discussed within this chapter. While Jack Torrance, Louis Creed, Todd Bowden, and Jud Crandall certainly appear to initiate a "pipeline to the infinite," what they open eventually closes in on them—their experiences result in personal annihilation and spiritual dissolution. All of these men are irrevocably changed—and doomed—by their common urge to violate moral perimeters, to intrude beyond each film's respective "barrier not meant to be crossed."

In the next chapter, we will consider the true heroes who emerge from films based on Stephen King's fiction. In contrast to the fathers and sons discussed in this chapter, there exist a group of cinematic characters that manage to endure in spite of overwhelming threats to their psychological stability and personal identities. They establish clear and defendable barriers to the encroaching madness that ends up engulfing Jack Torrance, Louis Creed, Judd Crandall, Kurt Dussander, and Todd Bowden. In sharp contrast to the protagonists featured in this chapter, they are likewise strengthened by their commitment to traditional moral virtues that affirm the sanctity of "life and goodwill and simple imagination" even in the face of their violation.

CHAPTER 5

DEFINING HEROIC CODES OF SURVIVAL:
THE DEAD ZONE, THE SHAWSHANK REDEMPTION, THE GREEN MILE

Most filmgoers tend to perceive *The Dead Zone, The Shawshank Redemption,* and *The Green Mile* as aberrations in the Hollywood film canon of work produced from Stephen King's fiction. I am beyond being surprised whenever strangers, upon hearing me link these films with King's name, comment in shocked disbelief, "Stephen King wrote those stories?" Such confusion is understandable, as David Cronenberg's *The Dead Zone* is more a tragic love story than it is a tale of terror, while *Shawshank* and *The Green Mile,* both directed by Frank Darabont, are essentially prison narratives. None of these films can be said to be typical of the horror genre, although all certainly contain sufficient elements of terror and graphic violence. And while *The Dead Zone* and *The Green Mile* rely heavily on supernatural occurrences, which are totally absent in *Shawshank,* their inclusion bear a greater affinity with religious, mystical, and folkloric phenomena than with the abject monsters of horror. All this notwithstanding, each of these films revolves around similar protagonists who occupy the respective centers of each narrative and serve to hold the plots together. Moreover, the unassuming central characters in these films—a schoolteacher, a former banker wrongly convicted of murder, and a prison guard—are immediately recognizable as prototypical Stephen King heroes. The films examined in this chapter are all, to greater or lesser extents, contemporary versions of Christian allegories. They speak to us of struggle and anguish, of isolation and human suffering. Yet the emphasis of each film is less on fear and despair than on the shared will and capacity to survive. In spite of tragic loss, these narratives are also reminders of what is good and noble and deathless in the human spirit. And this last point is a major reason why people who typically do not consider themselves as fans of Stephen King so often appreciate these three movies.

Direct references to Edgar Allan Poe's poem "The Raven" are made on two separate occasions in Cronenberg's *The Dead Zone*. The first allusion opens in an English class being taught by the film's central character, John Smith (Christopher Walken), immediately prior to a fateful car accident that will place him into a five-year coma and transform the remainder of his life. The second reference to "The Raven" takes place several years later, midway through the film, when Smith is again teaching. This time he is studying the poem with a single student, an adolescent boy whose life will be saved as a result of the psychic ability that Smith suddenly gains upon reawakening from the accident and coma. These two deliberate allusions to Poe's 1845 poem are impossible for a critic to overlook; Cronenberg employs the intertextual referencing as a means for paralleling—and then ultimately contrasting—the particular circumstances that confront John Smith throughout the movie.

Most obviously, Poe's most famous poem is about his favorite literary topic: The death of a beautiful woman and a first-person male narrator's inability or unwillingness to shed his romantic melancholia over her loss. Poe's speaker subsists inside a room where he studies and nurtures his pain. His isolation is interrupted by the raven, who appears only to increase his misery by ignoring the human command to "Leave my loneliness unbroken!—quit the bust above my door!" Poe's poem, like so many of his tales, is a study in what Poe himself called *perversity,* or the human desire for self-punishment. While at first the narrator is bemused by the raven's unexpected appearance, he quickly loses patience with the bird because its presence serves to deepen his human despair over his lost love, Lenore. Yet the narrator does nothing to force the bird into leaving, he never does summon a pest exterminator, and his questions about the destiny of the dead Lenore are rhetorically designed to end in the bird's negative comment, "Nevermore." Furthermore, the human knows that the raven is merely a bird; it could no more address his philosophical queries about the afterlife than could the bust of Pallas upon which the creature perches. But the narrator persists, attributing to the bird prophetic abilities: "Prophet! Thing of evil! Prophet still, if bird or devil!" At the conclusion of the poem, the reader understands that the raven has become a permanent resident of the narrator's room and soul. Moreover, the poet appears to find a real measure of pleasure in the additional gloom afforded by the raven's continued presence: "And my soul from out that shadow that lies floating on the floor / Shall be lifted—nevermore!" Throughout *The Dead Zone,* Johnny Smith finds himself in a position identical to the narrator in Poe's poem. He, too, has lost his love; his world's perimeters appear defined by tragedy and loneliness; and for a major portion of this film, Smith flirts dangerously with indulging a Poe-like propensity for cynicism and self-pity. At one point he even asks a student he tutors, Chris Stuart (Simon Craig), to read aloud the part of "The Raven" where Poe's narrator "talks about will I ever see her again," indicating that Smith finds the parallelism to his own romantic situation impossible to ignore.

Like so many of Stephen King's protagonists, John Smith is simply a victim of bad luck and unfortunate circumstances, and must find a way to cope with a personal upheaval beyond his ability to dictate. When we first meet him in this film, he epitomizes the normalcy of middle-class life (even his name highlights his ordinary status). He is a contented young schoolteacher, in love with a colleague who reciprocates his affections. Since they plan to marry in the near future, Smith forgoes the opportunity to spend the night with Sarah (Brooke Adams), saying "Some things are worth waiting for," and heads out into a terrible rainstorm. Because of bad visibility, Smith's Volkswagen collides with a milk tanker, and five years later he awakens from a coma to find his life completely upended: He has lost his job as a teacher, Sarah has married another man, and Smith is in possession of visionary insight—the ability to view certain trenchant past and future events that are connected to any person with whom he comes in direct physical contact. As a consequence of these abilities, which seem to be slowly killing Smith because of the intensity with which the visions are presented in his mind, he is beset with thousands of requests from "lost souls" to help others fill the void created by death and desertion. "I think Johnny Smith becomes a truly tragic figure in the movie," Cronenberg has explained. "He becomes completely alienated because of his abilities"

(Horsting 31). Smith tries desperately to avoid the popular fame that follows him; he even moves out of his parents' house to another town and takes up private tutoring to make a living. But he is pulled back into human society each time he encounters Sarah, whom he has never stopped loving, or a child who requires his aid. King's novel is a convoluted and expansive text that delves deeply into the lives of both Smith and politician Greg Stillson (Martin Sheen) up to and including their fateful meeting. Cronenberg succeeded in streamlining King's narrative—severely revising and editing four separate drafts of Jeffrey Boam's screenplay—until he nearly condensed the first third of King's book into the first ten minutes of the film. "I thought the way to be faithful to the story was to throw the book away and concentrate on being faithful to its tone, its feel," Cronenberg has argued in justifying why he labored to reduce the scope of King's novel (Horsting 31). The last third of the film effectively dramatizes the consequences of Smith's inability to avoid isolation and his commitment to others. Each time he uses his paranormal abilities to influence fate, John does so in an effort to help someone else. His intercessions, however, invariably produce mixed results, as his noble efforts to alleviate suffering often culminate in tragedy. At the end of the film, for example, he sacrifices himself in an assignation attempt to foil Stillson's campaign, leaving Sarah horrified and confused at the same time that he knows he has saved the future of the world by destroying the politician's career.

Smith's supernatural powers consistently link him directly to violence—particularly violence leading to death. Each time he enters the "Dead Zone," a realm that is centered in Smith's mind even as it radiates from his touch, he "feels like [he is] dying inside." The stark winter environment that dominates the film's backdrop from the moment Smith resurfaces from his coma is meant to suggest the pervasive theme of death. In fact, every major scene in the film ends either in death or with a direct reference to it. Afraid of fatally complicating the lives of others and of shortening his own life in the process, Smith tries to exist without human contact, to abandon his connections to the past and future, and to live in a "controlled environment" that recalls the deliberate seclusion of the speaker in "The Raven."

Although continually attracted to the solipsism found in Poe's poem, and particularly its tendency to wallow in personal loss, Smith's greater commitment is to the needs of others. And even while his great powers place him in intimate contact with the dead and dying, he ultimately sacrifices his own life to the world of the living. What saves him from the fate of Poe's self-absorbed narrator is Johnny Smith's contact with, and dedication to, children. Because he is a bachelor and has neither fathered his own progeny nor grown up in the company of siblings nor completely abandoned the realm of childhood himself, Smith maintains an idealized view of children. His contact with them bespeaks a mutual appreciation and respect unavailable to most adults. The fact that he is often called "Johnny" by other characters in this film signals his own degree of immaturity and lack of guile. Indeed, his gentle nature and soft-spoken demeanor make him an approachable teacher in whose presence young people feel comfortable. And these sentiments are reciprocated: Throughout the film adults are skeptical and suspicious of Smith's psychic abilities, worldly naïveté, and loner status; only children accept him unconditionally. When he tries to influence adults directly, Smith almost invariably fails. His virtues of humility and selfless love meet determined resistance from everyone except children.

Smith's uncomplicated view of life—he trusts Roger Stuart's (Anthony Zerbe) promise that no child would use the skating rink—coupled with his complete lack of worldly ambition—Smith never once is tempted to use his prophetic powers for self-gain—link him closely to the realm of childhood. Upon awakening from his coma, Smith elects to return to his father's house to recuperate, willingly placing himself in the role of an adult child. After he helps the sheriff solve the Castle Rock rapist case, Smith moves out to live on his own, but his life is still defined by the adolescents he continues to tutor. Smith's occupation as a schoolteacher prior to his accident is an important point of reference throughout the film: He prefers the company of young people because he has always possessed a special ability to work with them. Thus, each time Smith appears on the verge of withdrawing from society and into himself, an event forces him back into the world, and, significantly, each of these events is precipitated by Smith's direct involvement with children.

His first psychic vision centers on a young girl trapped in a burning house. Smith exchanges places with the frightened child so that he is not merely relating the events she is undergoing, but actively experiencing them himself. Yet perhaps the most significant example of his sympathetic bond with children takes place immediately after Smith has rebuffed Sheriff Bannerman's (Tom Skerritt) plea for help in discovering the identity of the Castle Rock serial killer. In his moment of deepest self-pity, Smith initially refuses to aid the sheriff, telling him that he has "made a mistake" in requesting such assistance and that God "has been a real sport" in destroying Smith's former life and then cursing him with prophetic insight. In the scene immediately following the sheriff's departure, Sarah arrives to visit

Smith with her young son. While the child naps, Sarah and Smith finally consummate the sexual interlude that was denied them years ago because of John's refusal to spend the night and his subsequent accident. In the scene that follows, the audience watches Sarah—aptly named after the woman in the Old Testament who is known for her domestic virtues—making dinner while her son plays on Smith's lap. The three form the family that would have materialized without the cruel intrusion of bad fortune. Even Smith's father is moved to comment that it is "good to have a family eating around this table again." Smith's afternoon liaison with Sarah and her baby reawakens his passion for life; it forces him out of his self-imposed cocoon of anger and regret. Minutes after Sarah leaves to return to her real husband, Smith watches a televised news report about the Castle Rock killer's latest victim, a fifteen-year-old girl. In the context of the afternoon he has just spent assuming the roles of husband and father, it is a child's suffering that again awakens him to action: The murdered girl inspires Smith to help the sheriff solve the homicides.

Film critic Bill Warren interprets this long sequence as pivotal to the movie: "By having Johnny's refusal to help Bannerman precede Sarah's visit to the farm, the latter scene is given as additional meaning: it brings Johnny back into the world again" (127). Warren fails to recognize, however, that the scene initiates a narrative pattern that recurs on several occasions throughout the cinematic text. Smith's propensity toward social withdrawal followed by reemergence into life remains the most distinguishing characteristic of the entire film. Actually, Cronenberg signals this potential in Smith the moment the latter looks out his kitchen window and apprehends that it is Sarah who has come to visit. Smith's next act—even before he opens the door to admit his former fiancé—is to hang up the cane he employs as an aid to walking, but which also serves as a symbol of his predilection toward self-pity and withdrawal. Significantly, the cane does not reappear while Sarah and her son are in the house; John brings it out only at the scene's conclusion, when he walks Sarah and her son to their car.

In *The Dead Zone,* Cronenberg is interested in testing and ultimately refuting Smith's commitment to a life lived without others. Like Poe's narrator in "The Raven," Smith feels a perverse sense of security and complacency apart from others. Living on his own or in his father's house, he is insulated from the betrayals of life—its cruel turns of fate and love's inconsistency. But in spite of Smith's urge to repudiate his bond with the rest of humanity, the vulnerability of children consistently forces him back into the social mainstream. Chris, the disaffected boy with the overbearing father, draws Smith out of a solipsistic closet that contains literally thousands of letters "from people I can't help." Near the end of the film, when Stillson employs Sarah's son as a shield (still-son) to protect himself from Smith's assassination attempt, John's refusal to sacrifice the child is a final indicator of his compulsion to place the welfare of children above his own self-serving impulses.

Ironically, Smith and Frank Dodd (Nicholas Campbell), the Castle Rock killer, are linked to one another not only through Johnny's psychic connection, but also in their bond to children. Smith, of course, is committed to helping children; Dodd pretends to help them in his role as a policeman, but actually employs his position to prey on them. The mutual links to adolescence that these two characters share is further deepened when the camera follows Smith and the sheriff into the interior of Dodd's home—his adult bedroom is filled with comic books, toy dolls, a rocking horse, and cowboy paraphernalia, and his secret life is protected by a mother (Colleen Dewhurst) who is acutely aware of her son's psychopathology yet does nothing to help him (the film even implies that she encourages it).

Both Smith and Dodd will die terrible deaths, Smith's choice no less suicidal than Dodd's. This, however, is where the parallel ends, for Dodd dies in order to avoid responsibility for his actions; Smith's death, on the other hand, is a Christ-like act of self-sacrifice made for the future welfare of humankind. In an interview with the director, Cronenberg suggested "Johnny's character in the film is almost Christ-like—he's the first character of mine who's almost a martyr—a reluctant martyr, of course . . . but he knows it's his destiny and he can't do anything about it" (Horsting 31). Christian imagery and icons follow Smith throughout the film, from the picture of Christ wearing a crown of thorns that hangs on his hospital room wall to his violent death with arms outstretched, bleeding atop the broken fragments of a wooden bench.

The strong Christian overtones of *The Dead Zone*, in addition to the fact that the film is really motivated by a sentimental love story under its preternatural veneer, distinguish it from most of the other films found in Cronenberg's oeuvre. The director has acknowledged: "It is certainly the least offensive film I've made; the only one where grannies come out crying about the tragic love affair at the end" (Rodley 114–115). Stephen King has likewise commented on the curious nature of *The Dead Zone*, particularly when it is paired against other more emotionally detached Cronenberg work such as *Dead Ringers* (1988*), The Fly* (1986*)*, and *Crash* (1996): "*The Dead Zone* is Cronenberg's only really human movie . . . it is very warm and loving. *The Dead Zone* was a perfect marriage, like two flavors that shouldn't mix but did" (Magistrale 14).

These are very interesting comments in light of the fact that the film's final scene is the violent conclusion to John Smith's tortured life. Moreover, the fact that he dies in Sarah's arms, aware of her confusion as much as her grief, underscores the film's relentless portrait of the complexities attendant to human love and self-sacrifice. But perhaps the most provocative element that King and Cronenberg share in their respective reactions to the film is that *The Dead Zone* defies easy generic classification. Although based on a novel by Stephen King and featuring a central protagonist who possesses paranormal abilities, the film is not a horror movie. The successful horror film presumably horrifies, shocks, or disgusts, reactions that are not persuasively ascribed to viewing *The Dead Zone*. And while this film contains some moments of graphic violence and is haunted by death from the moment John Smith awakens from his coma, the qualities of restraint and sympathy that Christopher Walken brings to the center of a drama about a common man struggling to reconcile his debt to humankind with his desire for a simple life distinguish this work from the rest of Cronenberg's oeuvre. "King's material is very different from mine," Cronenberg has acknowledged. "King's characters are usually very simple, open and honest, and the characters that I write are generally none of these things. They are urbane, sophisticated and complex—if not twisted. I'm more comfortable in dark corners" (Horsting 35).

Film critic James Verniere has argued that over the years Cronenberg has developed virtually his own "kind of cinema of pathology in which the ultimate horror is the horror of a diseased psyche" (55). This is an appropriate assessment of other Cronenberg films to date—for example, *Videodrome* (1983), *The Fly, Dead Ringers, Naked Lunch* (1991), *M. Butterfly* (1993), *Crash*—but I do not believe this definition works to quite the same extent in addressing the central consciousness of *The Dead Zone*. John Smith's link to other Cronenberg protagonists is indeed by way of a disease, but it is physical as much as it is psychological. At the conclusion of each of his films, Cronenberg's male protagonists comprehend the very limits of their own physicality—the body's deconstruction in *The Fly, Crash,* and *M. Butterfly* that parallels John Smith's headaches and deterioration—and these tragic realizations help to thwart the visionary potential to which his protagonists aspire.

The typical Cronenberg character is alienated, isolated, and on the verge of madness. John Smith certainly finds himself in a similar position, but not as the result "of a diseased psyche." Rather, Smith is surrounded by varieties of psychological pathology in Stillson, Dodd, and parents such as Dodd's mother and Roger Stuart, but the audience is meant to view the essential perversity of these adults in contrast to Smith's unwavering moral center. While it is true that Smith is tormented through most of the film, his ultimate horror comes not from a "diseased psyche," but from a healthy one that stands in opposition to those that are less healthy. In spite of whatever actions he takes to secure his isolation, the film undercuts his independent urge by documenting Smith's steady reintegration into life— even as each attempt to alleviate someone else's suffering propels Johnny further into his own "Dead Zone."

Consequently, by the end of the film, his quest to destroy Greg Stillson because of the politician's future threat to humanity is completely unsolicited. In a sense, history repeats itself: Sam Weizak (Herbert Lom) saves John so that the latter can prevent another Holocaust. Smith translates his powers into an understanding that people have responsibilities to one another that are difficult to fulfill and that often exist in opposition to personal survival. As a motivation for this sacrifice, the filmgoer must appreciate fully the self-insight that Smith reveals in a letter to Sarah prior to the Stillson assassination attempt: "I can't go on hiding any more. That's what I've been doing, running and hiding. I always thought this power of mine was a curse. Now I can see it's a gift. By the time you get this letter, it will be all over. You never will understand why, Sarah, guess nobody ever will. But I know what I'm doing, and I know I'm right." From these words, the audience senses a level of resolution and tranquility that is seldom available to other Cronenberg males and that has elsewhere been present in *The Dead Zone* only in those scenes where Johnny interacts with children. Smith knows himself well by the end of this film, realizes that he is doomed by a destiny that is beyond his control, and, unlike the major protagonists in Cronenberg's other films, makes the best of a bad hand.

Until the release of *Cujo* and especially *Dolores Claiborne*, the hero in most of the films that Hollywood has adapted from Stephen King's fiction is typically from the young, white, male middle class—a humble American Everyman, exemplified in characters such as Dennis Guilder in *Christine* or Johnny Smith in *The Dead Zone*. These individuals find themselves in situations where their ordinary lives have become suddenly extraordinary. A film such as *The Dead Zone* tests the mettle of its unassuming protagonist faced with circumstances that are largely beyond his capacity to comprehend, much less control. As a consequence of the struggle that ensues, the protagonist's personality enlarges to the point at which he becomes greater than he ever considered himself capable of becoming.

In this way, then, John Smith shares much in common with the falsely convicted felon, Andy Dufresne (Tim Robbins) in *Shawshank*. Both are modest men, in possession of above-average intelligences, who find themselves in situations that continually test their independence and powers of endurance. Andy and John experience severe disruptions in their lives, so severe that neither man is the same afterward. Yet each of these men is somehow protected from the madness and cruelty that surrounds them by a kind of inner shield. They are both survivors forced to adjust to radical change, and they have done so without succumbing either to cynicism or despair. Although neither man can be said to be a "loner," each exists at the perimeters of society, as both are isolated from mainstream life. More important, unlike most of the other characters that engage them, Johnny Smith and Andy Dufresne possess the ability to see themselves clearly and without illusions. There is a moral centeredness to both these characters that sustains them in the face of fate's vicissitudes. Red Redding (Morgan Freeman) recognizes Andy's uniqueness; even before he has the opportunity to befriend him, Red notes that Andy "had a quiet way about him, a walk and a talk that just wasn't normal around here . . . like he had on an invisible coat that would shield him from this place [prison]."

Speaking in a voice-over early in the film, Red, who is the narrator of a large portion of the movie, posits that the "fresh fish" inmates who arrive at Shawshank are "close to madness the first night. Somebody always breaks down crying." But Andy disappoints Red's bet that he will succumb to the brutality of his new environment. In fact, as I have already alluded, there is an "invisible coat" or a self-imposed "wall" surrounding Andy that is as impermeable as the stone walls of Shawshank prison itself. Andy possesses an existential quality of self-knowledge, a sense of himself and the fact of his innocence that makes his time in prison less desperate than it might have been for a weaker man wrongly convicted of murdering his wife and her illicit lover. Red initially misinterprets Andy's self-confidence for snobbery—"rumor has it that you're a real cold fish, think your shit smells sweeter than most"—for Andy is a man, like John Smith, who is self-possessed and who understands that the world will strip such a man of his essence if he is not vigilant and self-protective. Injustice follows Andy inside the prison; his intelligence and good looks are exploited by convicts and prison authorities alike when he is subjected both to sexual assault and the rape of his financial acumen by Warden Norton (Bob Gunton) and his guards. But Andy is never relegated to victim status: He uses his financial knowledge as a former bank vice president to obtain special favors from the prison authorities and, most of all, to gain survival time to tunnel his way out of Shawshank. After his brilliant escape, in which he also manages to steal back the illegal monies he has invested for the warden, Dufresne leaves behind his best friend, Red. Eventually, the two are reunited in Mexico, when Red joins him after obtaining a long-awaited parole from his life-term sentence.

In an interview with me several years ago, Stephen King acknowledged that he often chooses a character's name for a purpose, "here and there they appear like jokes" (Magistrale 3). The surname Dufresne is a French derivation of the word "mineralogist." Accordingly, throughout *The Shawshank Redemption,* Andy is associated with rocks and geology. He refers to himself as a "rock hound," made love and asked his wife to marry him at the base of a long rock wall in a Buxton, Maine, meadow, risks severe punishment at the hands of prison authorities in commissioning Red to procure a rock hammer, creates beautiful chess pieces from rocks that are brought to him by the other inmates, and escapes from Shawshank by tunneling for twenty years under its walls and depositing the debris each day in the prison's exercise yard. Not only is Andy an amateur geologist, as an inmate he lives a life literally enclosed in rock, as every perimeter wall of Shawshank prison is composed of imposing pieces of blue-gray granite assembled to resemble a medieval castle. In short, it is Andy's appreciation of rocks and geological processes that helps to make his stay at Shawshank psychologically bearable. But Andy's love of geology extends beyond mere hobby to become a dominant feature of his personality and, by extension, the film itself. Just as he appreciates the geodynamic processes that, through the constant imposition of pressure and time, break down the earth into individual rock fragments, Andy also intuits this action as a metaphor for life. In the cells surrounding him at Shawshank are examples of men who have acted on impulse—committing stupid and impetuous acts of violence with consequences that they now regret. Their long punishment in Shawshank—a kind of symbolic burial in stone—stands in stark contrast to the impetuosity of such youthful testosterone-driven behavior. To survive the interminable chronological sentence of prison life, these men must learn to adjust to what Red calls "all the time in the world," to assume a patience and self-restraint that was sorely absent in their decision to commit the crimes that put them in Shawshank in the first place. Through Andy's character, this film asks whether it is possible to make the necessary adjustments that come with the imposed time and pressures of prison life without also allowing one's spirit to calcify. We learn in the course of this film that Andy is simultaneously the representative of change and liberation as well as a symbol of rock-hard determination and endurance.

Most of the prisoners at Shawshank are forced to change themselves, to accept their condition as prisoners of the state—they adjust, in other words, to the constraints of punishment imposed on them. A steady record of Red's interviews with successive generations of parole boards measures his own distance in time and temperament from the rough adolescent punk who first entered prison. Midway through the film, Red acknowledges that the granite walls surrounding the prisoners change the people who are kept inside them: "These walls are funny. First you hate them, then you get used to them. Enough time passes, you get so you depend upon them. They send you here for life; that's exactly what they take. The part that counts, anyway." What Red calls "institutionalization" is really death-in-life, the inability to survive beyond the prison walls, as Brooks Hatlen's (James Whitmore) sad failure to create an existence on the outside so clearly illustrates. Prison, particularly a penal facility run with the disciplinary extremism of Shawshank, resembles the geodynamic process used to produce Andy's rock collection: Through the advent of time and pressure, it wears down the "sharp edges" of the men it incarcerates. Andy is kin to the harder rocks in geology—quartz or diamond—insofar as he refuses to give in to the eroding and homogenizing forces of long-term incarceration that wear down the distinctive personality traits of an individual. Unlike Hatlen and many of the other long-term prisoners at Shawshank, he will not lose himself to the system—to allow himself to become "institutionalized."

Filmmaking is largely centered on character portrayal and development. As a result, in any film a relationship is established between character and the mis-en-scène, or what is staged in front of the camera. As a prison movie, *Shawshank* necessarily operates within a deliberately restricted mis-en-scène; most of the scenes in this film occur within the prison walls. Even those interludes where we watch Red and Brooks Hatlen endeavor to function in the outside world merely underscore the psychological pervasiveness of the prison yard and the manner in which inmates are affected by prolonged incarceration. As a result of its deliberately circumscribed setting, the film relies almost exclusively on character and interpersonal relationships.

In a world where everything is tinted gray—the uniforms the convicts wear, the walls of the penitentiary, the exercise yard, even the air itself—Dufresne will not relinquish his optimism or allow himself to become dehumanized. Despite the various levels of abuse Andy experiences, he refuses to relinquish hope or his commitment to helping others. In one of the great moments in this film, Andy defies the prison authorities long enough to share the gift of music with other inmates. Instead of merely being grateful that his request for books and records has been so generously answered by the state legislature, their arrival encourages Andy to push the envelope even further in an act of spontaneous bravado that stuns the entire prison population. He plays a recording of Mozart on the penitentiary loudspeaker system. The aria that Andy plays is an excerpt from Act 2 of Mozart's *The Marriage of Figaro* (1786). The two women singing are a chambermaid (Susanna) and her mistress (Countess Almaviva). They are plotting a scheme to chasten as well as win back the amorous attention of Count Almaviva, the Countess's wayward husband who has lost interest in his wife and is currently focused on seducing Susanna. In a sense, the aria describes a situation that mirrors directly Andy's own personal circumstances: A spouse's sexual betrayal. But the aria also outlines a plan to empower the women by altering a condition that is frustrating for them both. In this way, their scheming is an act of defiance against the patriarchal authority of the count and the ancient privileged custom of *Le Droit du Seigneur,* whereby a lord possesses the right to sleep with any of his domestics. The rebellious plot that the two women articulate in song should be seen as paralleling and possibly even inspiring Andy's choice to subvert the warden's authority by refusing to "turn it off." "For the briefest of moments," Red informs us, "every man at Shawshank felt free." This is why Warden Norton reacts with such fury to Dufresne's seemingly innocuous stunt; he perceives it correctly as the most defiant moment in the entire film. In a microcosm composed exclusively of gray men and stone, Andy brings the beautiful and subversive voices of two female arias into the prison yard. As they listen to the singing, all of the men stand frozen in awe, transfixed by the lovely voices that shatter the dull routine of their daily existence.

As punishment for introducing Mozart's opera to the prison population of Shawshank, Andy ends up with two weeks in solitary confinement. He calls it "the easiest stretch of time I ever did" because music is a reminder to Andy, like his dream of a fresh start in Mexico, that the essence of the human spirit cannot be constrained by even the thickest walls. Brooks carves his name on a suicide wall above his head because he simply cannot cope with a world that has dramatically changed since his imprisonment in Shawshank. He has lost the ability to adjust to its increased levels of speed and anonymity because of the comfortable stagnancy he has found in prison. In contrast to this "institutional man," Andy embodies the monumental spirit of geological change itself—a patient faith born from the determination that even the greatest walls of stone eventually erode. Andy appreciates the sense of strategy involved in chess—the satisfaction of working patiently through a problem—and he prefers this game to Red's love of checkers. It is this same capacity that informs his willingness to work with inmates to help them achieve high school equivalency diplomas, to write two letters a week for six years to the prison board to obtain funds for a library, to endure successive periods of solitary confinement with only the memory of "Mr. Mozart to keep me company," and to spend decades tunneling his way underneath a wall. "Get busy living or get busy dying," Andy cautions Red. The phrase must be viewed as a challenge to *both* men as much as it is a sobering reminder that in Shawshank, if you do not keep moving through (or under) the walls of stone, you risk becoming part of the wall yourself.

With the possible exception of his wife's marital betrayal, for which Andy accepts at least partial culpability, women in *The Shawshank Redemption* are symbols of freedom and transcendence. Various photographs of Hollywood starlets hang on Dufresne's cell wall during the course of his incarceration—not only disguising his escape route, but also stimulating his imagination with a reminder of a world of sensual pleasures looming just beyond the walls that physically contain him. In one scene, the audience observes him staring at the classic photograph of Marilyn Monroe trying to maintain control over her white skirt as it billows around her thighs. In this particular mis-en-scène, the audience is unaware that Monroe is more than simply a black-and-white poster image fueling Andy's lascivious fantasies; she is also the keeper of his literal portal to freedom, and Andy is as much transfixed by that secret knowledge as he is by Marilyn's legs. The sopranos singing Mozart arias over the prison loudspeakers are likewise linked in Red's poetic voiceover to Andy's dream of freedom and individual self-expression: "some beautiful bird that flapped into our drab little cage and made those walls dissolve away."

The full title of King's novella, *Rita Hayworth and the Shawshank Redemption,* initially strikes the casual reader as an odd choice. But King's original title, shortened to *The Shawshank Redemption* for Darabont's film, implies the importance of connecting Rita Hayworth herself (as well as the various other women in the film who sing and appear in poster photographs) directly to the concept of redemption—the emancipation or liberation that comes through payment of a price—as it operates within Shawshank prison. Although there are no living women featured in *Shawshank,* all the women who are referenced in this film are versions of Rita Hayworth: Sexualized sirens of an unattainable femininity, of course; but these women likewise must be viewed as more than just torments for eternally incarcerated males as they reveal themselves also capable of transforming the prisoners' lives, however briefly, by bringing beauty and inspiration to men in danger of becoming "institutionalized." The film's women and Andy's inimitable personality are frequently linked throughout the movie and especially near the end when Red, while digging in sodden clay under the shadow of Shawshank's walls, muses sadly about his absent friend and uses the opportunity to remind us that Andy shares something in common with the exotic women opera singers he earlier unleashed in the prison: "Some birds aren't meant to be caged; their feathers are just too bright. And when they fly away, the part of you that knows it was a sin to lock them up does rejoice. But still, the place that you live in is that much more drab and empty now that they're gone."

As Andy's best friend and a long-term inmate, Red finds himself vacillating between the two extremes represented by Andy and Brooks. He chastises Andy for clinging to hope, "a dangerous thing that can drive a man insane, that's got no use on the inside." As a gesture of comfort to him after his thirty-year rejection by the parole board, Andy buys Red a harmonica. Red's refusal to play it indicates his fear and reluctance to embrace Andy's proclamation of music as a symbol of hope and freedom—a reminder "that there are places in the world that are not made out of stone, that there's something inside they can't get to, that they can't touch, that's yours." When Red does finally obtain parole after Andy has left, it is clear that he has become as "institutionalized" as Brooks and that he is "not going to make it on the outside." The film tracks Red as he pursues Brooks's identical path—he lives in the same apartment room, works the same job as a grocery bagger in the same supermarket. If not for Andy's influence, Red would have followed Hatlen's earlier death and chosen one of the guns in the window of a pawnshop instead of the compass that takes him to the rock wall in Buxton and then all the way to Mexico.

As the compass itself symbolizes, Dufresne supplies Red with moral direction, alternative bearings to Hatlen's journey toward self-destruction. While Red may be the "man who knows how to get things," it is his friendship with Andy that ends up salvaging his life. Andy's independence and escape from Shawshank has encouraged Red to question his own defeatist attitude toward prison institutionalization. Each time Red faces the parole board considering his case, he tries to appear as a model prisoner—humbly holding his cap in his hands, frequently averting his eyes downward, addressing the board politely, and assuring its members that he has indeed been rehabilitated. Over the years, this posturing has brought him nothing but rejections. In front of his last parole board, however, Red becomes a version of Andy—defiant in answering the board's officious questions, calling one of its members "Sonny," questioning their understanding of the word "rehabilitation," clearly unafraid of another stamped rejection. For the first time in the film he appears almost cocky, standing up for himself in the face of bureaucratic authority. Similarly, upon his release, Red rejects Brooks's choice of suicide and instead follows Andy's directions to the end of yet another rock wall, where he discovers a piece of volcanic glass covering a tin box with a boat on its cover. These rocks complete the geological symbolism of the film, suggesting the volcanic potential of hope (the box contains enough money to get Red to Mexico and to the boat Andy is restoring) and the life force itself. But this scene also links Red and Andy in an even more intimate fashion. At the base of this wall, years earlier, Andy first professed his love to his future wife, a woman who eventually betrayed him. In bringing Red to this same place, Andy risks failure once more. This is in keeping with his character all through the film, as we see his patience manifested in helping Tommy (Gil Bellows) obtain his high school equivalency diploma or in creating the prison's elaborate library facility for the enjoyment of his fellow inmates. Andy is a man who cares deeply for the people he loves, and he is willing to take the risks that love entails. Like the geological processes that have produced the rock samples he so admires, Dufresne's commitment to the projects he undertakes or to the people he loves is constant. Perhaps this is the reason why his wife's inconstancy so thoroughly unnerves him: Andy could never envision himself betraying her. His marriage may have ended prematurely and disastrously, but he hopes that his friendship with Red will not.

Shawshank owes a great debt to the eighteenth-century gothic narrative, with Andy in the role of the incarcerated yet intrepid maiden, surrounded by various masculine monsters that threaten to deflower him sexually and torture him psychologically. The themes of gothic art include a strong sense of environmental claustrophobia, the destructive imposition of the past on the present, and a metaphysical internalization of evil to which the gothic landscape and castle stand as objective correlatives (Simpson 29). Trapped in a gray, unyielding, castle-like fortress that is honeycombed with secret corners, cells, and passageways, Andy's combination of innocence—he is wrongly convicted of murdering his wife and her lover—and refined demeanor—he is a successful bank vice president incarcerated with hardened felons—further link him directly to the persecuted gothic female. Moreover, his feminine face and body (when he first notices Andy, Red calls him a "tall drink of water") and independent—even quixotic—personality are compelling features that both prison inmates and authorities find impossible to resist. Andy draws the entire prison population to him—out of a desire to befriend him, or to exploit his intellectual and financial acumen, or to possess him sexually. Whatever the reason, throughout the film, Andy, like the traditional eighteenth-century gothic heroine, is under personal siege and must constantly protect himself against intrusions that are physical (the sexual attacks from Bogs [Mark Rolston] and the Sisters) and psychological (the intimidation threats from Warden Norton), endangering his integrity and personal code of conduct.

Another way in which *Shawshank* owes a debt to gothic archetypes is in its reliance on moral ambiguity as a means to force readers into asking questions about the human condition. The individual in gothic fiction, according to critic G. R. Thompson, must rely not on institutional authority but the self for determining moral certitude. This is certainly the case in *Shawshank,* where Andy notes that "on the outside I was an honest man, straight as an arrow. I had to come to prison to be a crook." With its strict emphasis on universal conformity and the hegemony of the prison's authority over the individual rights and welfare of the convicts, *The Shawshank Redemption* dramatizes many of the same indictments that Michel Foucault raises about the history of penal institutions in his book *Discipline and Punish: The Birth of the Prison:* "The prison imposes violent constraints on its inmates; it is supposed to apply the law, and to teach respect for it; but all its functioning operates in the form of an abuse of power, the arbitrary power of administration" (266). Just as Foucault insists that the modern penal system undermines the very concepts of rehabilitation and justice it was constructed to promote, the power structure at Shawshank likewise proves to be more corrupt than the convicted felons it houses. In this film, as in many gothic texts, traditional orientations of good and evil are often inverted. The institutional authorities who operate Shawshank—from its corrupt warden to his sadistic guards—are the clearest representatives of evil in the movie, leaving Andy and the others prisoners to define their own moral code against the hypocritical Christianity of the warden. When Andy escapes from the prison, he does so with a conscience clear enough to steal the money he has been bankrolling for the warden. In fact, he performs perhaps the single most ethical act in the film when he sends evidence of the warden's illegal moneymaking operations to the Portland newspaper.

In keeping with a gothic code of challenging traditional moral formulations, Andy's morality is strictly personal. He knows that while he did not actually kill his wife with a bullet, his lack of sufficient attention to her in their marriage pushed her toward an illicit relationship with another man: "I didn't pull the trigger, but I drove her away. And that's why she died, because of me, the way that I am." Andy has endured his punishment at Shawshank for a personal failing, not a legal crime; he has always known he was innocent of the latter, but it took his two decades of prison incarceration to teach him about his own indirect complicity in the death of his wife. His incarceration helps him to accept his own role in his wife's infidelity and death, and perhaps this is the best explanation for his demonstrative efforts to express his feelings toward the prisoners he comes to love. On the other hand, Dufresne realistically comprehends the need to move on beyond his wife's memory and loss, and especially his own culpability. This is ultimately why his escape takes him to a Mexican town on the edge of the Pacific Ocean, a place where there is "no memory." Now that he has "paid for whatever mistakes I made and then some," he is prepared to get on with the business of his life.

While he cannot alter the past and the mistakes he has made, from the moment he arrives at Shawshank Andy begins a process of personal renewal. As a younger man, he failed to express adequately his love for his wife. Andy has learned something from that error, and he illustrates this most fully in his rescue of Red. Ironically, Andy ends up expressing himself best to another man, and a black man at that. We must never forget that his years in prison have enlarged Andy's spirit—by making him more profoundly aware of life's mutability and the ephemeral nature of freedom—so that through most of this film his character is seen in the role of aiding others. Perhaps he is motivated by guilt associated with his failed marriage, or maybe it is simply that his own level of personal suffering has opened his spirit to the suffering of others. Whatever the explanation, it is as if Dufresne's personal rehabilitation goal at Shawshank has been to transform himself from the "hard man, closed book" his wife "complained about all the time" into a man more than worthy of her love.

Earlier in this chapter, I noted several of the many allusions that *The Dead Zone* maintains between John Smith and Christian imagery. Another way in which Andy Dufrense can be further linked to Smith is with his own array of Christ-like associations. In *Shawshank,* Andy is an unassuming man of good works who is seen laboring continually with his hands, although as a stone carver more than a carpenter. He assembles quite a collection of apostles—with Red occupying the role of Peter—who are left to speak of his memory in quasi-religious terms after Andy has escaped (risen) from his symbolic burial beneath the stones of Shawshank. While Andy's otherworldliness distinguishes him from his fellow convicts, he is like Christ the eternal fisherman pursuing the salvation of fallen men.

Similar to the savior, Andy is betrayed by individuals he thought he could trust (Warden Norton) and persecuted by an unjust system that deliberately thwarts a miscarriage of justice because it threatens the perpetuation of a corrupt status quo. Moreover, Andy understands completely the social-financial system he ultimately subverts. He spends two months in solitary confinement after insulting Shawshank's "obtuse" warden, a stretch of time that roughly parallels Christ's forty days and forty nights alone in the desert. In each case, both men are tempted by evil (Norton and Satan) during the period of their isolation, and both emerge even more resolute from these encounters. Jesus often illuminated the hypocrisy of religious and civic leaders who employed their power for personal gain. In Andy's revelation of Warden Norton's corruption to the outside world, he shines a light on a man who professed to be a Christian, while only wielding power to his own advantage. Thus, the needlepoint biblical allusion that hangs in Norton's office—"His Judgement Cometh and That Right Soon"—speaks directly and ironically to Norton's own personal hypocrisy.

Shawshank is a narrative that begins in stone (Dufresne stares up at a granite wall that looms in front of him the first time he passes through the prison's front gate) only to end in water (on the edge of the Mexican Pacific). Throughout the film, water is a transformative agent, symbolizing rebirth and purification, as when Andy emerges triumphantly from the bowels of the prison sewer system in the middle of a thunderous rainstorm, or when Red greets his friend at the limitless edge of sky and ocean at the end of the film. Since so much of *Shawshank* is set in the confinement of stone, often emphasized by tight camera angles set in restricted spaces, it is highly significant that the movie ends with open-ended vistas in terms of both physical space (the Mexican beach) and in the fact that Andy is shown restoring a boat (bringing it back to life). Indeed, even the sandy beach on which Andy and Red embrace subtly underscores the ultimate breakdown of rock and stone to its final particulates.

One of the strongest arguments for considering Dufresne as a Christ-like figure is his intuitive ability to bring together disparate elements within the Shawshank prison population. The best illustration of this capacity is found in Andy's relationship with Red. Set primarily in the 1940s and 1950s, the film's chronology spans a time when black and white racial lines would have been most sharply demarcated. Even in Maine, where Shawshank is located, some semblance of Jim Crow segregation would have been in effect. Thus, the likelihood of Red and Andy becoming best friends during this historical era is highly unlikely. For some viewers, the easy bond that an uneducated black man and an affluent white bank vice president establish is the single most unrealistic aspect of this narrative, more fantastic even than Andy's long tunnel journey out of Shawshank through stone and offal. The film's oblivious treatment of race and class may indeed be fanciful and sentimental, but the harmony it purports also underscores the narrative's core theme of heroic survival. If personal isolation, as noted in the preceding chapter, is a cause for self-destruction and loss, then the bonds of friendship and simple love are its counterpoint, the means to salvation and transcendence. In *Danse Macabre,* Stephen King posits that despite its emphasis on terror and the abnormal, horror narratives often resemble more mainstream art insofar as they likewise include the importance of human fellowship: "If such behavior is to be, it cannot be as a result of an intellectual moral stance; it is because there is such a thing as love, merely a practical fact, a practical force in human affairs" (375). Above all else, *Shawshank* is a paean to friendship and love, and the film goes on to posit that these "practical forces" possess quasi-magical properties that make it possible to prevail over even the worst circumstances. After all, if love and friendship can survive in an environment such as Shawshank prison, then is it so inconceivable that these elements might also transcend the conventional restrictions of race and class?

Director Frank Darabont reprises many of *Shawshank*'s central themes—racial and class relationships, the redemptive power of love, the onerous burden of responsibility for another human being, shifting and blurring degrees of criminality and moral advancement—in his adaptation of another Stephen King novel, *The Green Mile.* Again set on a prison block, so named for the color of the floor that connects the individual cells on death row to the room containing the electric chair, this film also centers its major attention on the dynamics of an interracial male relationship. The two films likewise share similar narrative structures; much of *Shawshank* and the majority of *The Green Mile* are told in flashbacks. During the opening credits of *Shawshank,* the audience is encouraged to view Andy Dufresne as a convincing suspect in the murder of his adulterous wife and her lover; we see him drinking heavily from a bottle of whiskey, gun and bullets in his hands, waiting in a car outside the room where his wife and her lover passionately embrace. We next witness his formal sentencing in court that takes place in front of judge who is appalled by the cold-blooded nature of both the crime and the defendant. The rest of the film is spent systematically undercutting these first impressions of Andy as a plausible murderer. Similarly, in *The Green Mile,* when we first view the enormous John Coffey (Michael Clarke

Duncan) holding the mangled and bloodied bodies of two little girls under his arms, weeping and rocking back and forth in the woods, the audience is encouraged to make the same racist assumption that the Louisiana authorities employ in prosecuting Coffey: That at best, a simple, perhaps retarded black man has made a terrible error in judgment. The profundity of his agony and his repetition of the apparently self-condemning phrase, "I tried to take it back," further suggests that he may already be repenting his role in their deaths. Ironically, in both these films something of the audience's first impression turns out to be accurate: John may not have slain the children and Andy may not have killed his wife, but each man comes nonetheless to assume a unique level of responsibility for these respective murders. The hidden and complex truths contained in the deliberately misleading openings of *Shawshank* and *The Green Mile* are only made clear as the movies unfold—and as Dufresne and Coffey reveal themselves as men of goodness rather than as predators.

Additionally, both films carry strong religious overtones, as Dufresne and Coffey are uniquely different Christ-like figures. The spirituality of both movies is of central importance, and partially helps to explain their mass popularity, but it is not reflective of any organized form of Christianity. That is, both films imply that true spirituality is unlikely derived from any church doctrine; it is instead more of an organic presence that exists in loving human relationships and the world of nature. The divinely inspired John Coffey, for example, refuses the counsel of clergy on the eve of his execution, but he is not adverse to others saying "a little prayer" for him. Similarly, Dufresne's strong personal ethics stand in sharp contrast to Warden Norton's corrupt Christian fundamentalism; the latter employs the Bible as justification for his own brand of sadistic discipline, and conveniently hides his own moral and legal offenses behind the hypocritical guise of church-going righteousness. It is clear that in *Shawshank* and *The Green Mile,* Darabont offers a strong comment on Christianity and Christian values. In these narratives, however, Christ is not to be found residing in any church or in any easily recognizable religious dogma. Instead, in these films Jesus wears a human face, and evidence of His presence is best found in the friendships that men are capable of forming with one another.

In this aspect, Darabont subscribes closely to Stephen King's own attitude toward spirituality and religious institutions. As I have discussed in this book's analysis of *Carrie,* and as we will see again in *The Stand,* King is highly critical of religious zealotry, and he always locates true religious sentiment within a secular context. Whatever divinity coexists with humankind in King's world is dependent on the intrinsic worth of the men and women who give shape to its formulation. In contrast to his fictional fundamentalists, who sacrifice individual conscience and logic for an irrational zealotry, redemptive grace in Stephen King's world is neither predetermined nor locked within the exclusive domain of an almighty providence. True spiritual advancement in King's fictional microcosm—and *Shawshank* and *The Green Mile* are reflective of such sentiments—occurs only when a personal assumption of sin and guilt stimulates the actions of a heightened moral consciousness. Moreover, this progression is always humanly motivated and sustained; the changes necessary for this development are the results of a conscious and genuine alteration in the human heart that reflects the free exercise of an enlightened human will.

When the audience is introduced to Coffey's character (after the opening mis-en-scène when he is briefly pictured seated and holding the two dead girls), the camera is deliberately restrictive in its point of view: We see his massive form—the way he weighs down the prison transport truck, his muscled body, the enormity of his size compared to the other men around him—but only when he finally reaches his cell does the camera pan up to reveal his face. What the audience is permitted to see before encountering Coffey's face is the reaction of everyone else on the Green Mile to the black man's physical appearance and stature. The camera zooms in on the faces of prisoners and guards alike as Coffey enters their respective fields of vision. Each set of eyes looks up in silent amazement, forcing the audience to anticipate its own view, although it is deliberately restricted for several minutes. This introduction is a very effective setup to suggesting that Coffey is a larger-than-life personality. Moreover, at the conclusion of this scene, his hard body contrasts sharply with the softness of his demeanor in both speech and presentation. It is also deliberate that our introduction to Coffey is likewise the film's introduction to Percy Wetmore (Doug Hutchison). The latter, a small, effeminate-looking man, is not only a physical contrast to his black prisoner; Wetmore, one of the guards on the Mile, also uses the opportunity of escorting Coffey to his cell as a means for exercising his penchant for sadistic torment, announcing "dead man walking" as he leads Coffey in by his chains. The moment becomes, then, a dramatic exposition for revealing the essential character traits of two of the film's major personalities.

Convicted of raping and slaughtering two young white girls, John Coffey, the radiant presence in *The Green Mile,* is a study in contrasts. While he is a huge human being (7 feet, 350 pounds), whose physical presence fills up whatever space he occupies—from his faded blue denim overalls to the cell he inhabits on the Green Mile—mentally and spiritually he is as gentle and innocent as the girls he is falsely accused of killing. In childlike wonder, he is transfixed by the presence of star constellations at night, by the aerobatic mouse that lives on the Mile, by the smell of a damp clump of leaves, and by the angelic dancing of Ginger Rodgers and Fred Astaire in *Top Hat*. This is also why he remains so terrified of the dark and refuses to offer any of his home-baked cornbread to the malefic "Wild Bill" Wharton (Sam Rockwell): At heart, Coffey is a child, "a force of nature," and he remains an innocent in spite of the terrible levels of evil he has been made to experience.

While awaiting execution, Coffey reveals a supernatural ability to heal the sick, ease the sufferings of others, and reveal and punish the darkest secrets of corrupt men. All of the Green Mile prison guards are drawn to his personality, but particularly Paul Edgecomb (Tom Hanks), who supervises the inmates on death row at Louisiana's Cold Mountain Penitentiary. Just as Red narrates much of the action in *Shawshank,* it is through an extended flashback by an aged and retired Paul Edgecomb (Dabbs Greer) that Coffey's history is told. A bond of admiration and spiritual intimacy develops between the guard and prisoner, as Paul comes to realize that Coffey is not only unique among men, but also innocent of the heinous crimes for which he is destined to be executed. Unable to stop the process that has been ordained by the system of law and punishment that Paul serves, Coffey is put to death on Edgecomb's watch, leaving the guard simultaneously "cursed" because of his role in "killing one of God's true miracles" and blessed by the "gift" of his acquaintance. Both *Shawshank* and *The Green Mile* expand beyond the mere issue of surviving prison experience to focus on the spiritual rehabilitation of their main characters. Ironically, the penal and legal systems emerge as the truest criminals in both films, as innocent men are unjustly persecuted. However, extended incarceration does end up providing the opportunity for close introspection and the dramatic context necessary for self-reinvention. The issue of preserving personal integrity in the face of dehumanizing conditions is crucial to each film.

Just as *Shawshank* revolves around a Christ-like figure who influences all the other characters with whom he interacts, *The Green Mile* features a black Christ who bears the initials J. C. and who not only centers the major action of the film but is also condemned to be the savior of the white world. Like John Smith in *The Dead Zone,* John Coffey is simultaneously blessed and cursed with supernatural capacities that are activated when he comes into direct physical contact with another living organism. As is the case with Smith, this contact links him intimately to human sin; neither man ever gains insight into human goodness, only the secret evil in man.

This point seems important when referencing the various Christ analogs associated with each of these films, for in both *The Dead Zone* and *The Green Mile* human touch as a healing or visionary force is the exclusive province of John Smith and John Coffey. Moreover, the absence of human touch that characterizes most of the other relationships featured in each film highlights the superior humanity of Smith and Coffey at the same time as it indicts the political and social systems that persecute these Christian figures so relentlessly.

Despite John Coffey's utter selflessness, he endures a fate similar to that of John Smith in *The Dead Zone:* Both men are equally out of place as saints walking amid the wastelands of a fiendish place. The problem for these two protagonists is that they are merely individuals forced to work in a depraved and ravaged world. Like Smith, who is overwhelmed by the requests for help and the cries of anguish that fill up an entire closet in his apartment, by the end of *The Green Mile* Coffey is "dogged tired" of the human burden that he has been unable to avoid. As in *The Dead Zone,* while Coffey's efforts to restore innocence to a fallen world produce positive results, as when he cures the warden's wife, Melinda Moores (Patricia Clarkson), of brain cancer, or brings Mr. Jingles the mouse back to life, each of these restorative moments exacts a terrible price on Coffey's physical and psychological health. Just before he cures Melinda of her tumor, she asks Coffey, "Where did you get so many scars [on his body]? Who hurt you?" As an American black man living in the Deep South in the 1940s, Coffey has undoubtedly experienced personally the scourge of racism. Despite the protestations that Stephen King raises in this book's chapter 1 interview, the fact that Coffey's character is black adds a significant dimension to his role as a Christ figure. While suffering is certainly not exclusive to African Americans, Coffey is assumed to be guilty from the moment he is found holding the dead girls. A large white man caught in the same situation might have been victimized by the same prejudicial conduct of the white mob hunting for the girls. But how many times in America's racial history has a black man found himself in circumstances similar to Coffey's? The fact that he was not immediately lynched by the mob in the very woods where he is discovered is more surprising than his perceived association with the rape and murder of the two white girls. On the other hand, King's position that Coffey's race is irrelevant is plausible in light of fact that his scars are meant to be more than merely external and racial; John Coffey bears the symbolic scars of the world, the wounds of humanity. Coffey's "failure" to defend himself as innocent of his crimes at any point in this film is not just based on the image of the black man as a passive

Uncle Tom stereotype. It is also based on Coffey's personal exhaustion and resignation. He *wants* to die. He has seen enough of the depravity of man; even his massive shoulders are worn down by the weight and length of time he has had to assume the burden of humanity's sins. One might even go so far as to suggest that from John Coffey's point of view, there is no such thing as innocence left in the world; everyone is guilty.

After Coffey heals the warden's wife, she presents him with a silver St. Christopher's medal that Coffey wears around his neck for the remainder of his life. The choice of saint presents a particularly striking parallel to Coffey's role in this film, for the legends surrounding St. Christopher suggest that he, too, was a giant man who was persecuted and martyred. Furthermore, Christopher devoted himself to the service of others, performing acts of selfless charity, especially by carrying wayfarers over bridgeless rivers upon his strong shoulders. On one notable occasion, while ferrying a child across a river, Christopher staggered under what seemed to him a crushing weight. When he reached the other side, he upbraided the child for making him feel as though "I had borne the whole world upon my back." The child answered him, "Marvel not, for thou hast borne upon thy back the world and Him who created it" (*Encyclopaedia Britannica* 644A).

In *The Green Mile,* John Coffey bears the weight of the world—specifically, an intimate knowledge of its worst acts of sin and ugliness—upon his massive shoulders. It is noteworthy that Edgecomb truly begins a relationship with Coffey only after the latter cures him of a severe bladder infection by grabbing his crotch and magically relieving him of immediate discomfort. It is Coffey's magical touch, his simple supernaturalism that incites Paul's initial interest in his criminal case. But what exactly does Coffey mean by the cryptic mantra he keeps repeating—"I took it back"—to explain his restorative powers? Coffey wishes to do nothing less than "take back" sin from the human world; he seeks to restore and redeem the wretched who have been tainted or suffer because of human cruelty or illness.

Paul Edgecomb uses his prison work as a means to maintain a personal barrier against the same enormity of human evil that has overwhelmed Coffey's psyche. His empathetic professionalism as a man who must supervise the execution of felons in "Old Sparky," the quaint name given for the prison electric chair, inspires the guards who work with him to treat the prisoners with a similar degree of respect and dignity. Modeling Paul's behavior, the other guards, with the notable exception of the sadistic Percy Wetmore, never lose sight of the essential humanity of the condemned. This, of course, ironically underscores the film's indictment of capital punishment via electrocution as a cruel and inhumane method of execution. Darabont carefully constructs a subtle yet undeniable contrast between the state-sanctioned violence against the prisoners it condemns to death and the humane guards who are hired to carry out these executions. Paul "thinks of this place as an intensive care ward of a hospital," and therefore tries to bring whatever comfort he can to the convicts on the Green Mile. Most of the prisoners who inhabit his cellblock appreciate his attitude, especially in the terrifying context of imminent death. The audience witnesses Paul's increasing personal attachment to each of the convicts he must execute. The film's first victim, Arlen Bitterbuck (Graham Greene II), reveals to Edgecomb that he hopes his contrition is sufficient to provide him access to heaven, a place he dreams will be similar to a happy moment from his past. Paul helps to reassure the prisoner by concurring with Bitterbuck's speculation about the afterlife. With the execution of Eduard Delacroix (Michael Jeter), however, Paul must invent Mouseville, a mythological place for Mr. Jingles to reside after Delacroix can no longer care for him. Just before his death, Delacroix places Paul in charge of the mouse, clearly indicating the level of trust he has established with the prison guard. Paul helps Delacroix gain insight into the value of life; on the evening of his execution the latter tells Brutus "Brutal" Howell (David Morse) and Edgecomb, "I just wish I could have met you guys before I got in here," implying that Delacroix might have lived differently if he had.

Edgecomb has constructed a personal and professional demeanor that allows him to render comfort to the doomed men in his charge. But like the military general who sends his troops off to battle aware that many will not return, Edgecomb's professional placidity is part of a careful strategy to facilitate the orderly processing of executions demanded by the state and, just as important, to protect himself—as well as the condemned—from experiencing excessive stress and emotion. *The Green Mile* documents the steady erosion of Paul's efforts to maintain this necessary barrier between himself and the prisoners in Cellblock E, until finally the mystical nature of John Coffey, Edgecomb's last prisoner, results in the complete breakdown of Paul's disciplined professional conduct. By the end of the film, their roles have been subverted and reversed—the prison guard is asking his prisoner for instruction on how to conduct himself: "Do you want me to let you go, let you walk right out of here, see how far you can get? Is that what you want me to do?"

As the movie develops, Paul is drawn into a profound intimacy with John Coffey. At first, Paul is intimidated by the black man's imposing size and asks, "Am I going to have any trouble from you, John Coffey?" But after Coffey cures both Paul and Melinda of their respective maladies, the relationship between these two men changes dramatically, and Edgecomb is soon forced to acknowledge an ever-growing debt to the mystical black man. This debt is not merely because of the timely medical assistance Paul solicits from Coffey without adequate recompense (regardless of how well Mrs. Edgecomb bakes cornbread). Nor is it accrued in Paul's revelatory insight that it is actually Wild Bill who is guilty of Coffey's crime and that the guard must therefore execute an innocent man. The burden that Paul is forced to assume by the end of this film includes but is also greater than both these instances—more akin to the universal burden of guilt associated with the betrayal and crucifixion of Christ.

But why is Paul the only one "infected" with Coffey's divinity and human agony at the end of this film? Perhaps because Edgecomb is the one man who has befriended Coffey and finally releases him from a life of "people being ugly to one another, of the pain I feel here in the world everyday . . . like pieces of glass in my head all the time." Perhaps it is because Paul attains an intimate knowledge of the black man's divinity when he holds his hand and is provided access to "a piece" of Coffey's life experience. Or perhaps it is because Coffey intuits that Paul is a sensitive and moral individual and therefore capable of continuing his role. Like Coffey's willingness to try to rescue the dead girls in the film's opening scene, Paul takes a tremendous risk in taking Coffey into Melinda's bedroom. At the least, he risks his job and those of the two guards who accompany him; at the worst, he perpetuates the southern rape myth of the black man alone in the bed of a white woman and almost gets Coffey shot by Melinda's confused husband. In any event, just as the death agonies of the electrified Delacroix are shown passing through the divine conductor Coffey, Coffey's own electrocution, in turn, passes through Paul, causing Edgecomb and Brutal to quit their jobs on the Green Mile and to spend the remainder of their professional careers working with juvenile offenders. Instead of executing criminals at the end of their lives, the two men labor to save them at the beginning, "to catch them young" when there is still time to influence and redirect behavior. Their radical career changes suggest the full influence of Coffey, who likewise dedicated his own life to rescuing souls in jeopardy.

Furthermore, Paul has, at least for a moment, shared intimately the burden of John Coffey's vision. When the black man grabs his hand and reveals, in a flashback technique that is remarkably similar to those employed in *The Dead Zone,* Wild Bill's murder of the two girls, Paul is, like his blind biblical namesake, spiritually enlightened. He not only sees the identity of the murderer, but likewise learns what it is to possess Coffey's extraordinary powers of revelation. When their hands clasp together, Coffey provides Edgecomb "a bit of myself . . . a gift of what's inside me so you can see for yourself." As Paul enters into John's spirit, he sees for himself the visionary insights that Coffey can no longer bear alone: The anguished human condition—"the way it is everyday, the way it is all over the world"—epitomized in Wild Bill's senseless destruction of the two little girls.

What Coffey passes on to Paul in this moment of profound intimacy is both "the infection of life" (evinced in the latter's unwavering commitment to feed and care for the aged Mr. Jingles) and the worldly burden of guilt and sin. As his friends and loved ones grow old and die, Paul must live on—imbued with the spirit of ageless grace that has been passed on to him from Coffey. Like one of Anne Rice's existential vampires, tormented by the memory of the past and yet doomed to continue living with his burden for an indeterminate period of time, Paul wanders alone in an existence that corresponds exactly to Coffey's own time on earth. In the film's last scene, where Edgecomb reflects in bed on his long life and wonders about how much longer he will continue to walk his own Green Mile (this particular parallel is highlighted by the fact that Paul walks on a floor in the retirement home where he resides that is painted the same green color as Cellblock E's Green Mile), the nexus between Coffey and Paul is never more overt. Edgecomb exits this movie essentially on death row. He may not be awaiting execution in the electric chair, but he is nonetheless obsessed with his own death—how much longer before it will occur, how much more suffering must he endure, and whether he will die friendless and alone.

The ending of this film therefore presents a curious admixture of life's contradictions. Paul must carry the onus of his "curse of atonement, [his] punishment for killing a miracle of God," but, at the same time, he has also been transfigured by Coffey's living example of love—the "gift"—that has forever marked his life. At the end, Paul is truly no more afraid of death than was Coffey; in fact, they both appear to welcome its release. Additionally, Paul possesses Coffey's simple faith in the existence of a heaven. Early in the film the 108-year-old Paul Edgecomb weeps as he watches Fred Astaire dance in the film *Top Hat*. This odd moment initiates Paul's narration of Coffey's legacy to Elaine Connelly (Eve Brent). Only later on do we learn that Paul's reaction to Astaire's dancing occurred because he was reminded of Coffey, who also wept while viewing *Top Hat* just before his death. Astaire's gracefulness, Ginger Rogers's resplendent white feather gown, and the soundtrack playing Astaire singing "Heaven . . . I'm in heaven" come to symbolize for both men the glory of an afterlife and a peaceful conclusion to their mortal suffering. The musical score from *Top Hat* that unites Paul and Coffey plays a huge role as a source for emoting and connecting to the inner, spiritual self that endures even as the physical world does not. The earthly pain Coffey has borne is not in vain, for he leaves Paul and the film's audience with an object lesson that is as profound as it is simple. His message of love and faith is the same as Christ's, even if Coffey, like Jesus, is helpless to check the hurt we do to one another. His transcendent capabilities present to Edgecomb and to the audience a vision of magnificent potentiality. For a brief interlude, the suffering example of John Coffey silences the rage of human insult upon insult.

It is significant that of all the films that have been produced from King's fictional corpus, only *Shawshank* and *The Green Mile* have been nominated for Oscars in the Best Picture category by Hollywood's Academy Awards. I believe this reflects not only the Academy's ability to recognize excellent story lines, but also its propensity to reward films that are morally uplifting, featuring characters that manage not only to endure but also to prevail. In *Danse Macabre,* Stephen King provided language that should be kept in mind as an interpretive key for the films considered in this chapter: "I believe that we are all ultimately alone and that any deep and lasting human contact is nothing more or less than a necessary illusion . . . but feelings of love and kindness, the ability to care and empathize, are all we know of the light. They are efforts to link and integrate; they are the emotions which bring us together, if not in fact then at least in a comforting illusion that makes the burden of mortality a little easier to bear" (25–26). Codes of survival in these films center on the most valuable aspect of human life: The capacity to care for others. And heroic status is conferred on their central protagonists because of their resistance against selfish impulses, the will to control the urge for power, and, most important, the ability to extend sympathy and love. King's faith in the endurance of a traditional morality based on the values of love and the resiliency of the human spirit power whatever light remains in a world actively pursuing the destruction of itself and everything within it. Most of the examples of evil traced in this analysis operate from a principle of negation directed at everything that exists outside the self, ironically poisoning the very self at its center. Evil's opposite, then, is the force of selfless commitment to others—to close friends, to children, to anguished strangers. As the films examined in this chapter argue unequivocally, contact with worldly evil does not necessarily produce an infectious corruption of the same magnitude. The truest heroes in films made from Stephen King's fiction reaffirm the Christian maxim that we are finite as long as we remain isolated, but capable of greatness when we share in the "effort to link and integrate."

CHAPTER 6

TECHNOLOGIES OF FRIGHT:
CHRISTINE, MAXIMUM OVERDRIVE, THE RUNNING MAN, THE MANGLER, THE NIGHT FLIER

One of the more curious aspects about the films examined in this book so far is how few of them actually fit the mold of the "typical" horror movie. *Silver Bullet* is the only example where there is the threat of a recognizable horror monster—the werewolf—at the epicenter of the narrative. The monsters that most frequently emerge from Stephen King's imagination would appear to wear decidedly human faces: They form portraits of severe mental illness (Annie Wilkes, Louis Creed, Jack Torrance); out-of-control illustrations of bureaucratic perversion and violence (Warden Norton and his prison guards, commandant Kurt Dussander and his adolescent protégé, and contemporary versions of Nazi mentality employed by American governmental agencies such as The Shop); and postadolescent rage (Ace Merrill and his gang of thugs; Chris Hargenson and her fiendish allies, who are far more monstrous than their victim, "creepy Carrie"). It is not that King is averse to recalling from the shadows the supernatural archetypes of the horror genre—in fact, this chapter will acquaint the reader with several versions of the vampire in mechanized form—but more to his purpose is a fascination with probing the terrors of the commonplace and everyday, the horrors attendant with being human. Even the resident ghosts in *The Shining* and the werewolf in *Silver Bullet* ultimately serve as vehicles for underscoring a core King premise that supernatural phenomena are far less appalling than the distortions of an unraveling human psyche. In so many of Hollywood's translations of Stephen King's fiction, we are reminded of Emily Dickinson's assertion that "One need not be a Chamber—to be Haunted—" (333).

In addition to anthropomorphizing evil, the films of Stephen King establish various social contexts in which the apparatus of the supernatural or speculative worlds forms a direct correspondence with recognizable elements from the everyday or social realm. Collectively these films comprise a commentary on—and a critique of—postmodern America's value system: Our politics, priorities, interpersonal relationships, and our most revered and trusted institutions. King's work describes a particular matrix in time; it bears a direct association with significant aspects of American life and the types of human relationships and institutions that this particular culture has engendered. For instance, in *The Dead Zone,* the fact that John Smith, through the aid of his prophetic cognitive abilities, is the only individual capable of distinguishing the real Greg Stillson from his deceptive persona represents a clear indictment of an American electorate incapable of recognizing the separation between truth and illusion, the loud rhetoric of false patriotism and intellectual substance. That Stillson's despotic ambitions are foiled only by an accident of fate—a photographer captures him using a small child as a shield to protect himself against Smith's assassination attempt—highlights the degree of vulnerability in the democratic political system that Stillson comes close to duping. In another example, American class demarcations subtly contribute to Louis Creed's inability to accept the premise that "sometimes dead is better" in *Pet Sematary.* His recalcitrance is impossible to separate from the hubris of his being an American physician. Long accustomed to relying on scientific reasoning as a measure of control while also occupying a position of privilege in having his own personal desires gratified, Creed's immense grief as a parent is exacerbated by the godlike status his culture has conferred on him in his role as a doctor. His social class, in other words, is a factor in encouraging him to overstep his bounds, to defy barriers "not meant to be crossed." When his faith in scientific rationalism—his "creed"—confronts a mystical energy that stands in opposition to everything he has been trained to believe and that ends up fragmenting his world order, Louis Creed's psyche collapses. Of all King's characters, Dr.

Creed most epitomizes postmodern man's dilemma: Trapped in a universe where there is no longer a coherency at its nucleus, dislocated and decentered, he exits the film as a being utterly devoid of meaning. He has given his soul over to forces he neither comprehends nor commands; he is abandoned without hope of future or the ability to reference the past. His despair is only deepened by his stubborn efforts to make the miracles of the Micmac burial ground conform to his will.

The particular horrors present in King's films are thus closely aligned with, and often emerge from, culturally specific disturbances. These films signal that traditional bastions of social solidarity and identity are fraying or have dissolved. Beneath the surface of King's genial public persona and extraordinary popularity, his work is an expression of the major social, political, and personal anxieties of our time. The subtextual issues present in his films and fictions explore the landscape of the national unconscious, exploiting the personal and political adversary myths that Americans consciously repress. As a critical sociologist of his culture, Stephen King is concerned with creating cautionary tales about a nation under siege from within. Consequently, Hollywood's treatment of his detailed explorations into the devastating effects of alcoholism, drug abuse, perverted sexuality, familial tension, and malevolent or impotent patriarchal institutions suggest all the symptoms of community decay and all the modes of self-destruction that currently flourish, largely tolerated, in American society. Douglas Winter, whose perceptive criticism has interpreted King's fiction with close attention to its social-historical significance, offers this summary in *Stephen King: The Art of Darkness:*

> We pursue happiness, believe in progress, materialism, and the infallibility of science, but we doubt our success, our power, ourselves. As we watch the evening news, if we reflect even momentarily upon our social fabric, we begin to question the validity of the engine of progress. Our position as a society is a precarious one—and principally because of our misguided belief in the divinity of civilization and technology. When crime and inflation run rampant, when our nuclear reactors threaten meltdown, when our diplomats are held hostage in foreign lands, our doubts intensify. And these are the precise fears that Stephen King explores. (58)

In his introduction to *Science-Fiction: The Future,* Dick Allen maintains some valuable distinctions among various representative texts in the genre. The more pessimistic side of science fiction, he insists, "stresses the dangers of the machine age and how reliance upon science and technology weakens the basic human body and spirit" (7). The order that should govern the relationship between human and machine frequently collapses in science fiction and film, so that the humans—who have grown dependent on the faceless technology they have invented—find themselves no longer in a position of dominance. Indeed, in our quest to free ourselves by inventing the technologies of work and leisure, we literally have been forced to free the machine. King's ability to undermine American complacency and to question "the divinity of civilization and technology" find their way into a variety of Hollywood films, particularly those in which fragile humans must confront malevolent forces that are raging out of control. James Egan argues that "from the beginning of his career, King has concerned himself with the complex implications of science and technology, so much so that the horror he evokes often seems inseparable from the dangers of imperious science and runaway machinery of many sorts" (47). In King's films, the machine ends up manipulating this freedom into anarchy, resulting in the enslavement of humans and a relentless threat to their survival. An awareness of the dark underside of technological progress and the moral sacrifices that accompany its proliferation is an issue raised in several cinematic adaptations of King's narratives. Even the bastardized film *The Lawnmower Man,* which King denies as having anything in common with the published text on which it is based, shares at least the writer's antitechnological bias as a cautionary story about the nascent explorations of virtual reality.

King's 1983 novel, *Christine,* is about a haunted car. It also is about a haunted man, the automobile's first owner, an unsavory character named Roland LeBay, who maintains a mysterious connection with the car that extends beyond the title of ownership when he decides to sell it. In John Carpenter's cinematic adaptation, produced within months after the release of the novel on which it was based, LeBay's centrality is considerably more muted; in the film, it is actually Christine herself who radiates the bad karma, not LeBay. King's book effectively dramatizes Christine as a supernatural manifestation of LeBay's general misanthropy. He turns the machine into an obsession—even to the point where his wife and daughter are physically sacrificed to it—and Christine is used as a vehicle for directing his random fury against the world. In the film version, however, this relationship is substantially revised: LeBay (Roberts Blossom) has no personal history with the car; it was his brother who owned Christine, committed suicide inside the car, and then left the vehicle as inheritance property. Carpenter's LeBay is clearly privy to the malign energies inherent in Christine, but he is merely an extension of its dark power, an agent to her will, who sells the automobile to Arnie Cunningham (Keith Gordon) because "he [Arnie] had that same look in his eye my brother always had." Perhaps this is why Carpenter elects to place LeBay inside a grotesque full-corset back brace: The device signals the fact that he is a man without sufficient backbone, crushed by the weight of the inherited knowledge he shoulders.

The film's opening sequence likewise serves to deepen the affiliation between Christine and innate demonic properties. When the 1958 Plymouth Fury rolls off its assembly line accompanied by George Thorogood's rock classic "Bad to the Bone," one of the factory workers is killed behind the wheel, while another gets his hand crushed under Christine's self-animated hood. Later in the film, after crashing into a gas station, Christine's entire exterior frame is engulfed in flames, giving the Fury infernal affinities as it rolls down the highway en route to committing another murder. Thus, even more than the novel, Carpenter's film focuses on the machine as demonic technology. The Plymouth Fury is itself emblematic of an American myth and era. In the late 1950s, when Christine was forged in Detroit, the machine age was no longer an avoidable facet of existence. Americans had little choice but to adapt to the pace of the machine, as engines of technology transformed the social fabric of the middle class (the automobile made possible the mass exodus to the suburbs, while domestic gadgetry signaled the advent of a new lifestyle in the home). Central to understanding the relationship between men and machines, the conceit of the American automobile as a seductive object has its origins in the 1950s, but that concept has lost none of its persuasive influence over the years.

King has called the automobile "a symbol for the technological age or the end of innocence [since] it plays such a part in adolescence and growing up" (Jones 33). This symbolic context translates into the film as well. It both identifies and indulges the particularly male infatuation with the automobile, while at the same time underlining the fact that each of the adolescents who comes into direct contact with Christine is forced to forfeit his or her innocence. Because *Christine* is set in 1978, the era of cheap gasoline and the romantic lure of limitless space, speed, and open horizons is a long-distant memory, but as a machine that was born to run in 1958, these associations are immediately recalled in light of Christine's monstrous engine and frame and are particularly relevant when considering the radical personality shift that Cunningham undergoes. The main protagonist in the film, Arnie Cunningham, who is appropriately named after one of the characters and a restaurant in the television comedy *Happy Days*, which is also set in the 1950s, is fatally attracted to the promise of power and success just beyond his reach, resting comfortably in the confident hands of his friend Dennis Guilder (John Stockwell) or someone else. Perhaps Cunningham is initially drawn to the dilapidated hulk of Christine at rest in LeBay's yard because it resembles closely Arnie's own status as a loser. As he confesses to Dennis after purchasing the car, "Maybe for the first time in my life I found something that is uglier than me." While gazing at her rusted frame, however, Arnie can sense the car's potential: "Some work fixing her up . . . she could be great again." Once he becomes Christine's owner, both the machine and the man who owns her are supernaturally reconstructed. The car recovers its original luster and verve, while Arnie savors the freedom that has always represented the most seductive aspect of technology: He asserts his independence from his overprotective parents, from the high school bullies who have intimidated him; he comes of age romantically and sexually (even his terrible case of acne and black, horn-rimmed, nerdlike glasses mended with white tape disappear); and he remains brazenly unfazed when a series of mysterious murders occur that are directly linked to Christine. In fact, the mystery surrounding these murders creates an even more intimate bond between the car and the boy, as if the two share a lover's secret. Ironically, Arnie's freedom, and this is meant to symbolize King's perspective on the price of human emancipation when it is purchased through technological dependency, is in reality just another form of bondage. This explains why both King and Carpenter appropriately frame this narrative in terms of a love story: Christine is a metaphor for the American male's blind infatuation with technology—and the dangers that frequently accompany it. Late in the film, Arnie speaks of the illicit romance between man and machine, unaware of how much he is revealing about his own destiny, when he informs Dennis, "Love has a voracious appetite. It eats everything: friendship, family—it kills me how much it eats."

Christine possesses a strange, anthropomorphized energy that combines the various strains of an experienced older woman-mistress-vampire whose seductive repertoire warps Cunningham completely out of his mundane orbit. Perhaps this is one reason why so many of the rock songs King references in the novel are about love's betrayal and the fatal consequences associated with misguided passion. Because American males often refer to their cars as a "she," thereby revealing their dominance over the machine and women, the film poses an interesting inversion of this gender paradigm in pulling Christine and Arnie together, as the car is clearly the dominant female exerting her will over a passive male. (In King's novel, the relationship between human and car is often graphically demarcated in sexual terms, such as in the simulated act of sexual intercourse when Arnie must push his vehicle back to Darnell's shop after the car has been vandalized and the teenager achieves an orgasm inside Christine. Carpenter's picture, however, treats this topic with greater restraint.) As the film progresses and Cunningham's relationship to the car becomes more exclusive, his face drains of color and his eyes appear ringed with dark black circles, as if Christine is slowly vamping him of blood at the same time that it is transforming his personality. In fact, there is evidence that Christine has selected Arnie as its next owner as much as the teenager has chosen to renovate the old Plymouth. Unlike King's novel, where Arnie appears as an initially sympathetic character sharply unnerved by his startling identity transformation, Carpenter's Cunningham never really asserts himself against Christine's will; in the cinematic adaptation, he accedes with alacrity to the new personality his metal mistress provides.

Elsewhere in films made of King's fiction, evil wears sexually seductive disguises that pervert and distort vulnerable members of both genders— for example, the ghost woman who entices Jack Torrance in room 237 of *The Shining,* Randall Flagg's manipulation of Nadine Cross in *The Stand.* In *Christine,* however, we are presented with technology as the femme fatale, a cherry-red Plymouth that so thoroughly possesses the men she transports that human females are jealous of the machine's allure. Leigh Cabot (Alexandra Paul), Arnie's girlfriend, accuses him of "caring more for that car than you do for me," and he doesn't attempt to dispute it. Near the end of the film when he is driving at night with Dennis, Arnie's animated talk of love and the sacrifices it demands is not in reference to Leigh, as Dennis initially misinterprets, but to Arnie's relationship with the car itself. Christine definitely transforms Arnie's miserable life, pushing him beyond the perimeters of adolescent blundering and into the frontier of a jaded adulthood. But by the end of this metamorphosis the person he comes to resemble most in attitude, swagger, and even his choice of colorful language idioms is Roland LeBay. Contact with Christine makes Arnie "mature beyond his years," as Douglas Winter notes in *Stephen King: The Art of Darkness,* "a teenaged Jekyll rendered into a middle-aged Hyde, caught up in a masquerade where innocence peels away like burned rubber and death rides shotgun" (124).

Cunningham's deflowering comes at a steep price: He loses his best and only friend, all contact with his family, whatever potential existed to finding mature love with Leigh, and eventually his own life. In his last conversation with Dennis, Arnie removes his hands from the wheel of the car and begins to accelerate. He jokingly remarks to his former friend that he must bear witness to the superlative "alignment" of the machine, and the car responds accordingly by automatically hugging a sharp curve in the road. But by putting his complete faith in Christine's mechanics, in finally trusting her more than he does Dennis or himself, Arnie loses himself. For Christine is nothing if not a jealous and demanding mistress; she wants to possess her owner physically, psychologically, and spiritually. In return for Arnie's personal renaissance, Christine exacts from him his freedom and good-natured personality, turning him, like the cynical LeBay, into an extension of the automobile itself—a hard-edged and expressionless manboy whose cold and calculating choices make him ever more isolated and estranged from those around him. If the film has an extended moral lesson, it is that as man becomes more reliant on his technological creations, he comes to resemble them in his dulled sensitivities and moral indifference.

The vision of a motor vehicle invested with a demonic will of its own that informs the violence of *Christine* is pushed to its fullest possible extreme in King's directorial debut, *Maximum Overdrive* (1986). While *Christine* centers on the intimate relationship between an adolescent boy and his first car, and thereby instills romantic and melodramatic elements into its narrative, *Maximum Overdrive,* loosely based on King's short story "Trucks" published in the collection *Night Shift* (1978), is devoid of such distractions. In *Christine,* viewers are made to appreciate the lure of the machine even as we understand it hides an infernal presence. There are no similar qualifications in *Maximum Overdrive* as we are, like the characters taking refuge at the Dixie Boy diner, overwhelmed by the sheer power and size of the machine. *Maximum Overdrive* is *Christine* fragmented into hundreds of homicidal internal combustion vehicles and electronic gadgets and distilled into absolute mechanical mayhem. There is, in other words, no attempt to complicate its plot with an ambiguous love affair between a human and a vintage automobile.

This is simultaneously both *Maximum Overdrive*'s attraction and its undoing. The film's special effects animate ordinary machinery—a soda dispenser, an electric carving knife, a lawnmower, and trucks—into treacherous hardware. The effects are so convincingly rendered that I challenge any viewer immediately after watching this movie to remain unaffected the first time a tractor-trailer truck appears in his or her rearview mirror.

The demonic machinery of *Maximum Overdrive* completely dominates the narrative, and this is a good thing because the actors and their interactions are disastrously banal. Human beings occupy merely a peripheral focus as they are victimized by various machines and try to speculate about what is responsible for their current situation and how best to confront it. While Arnie Cunningham's personality is radically altered by contact with Christine, at least he retains a personality. In *Maximum Overdrive,* humans are displaced by the superior strength and intelligence of the machine. "I didn't know if I could work with actors," King admitted after the movie was made, "but I knew I could choreograph trucks and electric knives and stuff like that" (Jones 45). One could argue that the quest to destroy Christine elevates Dennis Guilder and Leigh Cabot to heroic status. In *Maximum Overdrive,* despite the reckless actions of Bill Robinson (Emilio Estevez), there are no real heroes because this picture belongs to the machines; moreover, there is no human solution to the problem these rampaging objects present. In essence, *Maximum Overdrive* is King's definitive statement about the destructive potential of machine technology and attendant level of human alienation, even as the film has little else to recommend itself as a work of art.

Not only is the machine world in active rebellion against the human world, *Maximum Overdrive* posits that the technology meant to serve man is both smarter than those who created it and also in possession of a wonderfully dark sense of humor exacted at their victims' expense. In a high comic moment early in the film, a soda dispenser transforms itself into a pitching machine, flinging beverage cans at children and their coach, and renders an entire little league baseball team helpless. The machines are certainly more noteworthy than the humans under siege; in fact, *Maximum Overdrive* might have been a better film if King had spent as much time investing his actors with personalities half as interesting as those that animate the machines.

Later in the film, a waitress named Wanda (Ellen McElduff), after watching restless trucks patrol for hours the parking lot of the diner where she and other humans have sought refuge, ventures out of the restaurant and screams, "We made you. How about showing us some loyalty?" Her lament echoes the title of the AC/DC soundtrack for the film, *Who Made Who?* Although obviously confused about the irrational events taking place in front of her, Wanda's reaction to the trucks is less anger or fear than a sense of betrayal, as if the machinery man has invented has somehow betrayed him personally. The issue of who is now in control—humans or their machines—questions not only the evolution of human immersion into the technological age, but goes on to reference perhaps the more immediately pressing logic: How is it possible to explain this revolt of the machines? Although King offers a specious accounting in the influence of a comet's tail upon the workings of the machine world, this extraterrestrial clarification does not explain the vile intelligence that coordinates the technological revolution of trucks and machines. *Maximum Overdrive* is not simply about machinery randomly malfunctioning; a design guides their revolt. The trucks speak a highly articulate demand for more fuel to the humans in Morse code, and when the diesel begins to flow, the vehicles signal one another to queue up and wait for servicing. A mounted machine gun is a lone sentry over its human hostages.

It is apparent that the humans who have taken refuge in the truck stop diner are at least partially responsible for their predicament. The "mechanized revolt" appears to be motivated as much by human stupidity, greed, and an overdependency on the machine as it is by the effect of a stray comet. Humans exploit and abuse one another all through this film; they treat each other with the same callous disregard that they apply toward the machinery that serves them. At the end of the film, when one of the survivors stops to steal a diamond ring off the hand of a dead woman, his avarice delays his escape and allows a truck to run him over. The owner of the Dixie Boy diner, a thoroughly odious man named Hendershot (Pat Hingle), has an armory in the basement. His collection of guns and high-powered weaponry indicates the level of distrust and lack of respect for human life underscored throughout the film. Whatever agency is in charge of steering the machines—for this is a highly orchestrated revolt—seems dedicated to exacting a severe punishment on humans, or at least emulating their callous behavior.

The worldview of *Maximum Overdrive* is repeated continually in the celluloid adaptations of King's descriptions of modern technology. The human world produces mechanical devices to serve it, but these machines usually fail to perform in the manner in which they were originally created. As allegories, these films suggest that as long as we trust in the evolution of civilization, which, for westerners, is viewed as synonymous with technological advance, this progression has and will continue to betray us to the point at which the perceived distance that comfortably separates master from machine may not be nearly as great as we might like to believe. Midway through *Maximum Overdrive,* the humans in the diner are forced to fuel the trucks that line up outside. Several of the characters are capable of recognizing, along with Wanda, that the machine has usurped the role of master, and the humans are left to do its bidding. The implication of this scene is that the machines *already* run our world, even without the intrusion of a comet from deep space, and Robinson underscores this very point when he wonders if humans were ever really in control.

The same technohorror critique found in *Christine* and *Maximum Overdrive* also pervades the first Richard Bachman book that was translated into a movie, *The Running Man* (1987). From 1977 to 1984 Stephen King published five novels under the pseudonym Richard Bachman. King's decision to employ a pseudonym was motivated primarily by curiosity: At the height of his popularity as a writer, he wanted to see if his fiction would still sell without his brand-name clout. *Thinner* (1984), the last of the Bachman titles, sold 28,000 copies when Bachman was the author and 280,000 copies when the ruse was revealed and King acknowledged authorship.

The Bachman narratives share a common tendency to portray men and women who are victims of a cruel fate. Sometimes this fate takes the form of bad fortune—for example, the accidental murder of a Gypsy woman in *Thinner* sets in motion the curse that will plague the attorney who kills her for the rest of the novel—but most often characters find themselves helplessly lost in an environment that is either indifferent to their welfare or actively opposed to it. The Bachman antiheroes are all distinguished by their sense of entrapment; no matter how they struggle, even those who are survivors in these tales are overwhelmed by inevitable forces, particularly those forces associated with technological alienation and encroachment. In *Roadwork* (1981), the most pessimistic of the Bachman books, George Dawes's obsession with the construction of an interstate highway that will destroy his home and community is a metaphor for the multileveled arena of social upheaval taking place all around him. In fact, everywhere Dawes looks he sees an America in transition, ultimately highlighted in the plastic and concrete of a new housing development. Even his favorite tavern replaces its old-fashioned pinball games with exotic computerized bowling machines. Bachman supplied King with a necessary alter ego, not just with a pseudonym in an age when publishing schedules make such artificial constructions convenient, but more important, with a voice to help King release some of his own literary demons. Bachman permitted King to indulge his darkest challenges to the individual poised against the onrush of an America progressing at any cost.

Two Bachman titles have, at this writing, been made into movies: *The Running Man* and *Thinner* (1996). Another film, *The Dark Half* (1992), is based metaphorically on the seven-year "relationship" King maintained with his pseudonymous twin, Richard Bachman. To greater or lesser degrees, these three films engage many of the same technological fears that characterize the other movies considered in this chapter. Sometimes it is an automobile that suggests the monstrous properties of a character, whether it be the sinister Toronado with the "HIGH-TONED SON OF A BITCH" bumper sticker that George Stark (Timothy Hutton) drives upon emerging from his burial crypt in *The Dark Half*, or the car that accidentally kills the Gypsy woman in *Thinner* when Billy Halleck (Robert John Burke) is distracted by his wife's sexual ministrations. The states of George Stark's and Billy Halleck's souls are mirrored in the cars they own and the manner in which they choose to drive them. As in *Christine*, the condition of the car speaks to the condition of the man.

In *The Running Man,* the medium of television and the various technological devices that characterize (and self-parody) the television personalities who appear on a nightly game show function exclusively as tools for a dictatorship of the future. These various technologies serve to divert the collective attention of an oppressed populace away from the state's daily acts of ethical misconduct and toward the grisly illustrations of what occurs to "criminals" who exist outside the mainstream. Anticipating a large crowd in the studio to watch the Ben Richards episode of the violent game show called The Running Man, a network agent remarks, "Better here than in the streets," indicating the level of distrust that demarcates the relationship between the film's police state and the population it seeks to control. Damon Killian (Richard Dawson) echoes these same sentiments when he tells the Justice Department that his game show helps to sublimate social unrest by providing "ratings instead of picket lines."

Even as *The Running Man* is a droll commentary on America's fascination with celebrities and televised violent sport, it is also a highly politicized narrative of helplessness born of poverty and social anomie. King's novel, although set in a futuristic America, accurately approximates current living conditions for many inner-city Americans. The "contestants" who participate in the televised game show risk their lives in get-rich-quick survival exercises that reflect the true level of their economic situation. Unemployed and destitute urban males participate in obscene state-sponsored contests where losers are killed and winners are permitted the opportunity to escape from gruesome lives of poverty. A huge American television audience subliminally vents its collective political frustration through the martyred persecution and death of one of its own. King's novel continually underscores the desperate economic and political circumstances that literally force young men into this violent "entertainment," while also suggesting a dark collusion between sport and capitalism. The national sporting contest featured in King's book has, of course, little in common with the true spirit of athletic competition and the civic virtues of good sportsmanship, as it more closely resembles the orchestrated over-the-top dramatics of professional wrestling. This is immediately evident in the fact that it is impossible to distinguish athletic survival from game show theatrics. *The Running Man* anticipates the so-called reality-television phenomenon that will emerge fifteen years later in programs such as Survivor, where contestants are required to endure intense physical torment at the same time as they engage in game show competition.

In considering the film interpretation of *The Running Man*, King has reasoned, "It was totally out of my hands. I didn't have anything to do with making it. . . . It doesn't have much in common with the novel at all, except the title" (Jones 54). What the film does reflect, however, is the real-life conservative vision of its central protagonist, played by Arnold Schwarzenegger, whom President George Bush Sr. once referred to fondly as "Conan the Republican." His character, Ben Richards, no longer the unemployed desperado of King's novel, is now a former police officer framed for and wrongly convicted of the mass slaughter of sixty innocent civilians. Gone is the poverty-motivated desperation of the Bachman protagonist; in his place, Schwarzenegger is a moral man manipulated by an immoral state bureaucracy. Also gone is the sharply delineated social-political context of economic inequality found in King's novel. Instead, Schwarzenegger's Richards embodies the triumphant spirit of American individuality, as he refuses either to serve the totalitarian regime that rules the United States in 2017 or to join the underground resistance movement dedicated to overthrowing it. In rejecting the nascent revolution, he informs one of the resistance fighters, "I'm not into politics. I'm into survival." Richards is indeed a righteous and singular voice of self-determination—a classic American action hero battling an oppressive government that, in collusion with an equally corrupt entertainment industry, seeks to regulate completely the daily existence of its citizenry. Captured by this political regime, Richards is forced to participate in the wildly popular Running Man game show that pits him against The Stalkers, a select set of athletic superstars who combine the state's own tendencies toward sadistic violence with a futuristic technology.

In the finale of King's novel, Richards pilots an airplane into the building housing the corporate headquarters of the ruthless television network that sponsors The Running Man; his suicide is an act of political terrorism as much as it is an expression of personal despair. In the end, the Bachman antiheroes all attempt some version of suicide. Richards's act of defiance is merely a gesture, a feeble effort to exert a modicum of control over a destiny that was clearly never really his to command. There are few moments of sympathetic identification between reader and protagonist in King's version of *The Running Man;* Richards's plight elicits only pity. In the more optimistic and melodramatic film adaptation, on the other hand, Arnold's Ben Richards defeats the superior weaponry of The Stalkers and demonstrates that one man is capable of facing down an entire evil corporate monolith. The viewer is encouraged to view the cinematic Ben Richards as a man whose virtues are never compromised even when besieged by a corrupt government. Richards's success inspires both the fledgling political underground movement as well as the cheering mob that earlier sought his death. At the end of the movie, he is vindicated and his reputation is cleared when the audience learns the truth about how the evil political regime has edited and reconstructed footage of Richards's earlier response to the food riot. The film version of *The Running Man* is thus a paean to the power of the individual—his self-reliance triumphs over all obstacles, political as well as personal.

The intersections between reality and the entertainment industry blur on several levels in this film, and this is in keeping with the movie's sobering parody of America's fascination with—and tendency to mix—violent sport, televised celebrity, and politics. In addition to making a film that significantly alters the divisive political ramifications of King's original text and, ironically, placates the right-wing ideology of the famous actor who plays its main character, *The Running Man* also features a variety of other actors whose Hollywood reputations become a kind of metacommentary on the roles they play in this film. Jesse Ventura, the professional wrestler and future governor of Minnesota, appears as the character Captain Freedom, a former Stalker who refuses to come out of retirement and aid the state in its efforts to subdue Richards. Jim Brown, the Hall of Fame NFL fullback and occasional movie actor, is also a member of The Stalkers. He plays Fireball, a pyromaniac whose televised persona relies on compressed gases that enable him to fly and project elaborate streams of napalm. The campy atmosphere of the picture is further enhanced by the hyperactive presence of Richard Dawson, who reprises his smarmy game show host persona from The Family Feud and adds to it a ruthless corporate demeanor as the master of ceremonies for The Running Man. The film's cast thus creates an ironic intersection with famous "real-life" entertainment figures. But it is Schwarzenegger's portrayal of Ben Richards who completes the movie's self-conscious parody of entertainment personalities and their famous personae. In King's novel, Richards is always overwhelmed by circumstances and fate's stacked deck. Schwarzenegger's character is quite the opposite. He is, instead, a take-charge action hero, resembling more the blend of paternalistic-warrior figure on whom the Hollywood actor has built his cinematic reputation, such as the kinder, gentler terminator cyborg in *Terminator 2* or the good-natured family man/highly competent undercover spy in *True Lies* (1994).

Despite its staged violence and Schwarzenegger's campy one-liners (he even gets an opportunity to inject his signature line, "I'll be back"), *The Running Man* is nonetheless a sharp-edged critique of a future, dystopic America where technology—and particularly the medium of television—is used to numb and subdue the American viewer. This is probably the closest parallel the movie maintains with King's text. An overt alliance is maintained among the totalitarian political regime, The Running Man game show, and The Stalkers. All three are connected by their reliance upon elements of an oppressive and violent technology used to suppress individuals who are deemed a threat to the regime. And, of course, anyone who fails to cooperate with the system or is insufficiently awed by the televised reality imposed by the state is deemed a subversive. Technology and political totalitarianism form an unholy collusion that is largely responsible for creating the film's stifling atmosphere of Orwellian surveillance and intrusive paranoia. It is clear that each feeds off the other and makes possible their mutual coexistence. We see this from the start of the picture, where videotape of a public food riot is edited and reconstructed to make Richards appear as the ruthless "Butcher of Bakersfield." The state then deploys a highly effective "prisoner restraint collar" locked around his neck that will detonate if he attempts to move beyond the invisible electronic fence meant to monitor his freedom. On the game show itself, The Stalkers are all associated in some fashion with artificial and mechanized energy sources. Each of the hunters dies when his respective technology either malfunctions or is used against its owner: Fireball perishes in a fiery explosion of self-combustion, Buzzsaw (Bernard Gus Rethwisch) is killed when Richards slices him in half with his own weapon, and Dynamo (Erland Van Lidth) electrocutes himself when his elaborate electrical circuitry comes into contact with water. Each of these technological men is destroyed by the very power source with which he is identified both by name and by reputation.

Contrastingly, Ben Richards is a "natural" warrior; he not only fights against the technologies assembled to destroy him by the state, he is also antitechnological himself, solely dependent on his wits and athleticism. While The Stalkers are provided unfair advantages through their technological weaponry, Richards defeats them without ever employing a weapon of his own. He thus subverts The Stalkers' violent machinery by turning it against the hunters themselves. Various machines—a motorcycle, a jet pack, and a metallic land rover—transport The Stalkers while Ben relies only on his legs to avoid their pursuit. The Stalkers hunt with technological weapons that disconnect them from their humanity (in spite of Killian's insistence that their identities are inseparable from the technology each employs) and are thereby divorced from their own bodies and the landscape they traverse. In contrast, because Richards is sent out into the world without a similar dependency, he maintains a more direct connection with his physical self and even the blasted urban landscape where he hides. Richards's character is effectively linked to pretechnological man—alone in the wilderness and forced to rely on his instincts and a natural affiliation with the animal world.

As in the conclusion of *Maximum Overdrive,* where the survivors are forced literally to leave technological America behind when they pilot a sailboat out into the Atlantic Ocean, advanced civilization likewise reveals itself in *The Running Man* to be beyond salvaging; it cannot be trusted and, in turn, the machinery that serves its design must also be abandoned. Within both these dystopian tales, however, are seeds of hope for survival and regeneration. But the legacy of *Overdrive*'s survivors is that of separation from, and rebellion against, overreliance on machines—a separation, in other words, from the very things in which postmodern man is most invested.

Like *Christine* and *Maximum Overdrive,* with which it shares a similar fascination with machines actively engaged in a relentless and obsessive quest to destroy humans, Tobe Hooper's *The Mangler* (1995) cannot be called a great film. The acting solicited from every character in the movie is exaggerated to the point of grotesque self-parody. For most of the movie, its characters suffer stomach distress, scream hysterically at one another, bleed profusely, and experience the most visceral of torments. And yet there are definitely several compellingly redeeming aspects about this enlarged adaptation of an early King short story first published in the early collection *Night Shift*. Originally intended to be a component of a tripart film featuring several machine-centered tales by Stephen King, *The Mangler* ended up being produced as an independent film.

The opening scene takes the viewer directly into the bowels of the Blue Ribbon Laundry, a terrible, gothic place where the omnipresent sound of machinery competes against the groans of female laborers who toil among dirty linen and the tyrannical exhortations of the shop's foreman, George Stanner (Demetre Phillips) and the laundry's brutal owner, Bill Gartley (Robert Englund). At the center of this earthly inferno is an enormous coal-black speed iron known as "The Mangler." As an undergraduate at the University of Maine from 1966 to 1970, King was himself employed as a laborer in an industrial laundry, and no doubt his experience there was the inspiration for this particular narrative. But in Hooper's film adaptation, everything in King's story appears out of proportion, so that even the speed iron itself is no longer merely a large machine with potentially dangerous moving parts that begin to move on their own. Instead, its apparatus has swelled into a mechanical behemoth, occupying nearly the entire factory floor. On either side of its elaborate cogs and greasy chains appear dozens of women pushing baskets of soiled laundry across the floor of the facility and feeding endless white sheets into the rollers of the speed iron. With bags of clothes floating on pulley systems suspended from the ceiling and frequent close-up shots of the steam iron swallowing sheets and belching vast plumes of steam, the film's opening sequence resembles a scene from a Hieronymus Bosch painting or, better still, a Charles Dickens or Thomas Hardy novel where humans have become enslaved to the primitive internal combustion machines that they must serve. Although the film is set in contemporary Maine, the Blue Ribbon Laundry, with its old cast-iron engine, subterranean interiors, female workers in drab uniforms, and general sweatshop environment recalls a Maine of the nineteenth century.

An exclusively female workforce services "The Mangler." The only males at the Blue Ribbon Laundry occupy managerial status or work safely at the perimeters of the speed iron, supplying it with frequent dollops of lubrication to keep its parts running smoothly. The men who are in charge of this profitable little inferno treat their female laborers as chattel. Upholding the work schedule is overwhelmingly more important than the safety and psychological well-being of the factory's workers. The laundry's owner, Bill Gartley, sports black leather gloves over his hands, silver braces on both legs, an eye patch, an artificial eye, a silver voice box embedded in his throat, and requires double crutches for locomotion. At one point in the film when he is preparing to have sex with one of his employees, Gartley strips off most of his metal hardware, piece by piece, and almost appears to fall apart before he actually reaches the object of his lust.

He is certainly more metal than flesh and is thereby linked effectively to "The Mangler" itself. The speed iron, in collusion with the men who manage the Blue Ribbon, form an unholy alliance that exploits women. "Understand this," Gartley announces gleefully late in the movie, "there's a little bit of me in that machine, and a little bit of the machine in me. We are the lifeblood of this town. We all have to make sacrifices." "The Mangler" is both at the literal center of the masculine alliance that controls both the town and the laundry and the embodiment of its most aggressively antifeminine principles: The machine feeds off women—their domestic labor as well as their blood—as do the human males who likewise profit from their work. The female laborers are of no more worth than the sheets they continually feed into the conveyor belt of "The Mangler": An endless river of white that is the machine's job to process.

The demon that animates "The Mangler" is apparently likewise masculine in nature, and as its blood lust deepens, it actively pursues the vulnerable women with its own supernatural animation. That this piece of machinery is demonically inspired conveniently explains its vampire-like hunger, but the film's misogynistic subtext poses a far more interesting explanation for the machine's particular choice of victims. Although the film unfortunately does not explain this very thoroughly, successive female sacrifices have sustained both Gartley's power and the devil within the machine. It is important to note that *The Mangler* highlights a gender bias that is just as pronounced as it is in *Christine*. In *Christine,* vulnerable males are manipulated and murdered when they engender Christine's feminine wrath. In *The Mangler,* both the machine and the men who built it exploit women. The physical abuse and violent death that women suffer while operating the steam iron merely extends the overt masculine fury that Gartley and Stanner demonstrate toward their female workforce at every opportunity. Gartley's disdain toward women runs so deep that he has sacrificed his own sixteen-year-old daughter to "the god of all machines" and likewise expects his live-in niece, Sherry Oulette (Vanessa Pike), to become yet another virginal sacrifice on the day of her sixteenth birthday. It is her blood—the "blood of a virgin"—that apparently reawakens "the beast in the machine." Even the conceptualization of a demon stimulated by a female "virgin's blood" only serves to strengthen Hooper's critique of the patriarchal design that is imposed upon the laundry and the town it sustains. Indeed, the town sheriff and state safety inspectors, all males, further deepen the film's collusion against women by conducting a sham of an inquest after the press kills and mutilates another worker. Their immediate decision to rule Mrs. Frawley's (Vera Blacker) murder an "accidental death" allows the speed iron to remain in operation and to perpetrate its murderous rampage. King's primary source material completely avoids the acute gender subtext present in this film, which suggests that Tobe Hooper—who both directed and wrote the movie's screenplay—envisioned *The Mangler* as something more ambitious than merely the story of a demonically possessed industrial machine.

The Night Flier is based on a King's short story that was originally published in Douglas Winter's 1988 anthology *Prime Evil*, a collection of tales featuring new work by contemporary writers in the horror genre. As in *The Mangler*, King's original narrative is greatly expanded in the Mark Pavia and Jack O'Donnell screenplay, especially since they initially envisioned the project as a two-hour made-for-television movie. Although the film elaborates on events in King's tale—including, for example, the addition of a major character, Katherine "Jimmy" Blair (Julie Entwisle), who plays the role of a neophyte investigative reporter—Pavia and O'Donnell tried to "remain faithful to [King's] feel of the story and the characters" (Jones 115). The film premiered on HBO in November 1997 and received theatrical release across the United States in February 1998.

Just as Christine maintains a vampiric association with the men that own and drive her, gradually turning them into extensions of the car's innate evil, *The Night Flier* poses another unholy union between malevolent spirits and the machine. The film's vampire, ironically named Dwight Renfield (Michael H. Moss), alludes to Dracula's asylum-bound acolyte in Bram Stoker's 1897 novel. Fascinated by flies and other airborne insects, Stoker's Renfield remains confined throughout the novel and upon Dracula's arrival in London is permanently grounded by his master's cruel and vicious silencing. The Renfield in *The Night Flier*, on the other hand, has finally found his own wings—or, more precisely, the wings of a black Cessna airplane that he uses to transport himself to various small towns along the East Coast where he disembarks for nocturnal feedings. Like Christine's relationship with the men who own her, the airplane maintains an intimate bond with the vampire that pilots it. The Cessna flies only at night, invisible to radar and the human eye alike, and the machine itself appears to partake literally in the bloodletting activities of its pilot.

When Richard Dees (Miguel Ferrer), the unscrupulous reporter for the tabloid *Inside View*, examines the interior of the cockpit, he discovers the instrument panel covered in dry blood and gore, as if the vampire somehow has shared his bloody feasts with the airplane itself. Indeed, the close reciprocal relationship between beast and machine can be traced in the color of the Cessna itself, as it is painted to match the colors of the vampire's wardrobe—basic black, similar to Renfield's omnipresent cloak, with red piping on the plane's wings and back rudders that matches the lining of the vampire's coat. Even the inside window frame around the airplane's door is tricked out in purple curtains with tassels that resemble the inner lining of a coffin. Indeed, the vampire's Cessna is both a means for transportation and a mobile coffin. On two separate occasions, a large mound of dirt appears on the ground beneath the airplane, indicating that this particular Cessna leaks cemetery soil instead of oil. Like other infernal machinery discussed elsewhere in this chapter, the Cessna is an extension of its owner as well as an independent agent. In the film's opening sequence, Renfield's first victim, Claire Bowie (Richard Olsen), is knocked unconscious when the door of the Cessna slams itself violently against his head several times without the aid of any apparent accomplice.

Several aspects about *The Night Flier* offer a unique contribution to the vampire tradition while also distinguishing it as a Stephen King film. For example, the vampire itself is a contradictory blending of hideous monster, in possession of a single elongated fang rather than the dual incisors of the typical vampire, and handsome outcast, who is apparently haunted by at least an aspect of his former humanity, as evinced by the unexplained wedding album kept inside the airplane that Dees uncovers late in the picture. The film's main character, Richard Dees, who spends the entire movie tracking the vampire, is no typical King hero. Dees shares much more in common with the hard-drinking, cynical antiheroes of film noir. His job as a reporter at a sleazy tabloid is a perfect complement to his disagreeable personality; he is a man who has no qualms about exploiting the tragedies of others—his intrusive camera photographs grisly car accidents and the carnage of the vampire with equal dispassion—or violating the codes of ethical and legal conduct. The film carefully documents that Dees shares much in common with the vampire he is pursuing, as both view humans as stupid prey for their respective needs. Like the vampire, Dees is an antisocial loner who owns his own airplane and uses other people and their money to satisfy his personal and professional requirements. As the vampire drinks the blood of his victims without remorse, Dees uses their bloodletting to sell copies of his newspaper and to increase his own notoriety.

This is why at the end of the film Renfield decides not to kill Dees—because he recognizes a monstrous kinship: "Your appetite for blood intrigues me. We have a lot in common, you and I. Perhaps you need me,

Dees. We are brothers in blood." Even the initials of their names—*R*ichard *D*ees and *D*wight *R*enfield—suggest that the reporter and vampire are inverted mirrors for one another. When the two finally meet, it is in an airport bathroom in front of a line of mirrors suspended on the wall. Renfield's face remains invisible, and in keeping with classic vampire lore, his body is likewise not reflected in the mirror's glass. (In a nice special effects moment, the invisible vampire makes his presence known to both Dees and the audience by urinating blood into a white urinal.) Taken as a whole, the scene vividly recalls the oft-cited moment in Bram Stoker's *Dracula* where Jonathan Harker looks for Dracula's reflection in the mirror, but sees only himself: "The whole room was displayed; but there was no sign of a man in it, except myself" (31). Immediately after this, Dees appears to be talking to himself in the mirrors, thus encouraging the audience to establish a point of connection between the two men. Because of the particular camera position—viewing Dees straight on with Renfield behind him but also off to his right—Dees's head appears to be superimposed on the now suddenly visible body of the vampire.

The blurring of their identities is crucial to the ending of the film when Dees demands to glimpse the face of the revenant and the latter responds by revealing not only his hideous face and gaping maw of a mouth, but also a vision of "what hell looks like" in the mutilated human corpses strewn across the airport lounge. Until this sequence, the vampire and the investigative reporter have shared a similar mechanistic coldness in viewing human death. When Dees takes in the expansive violence in the airport, however, he looks on it with a degree of honest horror that has been absent in his previous dealings with human tragedy. At any other time in this film, Dees would have been busy photographing the crime scene with detached enthusiasm. But on this occasion, as the film's camera lingers over Renfield's massive carnage, detailing its bloody aftermath in unflinching close-ups and with an unwavering gaze that both parallels and parodies Dees's own photographic work for the tabloid, the reporter finally responds with genuine emotion. After encountering the vampire, the zombielike reawakening of the slaughtered dead and their assault on Dees is in retribution for his career-long failure to behave humanely. When he is attacked by the undead surrounding him (one zombie mocks the reporter's obsession with flashing light-bulb eyes and asks if he can take Dees's picture), Dees responds with a violence that is equaled in intensity to that of the vampire himself, hysterically hacking bodies with an ax. Consequently, when the police arrive at the crime scene and kill Dees because they believe he is responsible for this horrible crime, the kinship steadily developed throughout the film between the vampire as a killing machine and Dees as an unemotional exploiter of human violence is completed.

The final scene in *The Night Flier* is perhaps the most provocative aspect of the picture, and worthy of commentary. Katherine Blair, Dees's protégée and neophyte reporter at *Inside View,* passively watches as two policemen erroneously conclude that Dees is responsible for the murders actually commissioned by Renfield in the airport lounge. It is interesting that in King's fiction, Richard Dees never dies, nor does he experience the vision of hell in the airport that concludes the film. The short story ends with the vampire's escape; the police arrive unaware of Renfield's existence and arrest Dees in his place. The movie, on the other hand, provides a more elaborate punishment appropriate to Dees's own acts of vampirism, and this extends to include Katherine Blair's character as well. Instead of coming to Dees's defense and informing the police about Renfield, whom Katherine knows is the real killer, she remains silent and thereby is indirectly implicated in his execution by the police. Not only does she become an accessory to his death, she also allows the vampire to escape (the two share a long moment of visual collusion across the airport tarmac just before the revenant takes flight in his airplane). Immediately afterward, we learn that she has become the tabloid's front-page reporter, capitalizing on Dees's destruction and further exploiting the lie that he, and not Renfield, is the Night Flier. This engaging twist at the film's conclusion is much more in keeping with the self-duplicating legends associated with the vampire than is King's short story. Just as Dees reveals his bond with the vampire in his attitude toward human suffering and bloodshed, Blair's calculated silence suggests that she has been similarly tainted by her prolonged exposure to these two vicious males. Completing her education as Dees's protégée, she even repeats his career "philosophy"— "Never believe what you publish, and never publish what you believe"—indicating that she herself has adopted it. No longer the naïve cub reporter ("Jimmy") who began the film, her final actions (and that single moment of visual collusion with Renfield as he prepares to escape) indicate that she leaves it kin to the vampire: A career-savvy creature willing to sacrifice her scruples and even other human life for the sake of an insatiable ambition. Although physically untouched by the vampire, contact with Dees and Renfield has been sufficient to turn Katherine into a monster. Even our last shot of her—a photograph on the tabloid's front page—shows Katherine occupying the place that was formerly the exclusive domain of Richard Dees. The hardened look on her face in this picture completes the parallel.

The machinery of destruction featured in Hollywood's interpretations of Stephen King—from rampaging automobiles and trucks, to a superannuated industrial speed iron, to a sinister airplane that flies only at night—share a common link to the vampire tradition in the featured machine's hunger for human blood. Many of these steel objects are alive, infused with energies that allow them to think, monopolize, quest, kill, and possess. Unlike the traditional vampire, however, this technology does not appear to possess the power of re-creation; when people die as a result of direct contact with this machinery, they stay dead. But the ghosts inside the machines, like the vampire, are somehow sustained, physically and psychically, by a hunger for human blood. Additionally, just as the vampire possesses an immortal existence and cannot be dispatched by conventional methods, the human protagonists battling a King machine find it increasingly difficult or impossible—for example, "The Mangler" and Christine—to vanquish their metal nemesis, as it has both the ability to alter its shape and to regenerate itself spontaneously.

Why or how this machinery of technology became demonically spirited is often ridiculously explained (a comet's wake) or unclear and essentially irrelevant, but the particular social constructions associated with these celluloid monsters invite quasi-Marxist analysis. Karl Marx often referred to the economic relationship between the worker-proletariat and the bourgeoisie-capitalist as vampiric. The capitalist needs and appropriates the life and labor of the worker; the latter is employed to sustain the lifestyle and privilege of the bourgeoisie: "Capital is dead labour which, vampire-like, lives only by sucking living labour, and lives the more, the more labour it sucks" (342). In the films considered in this chapter, it is difficult to avoid social and economic subtexts in interpreting the machine's strange operational "priorities"—for this technology is often identified with distinct work and class identification. Like the cyborg replicants in the film *Blade Runner* (1982), designed to be socially and economically exploited by their human creators, King's machines radically invert their original epistemology, blurring the distinctions between slave and owner, exploiter and exploited. As the particular technology featured in these films gains in power and control, it assumes traits closely aligned to those that Marx affiliated with the capitalist-vampire. The anthropomorphized machine is similarly devoid of social conscience, and its only concern is the perpetuation of its own demonic tyranny through the exploitation of the humans that serve it. Once a King machine is invented and fine-tuned both to serve the needs of man and to turn a profit, the product somehow turns itself into a devastating exploiter of those who would have it serve them. Technological and industrial progress has given birth to a monster— a nonorganic being as powerful as it is uncontrollable. The very logic of capitalism has thereby ironically created the means of its own destruction: Technological advancement, so necessary to the maintenance and expansion of capitalism, subverts itself. Mechanical objects may have been initially forged to serve the social and economic will of their human creators, but somehow in these films this technology is in rebellion against its human masters. The human inventor's worst paranoia is brought to fruition in these narratives of misadventure: The inventor's own tools, like those that appear in *The Sorcerer's Apprentice,* have, without warning, turned against the inventor.

In an age where computers and high-tech equipment have provided humankind with advanced security devices for our homes, automobiles, and businesses, ironically we feel no more secure than we did before these devices were invented—in fact, perhaps we are less secure than ever. Threatened daily by the danger of mechanical breakdown or security breeches by a more advanced form of technology harnessed by our adversaries in business and war, postmodern men and women must learn to function in an atmosphere of anxiety. King himself has posited that the cultural subtext of the technohorror film is a constant reminder "that we have been betrayed by our own machines and processes of mass production" (*Danse Macabre* 156). As projections of human hubris, these machines reflect levels of strength and endurance that man himself does not possess; this superhuman power, coupled with an infusion of demonic evil, makes this technology a deadly and resilient foe. In films adapted from King's narratives, as in many other science fiction novels and movies, technological advancement, while it initially represents improvements in living and working conditions for humans, invariably results in the machine rebelling against those who created it. Just as the Frankenstein creature pursues relentlessly the human who gave it life, in *Christine, Maximum Overdrive,* and *The Mangler,* the machine usurps the role of master, leaving the remaining humans, when they are permitted to live, in servitude to the will of the machine.

The general history of the technohorror film has tended to illustrate the impotence of science in the face of monumental problems it has tried to solve, but only succeeded in exacerbating further. The best of these movies pose some unsettling answers to the distinctly modern question of whether man—the great destroyer of the natural world—is of nature or above it.

The technology we employ to overcome nature also separates us from it. In films such as *The Running Man, The Stand,* and *Firestarter,* governmental bureaucracies and science are linked in an unholy tryst: Both tinker blindly and immorally with aspects of nature they neither respect nor comprehend. There are no golden futures in King's dystopian portrayal of contemporary technologies, no scientists who come to the rescue of a beleaguered humanity, as was the case in many of the science fiction films during the halcyon years of the 1950s. Too many cracks in technology's Crystal Palace have emerged in the past half century to sustain our faith in such idealistic resolutions. A nuclear weapon that ten years ago could only be delivered on the tip of a missile can now be strategically transported from country to country in a suitcase. The possibility that technology can destroy civilization as we know it is no longer a dirty boast used exclusively by politicians and mad scientists; it is a reality that now includes even splinter groups in possession of the right equipment and expertise.

Moreover, the movies made from Stephen King's fiction argue that calamity rather than enlightenment will result from the erroneous utopian premises of the technoscientific worldview (Egan 47). The more sophisticated our machines become, the greater the potential of our losing control over them. And should this occur, as the examples of Arnie Cunningham and Bill Gartley illustrate, we stand in jeopardy of also losing ourselves. This is reflective of King's generally pessimistic technological outlook; from the beginnings of his writing career to his most recent comments in this book's chapter 1 interview, he simply has never identified with General Electric's unqualified faith in a limitless scientific future. In the big, explosive action movies that characterize the films examined in this chapter, King shares his technophobic anxieties with a prosperous and complacent American public that, in words of David Rosner, "tends to see illness and suffering and death as anomalies. We think we can somehow outlaw and conquer death. We have tremendous faith in technology, and are used to controlling events" (Barry 37). Perhaps this America is now in a better position to wrap its mind around the dangers implicit in these films. The "betrayal of technology," symbolized in the imminent threat of bioterrorism, commercial airliners transformed into missiles, and the imploding skyscrapers of September 11, is no longer so far removed from the surrealistic image of motor vehicles randomly attacking an innocent and stunned populace.

A natural world stripped of its mysteries, either through technology or self-conceit, only reinforces our sense of being alone in the universe, our fear of mortality, our feelings of insignificance. In his discussion of Mary Shelley's novel, *Frankenstein,* Warren Montag posits: "Scientific and technological progress does not strengthen human institutions by reaffirming the community of free and rational individuals but instead introduces separateness, division, and antagonism into the social world" (391). Technological development, in other words, does not necessarily coincide with human progress; technological worship may in fact result in a crippling of man's awareness of his own mystical and transcendent powers. This is certainly the case in those King films where a machine is as a central concept. Its appearance is cautionary evidence against the pursuit of selfish human pursuits and our collective willingness to allow machinery to create a mythology of its own—of the dangers inherent in opening doors to an unpredictable world and of making Faustian pacts with workplace and domestic technology.

Perhaps the only minor qualification, if we can even call it that, to King's dystopian vision of technology is a short, obscure film entitled *The Word Processor of the Gods* (1984) that originally appeared as a half-hour episode of the *Tales from the Darkside* syndicated anthology series broadcast on the USA television network from 1983 to 1988. Based on a King short story, it features a personal computer that is capable of transforming the life of a besieged husband by "deleting" his annoying wife and son and replacing them with a more harmonious family. The computer possesses supernatural capabilities that benefit the main character, Richard Hagstrom (Bruce Davison) in his Walter Mitty–like efforts to escape the domestic confines of a bad marriage, and thus technology is used as the tool to relieve Hagstrom from his immediate unhappiness. But even *The Word Processor* is not entirely without a certain level of moral ambiguity, as Hagstrom's selfish freedom comes at the expense of sentencing his wife and child into the netherworld of cyberspace. Certainly his family is obnoxious enough, but their eternal banishment is finally too severe; it is the work of a machine that is more animated by malignant energies than divine. The threat in films such as *Christine, The Mangler,* and *The Word Processor* is not only in the machines themselves, but also in human vulnerability to dehumanization. The alienation of the assembly line has emerged from beyond the factory wall to become an active presence in the lives of consumers. Indeed, all of King's technohorror films seem to promise that whenever and wherever man seeks to harness the mysteries of nature—to imitate God—he leaves himself open to some kind of encounter with God's opposite.

CHAPTER 7

KING OF THE MINISERIES:
'SALEM'S LOT, IT, THE STAND, THE SHINING, STORM OF THE CENTURY, ROSE RED

Since the late 1970s, celluloid interpretations of Stephen King's fiction have premiered on large screens in theaters all over the world as well as on the smaller screens of household televisions. The films of Stephen King translated into made-for-television adaptations—the longer teleplays belong to a television genre called the miniseries—typically have appeared on successive evenings, usually ranging from two to three nights. Not incidentally, the American broadcasts of these films often have coincided with a national holiday and/or appear during one of the four "sweep weeks" (a week in November, February, May, and July where A. C. Nielsen collects data that measures and evaluates audience demographics and the comparative popularity of the commercial television networks).

Although this chapter will consider several of the more notable efforts from this category of made-for-television movies, my efforts here will provide neither an exhaustive interpretation nor a comprehensive summary of the dozen-plus King telefilms that have aired in the past twenty-five years. Because of this book's limitations of space and design, another volume, dealing exclusively with the enterprise of made-for-television Stephen King, awaits an author. These circumscriptions notwithstanding, this chapter seeks to acquaint the reader with the most significant—both in terms of artistic quality and popularity—illustrations of the made-for television Stephen King films. What follows now are some general starting points to consider as background information relevant to such a discussion:

- Various commercial and cable networks have broadcasted King made-for-television movies, including CBS (*The Golden Years,* a seven-part miniseries, and *Sometimes They Come Back,* both televised in 1991); Fox Network (*Quicksilver Highway,* 1997); HBO (*Night Flier,* 1997); and USA Network (*Trucks,* 1997). However, ABC has presented the vast majority of the King teleplays, particularly in the last decade, and, notably, also has served as the production company for the most ambitious of the miniseries: *IT* (1990), *The Tommyknockers* (1993), *The Stand* (1994), *The Shining* (1997), and *Storm of the Century* (1999).

- Several of King's most famous best-selling novels have been translated into miniseries rather than into feature-length films. The sheer size and scope of projects such as *The Stand, The Shining,* and *Storm of the Century* required a minimum of three nights to screen, as each of these epic dramas, running five to six hours in total length, is nearly three times as long as the average Hollywood film. While King himself has not authored the screenplays for most Hollywood feature film adaptations of his own fiction, he has composed the majority of the teleplays for the miniseries, including the three titles cited above. Following their successful collaboration in *The Stand* and *The Shining,* Mick Garris is often King's first choice when selecting a director for a television miniseries. Garris first teamed with Stephen King as the director of *Sleepwalkers* (1992).

- A miniseries adaptation of a best-seller or a made-for-television movie on the disease of the week are usually money losers for a network because they are simply too long to be rebroadcast, but they remain staples of the sweep weeks because they can be hyped with advertising (Twitchell 223). This, however, is not always the case, particularly when King's name is associated with a miniseries production. Although *Storm of the Century* produced Nielson numbers lower than any previous King adaptation on television (Jones 123), *IT* and *The Stand* were commercial successes. *The Shining,* originally telecast in 1997, has since been rebroadcast in its entirety twice, in July and December 2002, and *IT* and *The Stand* also have been appeared periodically on both cable and national networks.

- Each evening's installment is separated into two-hour, prime-time segments. Expensive commercials appear every eight to ten minutes following the first twenty-minute opening sequence. The viewing public is encouraged to connect the project being advertised with King's previously established reputation as "America's master of horror." King appears to be one of the few writers in America whose name is infinitely more important, in terms of popular identification, than any of the individual titles from his canon. In a blatant effort to capitalize on Stephen King's instant name recognition and success, the network sponsoring a King telefilm typically begins an advertising blitz weeks before its premiere, always identifying the story title with King's name, the latter often given prominence (e.g., *Stephen King's Rose Red*). In publicizing the miniseries *Storm of the Century,* ABC initiated a promotional blizzard five months before the drama actually premiered.

- A highly successful telefilm can attract approximately 40 to 70 million viewers at any one time (Edgerton 151). Further revenue is generated in its sale to overseas broadcasters and in videocassette rentals and purchases months after the miniseries premieres. Stephen King titles thereby represent a unique phenomenon in the marketing of made-for-television movies, as they take on a life of their own. Their deathlessness stands in sharp contrast to the vast majority of televised miniseries, which die upon their birth, as they are infrequently rebroadcast and even less seldom transcribed into video or DVD formats (usually because of length and topical interest) once they have aired on American television.

- The deeper its commitment to a multievening miniseries, the more the sponsoring network has reason to be nervous. If the adaptation inspires viewer interest on the first night, these viewers likely will return for at least a portion of the subsequent broadcasts. But even then the television audience can be fickle. The first two installments of the miniseries *Storm of the Century* drew respectable numbers, but its third evening was a demographic nightmare because it appeared opposite George Clooney's final appearance on *E.R.* On the other hand, if the initial material fails to sustain viewer interest, the network risks losing prime-time viewers for the next two or three nights until the miniseries plays itself out. Since the first miniseries were aired in the 1970s, the commercial networks learned that the key to a successful telefilm is to create the idea that it is "special" in the "collective mind" of the viewing public. This strategy then fosters a commitment on the part of the spectator to keep coming back as the story unfolds nightly (Edgerton 163). Perhaps this helps to explain ABC's decision to air all through an evening's telecast selected preview clips of forthcoming scenes immediately after each commercial break and before recommencing the narrative itself. Additionally, during each of these clips, King's name is always associated prominently with the miniseries in order to attract those viewers who may be unaware of the association between title and author or channel surfing their way to another network. Before beginning its nightly portioned telecast, ABC also supplies viewers with elaborate and graphic summaries of the previous evening(s) narrative. I have not been able to ascertain if these promotional strategies were initiated exclusively for the King miniseries, or if ABC adopted them as a result of its experience with other, non–King-related telefilms, but they have been employed for the premiere of every King miniseries that has aired on ABC since *The Tommyknockers* (1993). Moreover, they must be effective, as they have been used to promote other ABC miniseries and various programs broadcast on other stations, such as *Six Feet Under* on HBO.

- While the televised miniseries has supplied a forum for King projects too expansive for conventional theatrical release, and occasionally has produced work that is as good as any to be found in Hollywood's feature-length films of Stephen King, there are nevertheless several drawbacks associated with the genre. Since 1972, operational budgets for made-for-television films have been generally five times smaller than the average Hollywood feature film (Edgerton 169). Consequently, there is less time for rehearsal; sets are less elaborate; special effects are less than "special," making the viewer conscious of their contrivances and intrusions into the narrative (e.g., the special effects in the last part of *The Stand* are an embarrassing distraction); the actors, while often quite accomplished, are more likely to be associated with television work rather than Hollywood feature films (e.g., John Ritter in *IT,* Steven Weber in *The Shining*); story concepts, particularly in the multiple-night miniseries, are bloated and sluggish in their exposition and are subject to annoying commercial interruption at their most dramatic moments; and filming schedules are approximately four times shorter than in a conventional Hollywood release. Several or all of these restrictions frequently combine to hamstring made-for-television movies, regardless of their length or subject matter. And when the film deals with the typical themes of horror art—death, violence, gore, and supernatural mayhem—oftentimes the usual problems associated with made-for-television movies are complicated with issues of censorship. King himself expressed a notable reservation about the genre when *The Stand* was being considered as a miniseries in 1992: "I just can't see the end of the world being brought to you by mouthwash and toilet tissue" (Jones 88).

- Despite their many stylistic improvements over the last three decades, telefilms typically appear "less authentic" than films made for theatrical release. The viewer is too frequently reminded—in the acting, in the degree of verisimilitude, and in the cinematography itself—that made-for-television movies still remain Hollywood's "stepchild," a contemporary version of the B-picture that cannot be taken quite as seriously as Hollywood feature films. Most damaging, the advertising factor is a far more invasive presence on television than it is in theaters, where, for the price of a ticket purchased beforehand, the theater audience is subjected to all advertising prior to the film's beginning and then views the movie uninterrupted by commercials. The advertising component of television—and its concern with popularity and ratings—cannot help but create an adverse influence on the quality of televised art and its mode of presentation. That is, even the best miniseries must manipulate its narrative sequencing so that viewers encounter "miniclimaxes" every ten minutes prior to a commercial break. Making certain that the television audience sits through the commercials is, after all, at least as important to the success of a broadcast miniseries as the story itself.

'SALEM'S LOT (1979)

King's 1975 novel doesn't actually mention the existence of vampires in the town of 'Salem's Lot until better than one hundred pages into the book. Ben Mears returns to the town ostensibly to write a novel about it, but his real motivation is a compulsion to return to the place of his childhood. He is haunted by memories of a mother who committed suicide when he was fourteen; by the "sudden blackness" pursuant to his wife's death while riding a motorcycle; by the Marsten House, epicenter of evil and former residence of suicidal Satanist Hubie Marsten; and by the town itself, with its history of licentious liaisons, alcoholism, child abuse, and violent blood lust. Both the film and novel make the Marsten House—scene of marital discord, murder, suicide, and ultimate symbol of human corruption—into an imposing presence that broods over the rural landscape. In the film, Ben Mears (David Soul) drives directly up to the house upon his return to 'Salem's Lot, whereas the novel is more subtle in highlighting his obsession: He begins to notice that the Marsten House is omnipresent, a section of its roof or one of its lighted windows peeking out from beneath the heavy shadow of trees. In novel and film, however, the house grows in stature and dominance, becoming one of the great haunted houses on the American cultural landscape.

King's third-person narrative is a scathing portrait of small-town middle America. 'Salem's Lot is located on the same Maine road map in King's imagination that includes the towns of Castle Rock, Haven, Little Tall Island, and Derry. In fact, 'Salem's Lot will serve as the prototype for the small Maine town to which Stephen King will return continually during the next thirty years of fiction writing. It is a place that barely hides its collective sins under the rubric of a picturesque village: "A person from out of town could drive through the Lot and not know a thing was wrong. Just another one-horse town where they roll up the sidewalks at nine. But who knows what's going on in the houses, behind the drawn shades" (266). As such, much of King's novel links the invading vampires, Straker and Barlow, who are European foreigners, to a society already so manipulative and violent that it makes the iterant revenant feel comfortable, if not tame by comparison. Vampires choose this town deliberately because it is sympathetic to the secretive malevolence they require to flourish.

The vampires who prey on the inhabitants of 'Salem's Lot discover a community that is more than just hospitable to their soullessness; the denizens of 'Salem's Lot appear ready to accept and to welcome the evil darkness of the vampire as a vehicle for escaping the financial, marital, and communal misery that typifies everyday life in this American town. The spread of evil in the Lot, although diminished by Barlow's eventual destruction, is due in great measure not to Barlow's introduction of catastrophic Evil to the town, but rather to the omnipresent evil that has always existed as a shared condition among the Lot's human community. King makes the point of illustrating the difference between Evil and evil in the character of Father Callahan, who embodies the contradictory impulses of resistance and capitulation that can be found within individual inhabitants of the Lot. Callahan (James Gallery), who unfortunately occupies a far more abbreviated role in the film than he does in King's novel, is in both the link to the spiritual energies of Roman Catholicism. King's priest is a complex individual who means to do well, but has become mired in the minor sins that surround him—in the town itself and in his own addiction to alcohol. It is these lesser evils, which infected the town long before Barlow entered it, that result in the priest's loss of focus and impotent failure when confronted by Barlow's spiritual challenge. The everyday evil in the Lot has worn him down to the point that when apocalyptic Evil of the type he has read about and professionally prepared himself to encounter does finally appear, Father Callahan is not strong enough to confront it. In the novel, this confrontation takes on tragic import because King has prepared the reader by supplying the details of Callahan's spiritual crisis; in the film, the brevity of the priest's single scene never permits the audience an opportunity to view his struggle with much sympathy or depth. Father Callahan emerges as one of the book's most engaging characters. He is cast out into the world by Barlow to wander it alone, bereft of the church by virtue of having been tainted by drinking the blood of the vampire, but dispossessed of the identity that comes in becoming a vampire himself. In Hooper's film, none of these elements is present; Callahan's personality and contact with Barlow are both grossly simplified.

The rural town in America, and the pastoral myth that is associated with it, represents the last bastion of American values and patriotism. At the time King was writing this book, President Nixon was fond of referring to the "silent majority" who supported his presidency—those Americans, like the citizens of 'Salem's Lot, whose silence signified their allegiance to traditional and conservative moral and political values that were under siege during the 1960s and early 1970s. Consequently, when the vampires conquer 'Salem's Lot without much resistance, it is possible to interpret this as a sign of the silent majority's essential resignation and corruption; indeed, that the moral values they purportedly held sacred had lost both their potency and their resiliency. In an interview with critic Douglas Winter, King specifically historicized his text: "I think the unspeakable obscenity in 'Salem's Lot has to do with my own disillusionment and consequent fear for the future. The secret room in 'Salem's Lot is paranoia, the prevailing spirit of [the 1970s]. It's a book about vampires; it's also a book about all those silent houses, all those drawn shades, all those people who are no longer what they seem" (41). Just as the silent majority had failed to intercede against an immoral war and an immoral president who was a crook, the majority of citizens in the Lot capitulate to the zombielike malaise that the vampires inflict upon the town. Moreover, the spread of the vampire plague consumes whatever individuality is left in this village. In Bram Stoker's 1897 novel *Dracula,* vampirism is essentially a subversive act— Dracula's bite transforms his victims into aggressive, highly sexualized and transgressive beings. King's treatment of the phenomenon is nearly opposite in its effect: In *'Salem's Lot,* the vampire's kiss is the equivalent of a lobotomy. As in Richard Matheson's novel, *I Am Legend* (1954), which King has acknowledged as a tremendous influence on *'Salem's Lot,* the transformation into a vampire merely serves to complete the mass homogenization of small-town America that King suggests had occurred long before the vampire took up residency.

King's tale is definitely a contemporary homage to Stoker's *Dracula,* but its distinctly *Americanized* features suggest that this novel as much resembles the fictions of Sinclair Lewis, Sherwood Anderson, and the suburban terrors of John Cheever as it does its Victorian predecessor. Emerging at the end of an era that delivered Americans from their collective innocence in the aftermath of the Watergate scandals and the Vietnam War, *'Salem's Lot* subtly references those somber historical moments in its critique of a closed society that does nothing to combat the evil that originates from outside sources as well as the corruption that emerges from within the town itself. In one sense or another, the whole community hides behind a collective false front that parallels the "antique business" Barlow and Straker employ in the daytime to disguise their nocturnal activities. The revenants overwhelm the numb and disbelieving citizens of 'Salem's Lot without much difficulty or resistance, and it is important to note that in the novel, in order to escape this threat, Ben Mears and Mark Petrie (Lance Kerwin) are forced not only out of town but also out of the country, only stopping their flight once they have crossed the border into Mexico.

The subtle yet pervasive social-political subtext to King's novel is virtually abandoned in Tobe Hooper's directorial account. The telefilm originally premiered as a two-night, four-hour miniseries in November 1979. It represented the first appearance of a King novel on commercial television in front of a national audience. Although several versions of the film were eventually produced—the televised miniseries, a European release, and a home videocassette—only the last, a severely edited two-hour adaptation of the original miniseries, is still readily available under the title *'Salem's Lot: The Movie.* George Beahm, one of King's more recent biographers, accurately notes the film's steady erosion in each subsequent edition: "The better versions tend to be longer. The story is rich and complex and requires time for its telling. Clearly, when shoehorned into a two-hour home video version, the story suffers" (186). Additionally, the telefilm elects to stay within only the most superficial perimeters of the novel's basic plot. The elaborate portrait of the Lot's sociology, which constitutes such a major portion of King's novel, is lost in Hooper's nearly exclusive focus on the machinations of Straker (James Mason) and Barlow (Reggie Nalder) to vamp the small town. The film might as well be set anywhere and at any time in the twentieth century; the only suggestions that hint at a more definitive historical context are the long haircuts most of the males wear and the recognizable model year of the cars that they drive. Additionally, *'Salem's Lot: The Movie* fails to detail the importance of King's own "Crew of Light," the novel's small group of resistance fighters that is led by Ben Mears. In the film, the heroic efforts of this assembly is reduced primarily to work of Ben and young Mark Petrie, and their painstaking battle against the vampires taking over the town is further reduced exclusively only to those revenants—including Barlow—that inhabit the Marsten House root cellar.

In the cinemagraphic adaptation, Barlow is no longer the highly articulate and sophisticated demonic energy he is in King's novel. Instead, Hooper makes him into the silent nosferatu, a revenant that is more beast than human and whose blood lust is motivated by animalistic compulsion. Hooper pays homage to F. W. Murnau's classic silent movie, *Nosferatu: A Symphony of Horror* (1922), by creating a monster that resembles Murnau's vampire in both looks and behavior. King himself was not very pleased with the re-creation of Max Schreck's Count Orlock: "The fact that they wanted to make [Barlow] truly horrifying rather than charming and sophisticated didn't bother me, but they made him look too much like the vampire in *Nosferatu*. This is the third time that particular makeup concept has been used, and I think they could have been more original" (Underwood and Miller, *Feast* 92).

Barlow likewise shares many the Count's ratlike affinities: a white hairless and misshapen skull, elongated fingertalons, and protruding fangs in the front of his mouth. Barlow appears in only three scenes in the course of the film (Collings 46), but his horrific presence leaves an indelible mark, especially for miniseries viewers who had read King's novel or were expecting a vampire similar in looks and demeanor to Frank Langella's *Dracula* (1979). Accordingly, Straker is left as the character that maintains the tradition of the vampire as urbane sophisticate; he is the film's link to Bela Lugosi's portrayal of *Dracula* in Tod Browning's 1931 black-and-white adaptation. Richard Kobritz, the film's producer, finds a parallel between Straker and the dualism of the Marsten House: "Straker is pristine like the outside of the house. Inside it is a chamber of horrors, representing Straker's inner self. The house is beyond your wildest nightmare; everything is rotten, no furniture. Everything falling apart" (Casey 39).

The strengths of Hooper's film interpretation are unfortunately few, and overall the picture has not aged well even as a B-grade horror movie. But Hooper, who five years earlier created one of the truly great American haunted houses in his movie *The Texas Chainsaw Massacre* (1974), does provide an excellent physical rendition of the Marsten House as a haunted dwelling that draws evil men to its evil history, "a beacon throwing off energy." Its empty interior shots create an ambiance of ruin with white feathers floating in the air and blowing along the floor, its elongated staircase and hallway filled with closed doors on the second floor, and its walls adorned with the stuffed carcasses of dead wild animals (which, incidentally, anticipates the bizarre taxidermy of *The Lost Boys* [1987]) complement perfectly the mansion's elevated exterior, replete with gables and single light in an upstairs window. But none of these structural echoes to the far superior *Chainsaw Massacre* can rescue *'Salem's Lot*. The latter's plot fails to develop individual characters and the necessary relationships that must exist among them. At the end of *'Salem's Lot: The Movie* (in the originally telecast miniseries Susan is transformed into a beautiful vampire that Ben must rebuff and kill), the audience has no idea what happens to Susan Norton (Bonnie Bedelia), Ben Mears's lover, who is captured by Straker and presumably perishes in the Marsten House fire that Mears and Mark Petrie set even before attempting to look for her. Although it is clear that Barlow has not yet vamped Susan prior to his destruction by Ben and Mark, and that therefore she is being held somewhere in the house, Mears merely mumbles a lame apology to her forsaken spirit and then goes ahead with the torching. As in the superficial cameo role that is assigned to Father Callahan, Susan Norton's unsettling disappearance highlights the major flaw of *'Salem's Lot: The Movie:* Hooper simply fails to spend enough time and energy deepening and resolving either the film's plot or the fates of its central protagonists.

Film critic Michael Collings argues that Hooper's *'Salem's Lot* essentially fails as a result of "the constraints of television. From the beginning, the project ran afoul of network standards, including prohibitions against overt violence (an element endemic to vampire films), against showing children threatened (a theme consistent throughout practically everything King has written), against the kind of innovative approach that would have made the film noteworthy against the backdrop of the hundreds of vampire films produced over nearly eight decades" (49–50). King was also concerned that the film would be constrained by the medium, a position that he has since qualified in light of his more recent television work (see the interview in chapter 1): "TV is death to horror. When *'Salem's Lot* went to TV a lot of people moaned and I was one of the moaners" (Underwood and Miller, *Feast* 82). King's and Collings's criticism of both the film and the medium that delivered it are difficult to refute. And one might also add that because *'Salem's Lot* was a made-for-television miniseries, and therefore consistently punctuated by commercials, most of the occasions when the vampire does spring forth to create a dramatic moment of fright are annoyingly curtailed when the movie abruptly freeze-frames or fades out to signal a commercial break. Moreover, in 1979, early in the history of the televised miniseries, *'Salem's Lot* was telecast in two installments that were aired a full week apart (November 17 and 24, 1979). As a result, audience interest was allowed to dissipate by the time the second half of the film was telecast.

Collings's observations are particularly interesting, however, when considered beyond *'Salem's Lot* to include the many film adaptations of King novels that have since premiered on television. Over the years, the medium has improved in its production approach to advertising and televising the genre of the miniseries as well as portraying horror in general; and, as a consequence, certain King texts have translated better than others. It is also clear that the difference in quality among these various adaptations suggests the possibility of producing quality work that transcends, or at least manages better, "the constraints of television."

One element that appears critical to this discussion is the level of seriousness that individual filmmakers bring to a particular project. Adapting Stephen King's fiction to film—and especially to television—is not like making a movie of a Jane Austen novel. In the case of translating an Austen text, it is always assumed that the filmmakers will treat it as high art and endeavor to accord it such status on celluloid. When dealing with Stephen King, on the other hand, the issue of his extraordinary popularity often factors into discussions of his work as high art, revisiting the issue of whether or not a popular artist can be treated seriously as an artist. The most successful approach to making movies from Stephen King's books has always first necessitated the filmmaker's willingness to acknowledge King as a serious writer, to accord his source material the level of richness and complexity it so often deserves. Hooper and teleplaywright Paul Monash reduced a novel rich in characterization and subtle sociopolitical subtexts into a campy, minor vampire story. The gothic elements in King's novel—vampires, ghosts, a haunted house—serve to highlight and comment on the distinctly *human* terrors that pervade the town. Hooper's film sacrifices its humanity in deliberately emphasizing only the most superficial aspects of gothic dread. The makers of *'Salem's Lot: The Movie* never envisioned the possibility that their movie, like the novel from which it came, could have become a "film noteworthy against the backdrop of the hundreds of vampire films produced" (Collings 49–50).

IT (1990)

Just after the 1986 publication of this novel, Stephen King called *IT* "the summation of everything I have learned and done in my whole life to this point" (Winter 184). Indeed, the novel embodies many of the issues, concepts, and narrative stylistics King has been employing since *Carrie*. Even characters and objects from earlier books recur or are resurrected for cameo appearances—the 1958 Plymouth Fury from *Christine,* a younger version of *The Shining*'s Dick Hallorann. The core subject matter of *IT*— that an entire town can become a haunted landscape—surely owes its origins to *'Salem's Lot* and *The Body* (*Stand by Me*). But neither *'Salem's Lot* nor *The Body* delves into the elaborate historical and sociological evil that is represented in Derry, Maine. *IT* is a far more ambitious effort, the work of a writer who has been preparing for such an in-depth and integrated analysis in previous narratives, but has finally reached that point in his career where he possesses the tools to undertake the challenge. To illustrate this point, the reader needs only to refer to King's comments in the chapter 1 interview of this volume regarding the importance of selecting Bangor as the urban prototype upon which Derry was based. The novel details the interrelationship between the town of Derry and the monster known as It, a creature that helps to sustain the town's economic viability in exchange for Derry's willingness to allow the monster to prey on its children.

Even as the novel is a historical portrait of a small town, and It an evil force linked to human depravity, *IT* is primarily a novel about child abuse. As such, this issue connects most intimately to so much earlier work in King's canon, for the theme is an obsessive one in his universe. In the novel, child abuse is an effective means of highlighting the gap that separates adults from children, a separation that the seven adult members of the Losers' Club must close by returning to the town where as children they shared a collective experience of battling It years earlier. As in *Stand by Me, Hearts in Atlantis,* and *Dolores Claiborne,* the reactivation of memory, centered upon a return to childhood, is necessary to vanquish or at least to balance the destructive energies operating in King's universe. In

IT and throughout most of King's fiction, youth is not just a force of physical vitality, but also a psychic reservoir. To do battle against It as adults, the Losers must rediscover their connection to adolescence, becoming, at least in their imaginations, children again. In an interview question that King answered about the time he was writing *IT,* he summarized his attitude toward children: "I've written a couple of stories on the 'evil children' idea, but mostly I see children as either victims or as forces of good. I think children are lovely people. They are innocent, sweet, honorable, and all those things. I know that's a romantic ideal, but to me they seem good" (Underwood and Miller, *Feast* 18–19).

The two-part teleplay, written by Lawrence D. Cohen (Parts 1 and 2) and Tommy Lee Wallace (Part 2) and directed by Tommy Lee Wallace, eschews the vast historical and sociological sweep of King's novel, choosing instead to focus individually on the seven grown-up members of the Losers' Club—who acquired this group name because of their status as childhood misfits and outsiders—and their personal recollections of an oppressive collective past in Derry. Derry's adults profess a love for their children, but aside from imposing a seven o'clock curfew, there are no concrete examples of adult panic or serious resolve surrounding the disappearance of so many young people. As horror novelist and titular leader of the Losers, Bill Denbrough (Richard Thomas) recognizes, "This whole town is It in some way, all of them." Early in the film a police officer investigating one of the child murders reminds a concerned Mike Hanlon (Tim Reid) that the latter is a librarian, not a cop, and that he should therefore mind his own business when Hanlon expresses his concern about the number of unsolved murders and disappearances involving children. Indeed, one way in which the seven children are brought together in this film is by virtue of parental neglect or cruelty. Ranging from dead or abusive fathers to hysterical and indifferent mothers, there is not a single positive portrait of a father or mother in this telefilm. The fact that no parent can see the blood in Beverly Marsh's (Emily Perkins) bathroom coughed up by the various youthful victims of It highlights the isolation and estrangement of the children who are under assault. Denbrough realizes that the imaginative gap separating children from their parents is responsible for their blindness: "They don't see what we see. They grow up and stop believing."

The association between the adult world of Derry and It is further established in the masterful choice of a carnival clown as a unifying symbol for the various creatures representing the monster It. Pennywise the Dancing Clown (Tim Curry) purports himself as a character created for the amusement of children—part cartoon, part emanation from a comic book. When adults think of clowns, they often associate them with childhood, but the children in this movie always view the clown as an "adult" that preys upon children. Pennywise's jocular persona first lures the unsuspecting child with the promise of pleasure and fun, and then turns on her, revealing that underneath the greasepaint and lurid colors the clown is actually an adult wearing a disguise. Pennywise's dark sense of humor, always bordering on the obscene (it is impossible to separate this character's grotesque humor from his terror), is lost on the children he seduces, just as his sharp set of teeth only emerge once the child is entrapped and the clown's true intentions are revealed. That Pennywise is not what he seems underscores the fact that Derry is not the safe small-town community it appears to be and that the town's parents are neither truly concerned nor nurturing toward their children. Emerging from "down here [where] we all float" in the Derry sewer system or out in the desolate marshes of the Barrens, Pennywise represents the dark underside of Derry itself, forging a symbolic connection between the town's corruption and invisibility and the secreted violence that lurks just beneath the placid surface of familial relationships. The sewer system, which is It's lair, is supposed to carry away the town's waste; instead, with Pennywise nesting in it, the system remains clogged and unable to purge itself of its own offal.

It is important to highlight that all the childhood members of the Losers' Club grow up to be "unusually successful" professional adults, contrasting sharply with their status as adolescent Losers and misfits. Their success and accompanying affluence appear to have been the result of some supernatural tinkering, as their collective success has insured their physical distance from Derry and thereby aided It in setting up barriers to the memory of their adolescent summer together. Only Mike Hanlon has remained behind to "keep the lighthouse for us," taking up his own father's role as amateur historian for Derry, and It in particular. When he notes that Pennywise operates in thirty-year feeding cycles and that the worst tragedies in Derry have always coincided with one of these cycles, he summons each of his childhood friends with the same question: "Do you remember?" Reunited thirty years later, the adult Losers realize that their collective memory is only partial, that recollections of events fade over time as a child moves on to adulthood and forgetfulness. Pennywise uses this to intimidate Ricky Tozier (Harry Anderson) in the Derry library the day of his return: "Get out of town by sunset. You don't remember enough. You're too old."

Just as the Losers are terrified of returning to Derry to face It once again as grown-ups—one of the seven, Stan Uris (Richard Masur), is so traumatized that he elects to commit suicide rather than to go back to the town—those who do return also rediscover the power that is inherent in simple childhood faith and the loyalty of friendship. Pennywise preys on isolated children; long accustomed to being ignored by the adult denizens of Derry, he is, on the other hand, nervously intimidated when confronted by the collective energy of a unified group. As Hanlon speculates early in the second half of the film, "There was some kind of force guiding us that summer. I don't know if it came just to help us, or if we created it. But maybe it's still here." A wellspring for the collective influence that radiates from the Losers' Club is their shared commitment to one another and to the other children of Derry. The strength of the adult-children who struggle against It lies in their ability to meld their individual imaginations into the psychic potency of a group dynamic. When the group holds hands and forms a circle in the library in the midst of Pennywise's supernatural assault, they are able to stop the clown's attack. Similarly, when all the Losers help to clean up the blood that keeps exploding from the sink drain in Beverly Marsh's childhood bathroom, the blood never comes back. Individually, they are vulnerable, as when Mike Hanlon is wounded by Henry Bowers (Michael Cole) wielding a switchblade in his hotel room, but together they possess the power to counterbalance It's destructive and isolating energies. The reactivation of memory, centered on a return to childhood, is often a necessary prerequisite in King's universe to the adult reimposition of mental balance over threatening forces, both natural and supernatural. Youth is not just a force of physical vitality, but also a psychic reservoir. Thus, the collective power of the adult Losers can be defined as the sum of the members' individual memories from childhood. This helps to explain why most of these memories recur to individuals in the company of the whole group. Each personal memory becomes a piece of the group's shared history, allowing the individual narrator to help fill in gaps belonging to others in the collective.

In an essay entitled "Good and Evil in Stephen King's *The Shining,*" critic Burton Hatlen posits "the Good in King's world is represented only by small groups of people who (barely) cling together in the face of encroaching darkness, rather than by any supernatural power which can serve to counterbalance the forces of destruction" (85). This is a very trenchant observation that operates throughout King's canon. In *IT,* the recognition of, and bonding with, the personal suffering of others allows the members of the Losers' Club, as adults as well as when they were children, to enlarge their own spirit of redemptive sympathy. The group opens to accept Mike Hanlon when he is pursued by Bowers and his gang of thugs, and then risks the welfare of its individual members in a rock fight to protect Hanlon. The individual and the collective grow stronger as a result of their shared connection with one another; this was true when the Losers were children, and it is also true when they reunite as adults.

The circular imagery that highlights the film's emphasis on adults re-experiencing childhood is repeated in various forms throughout the film. The concept of the magic circle is evoked each time the Losers join hands. It's underground lair features a topography of circular drains on the sides of the walls and ground. Certainly another of the film's most important circular symbols must be the wheels of Silver, Denbrough's repossessed bicycle, which he rides as a child to save Stan Uris from Pennywise and then again as an adult to rescue his wife, Audra (Olivia Hussey), who has been traumatized by It. Silver's name not only suggests the Lone Ranger's trusted steed, but also is likewise the substance in the slingshot projectile used twice by Beverly to wound It. Riding atop Silver, Bill appears as a gallant warrior; he summons the imagery of a god, perhaps Mercury or Bellerophon, the rider of Pegasus. It is particularly important, in light of the film's plethora of circular shapes and recurring patterns, that Silver's wheels propel Bill and the catatonic Audra on the bar in front of him on a journey back through the streets of his youth. Even though he and his wife are physically too big for the bike, he chooses to ride it like the adolescent boy he remembers—recklessly, "to beat the devil." Weaving in and out of traffic, he and the wheels of Silver complete another magic circle and rescue Audra from the abyss of her own terror. Like some fairy-tale princess under a monster's spell, she is awakened from her artificial sleep because her childlike hero possesses great courage and the willingness to risk his life for hers.

Of all the telefilms adapted from Stephen King's fiction, *IT* is arguably the most faithful rendition of the novel that inspired it. Consequently, *IT* the miniseries also suffers from the same flaws that are to be found in King's magnum opus: The long narrative builds to a final climatic confrontation between It and the adult Losers in the sewers beneath Derry, but then simply implodes. The Wallace-Cohen teleplay is wise enough to exclude the awkward and controversial sexual intercourse scene in King's novel, where Beverly loses her virginity to each of the twelve-year-old boys in the Losers' Club just after their first confrontation with It. However, in the decision to substitute a cheap special effects monster in the form of a chicken-wire–framed giant brown spider in place of the brilliantly sardonic Pennywise, the film repeats King's own regrettable finale. Because Pennywise establishes such close and terrifying bonds with each member of the Losers' Club and with the group as a whole (as well as with the movie's audience), eliminating the clown from the ultimate battle scene undercuts the acute dramatic tension that the miniseries has steadily been developing. In place of this tension, when the Losers finally vanquish the spider monster It by kicking it to death and tearing out its slimy arachnid heart with their bare hands, the film descends to a level of puerile ridiculousness. After It is destroyed, the last fifteen minutes of the telefilm conveniently resolves the few remaining conflicts and neatly shuffles the central characters off into a quick happy ending. It is unfortunate that a television movie that wrestles so convincingly with topics such as child abuse, the compulsive urge of certain children to bully others who are perceived to be weak or different, the bonds of redemptive sympathy that develop among adolescents who share the struggle to overcome the labels of loser and outsider, and the effort to reinvigorate adulthood with the recollected spirit of childhood essentially abandons these issues in a conclusion unworthy of the seriousness these topics inspire.

THE STAND (1994)

Bringing *IT* to cinematic fruition was, above all else, a superb act of compression. How else to describe the condensing of a thousand-page novel into a coherent four-hour miniseries that remained incredibly faithful to the original source? The making of *The Stand* into a miniseries posed some of the same problems in dealing with the epic design just described, but even more exacerbated. *The Stand* is, narratologically as well as philosophically, a more complicated text than *IT.* Although split between two distinct time epochs that gradually merge at the climax of the novel, *IT* still evokes a linear plotline: The children in the Losers' Club battle It as children and then again as adults. Editing down the length and scope of the novel required a judicious selection and conflation of scenes and the rendition of the teleplay into two halves—one night belonging to the children, the next night to the adults—and the main plot problem was solved.

The Stand, on the other hand, presents the separate and sometimes interactive storylines of more than a dozen westward-migrating individuals that gradually converge into two camps—one group located in Las Vegas under the dictatorial rule of the Dark Man, Randall Flagg (Jamey Sheridan), the rest of the cast drawn to Boulder, Colorado, and the Free Zone established by an aged visionary named Mother Abigail Freemantle (Ruby Dee). Eventually, representatives from the two oppositional forces confront one another in Las Vegas, and readers and viewers are left with the only surviving protagonists who began the tale, Frannie Goldsmith (Molly Ringwald) and Stu Redman (Gary Sinise).

The Stand offers itself as a funnel-shape narrative: Beginning with a huge cast of survivors who share very little in common and gradually narrowing down to focus on a core collection of individuals who are all engaged in the same task of survival in a postapocalyptic America. The journeys that the central characters undertake physically re-create another funnel-like image, as their westward journeys from starting points across the eastern half of the United States tend to coalesce along the same routes leading to either Las Vegas or Boulder. These two narrative constructions are interestingly inverted by the spread of the superflu itself. What begins as an isolated, nearly contained accident in a small government installation in rural California quickly opens out, widening eastward—like some kind of continental sneeze—effectively contaminating the rest of the United States within a two-week period.

Putting all this material into a workable script was a major reason for the long delay in compressing what is arguably King's most popular novel (both the 1978 version and the 1990 complete and uncut edition remained on *The New York Times'* best-seller list for months after their publications) into a film. George Romero, who had directed King's screenplay *Creepshow* (1982), a collection of five short horror tales, was the author's initial choice to cowrite the screenplay and then direct *The Stand.* King and Romero intended to produce a two-part film—the individual two-hour halves separated by about a year's production time—as a theatrical release. But the epic length and scope of *The Stand*'s plot kept frustrating their collaborative endeavors. As King acknowledged in a 1983 interview: "Length is a problem. It's been through two [screenplay] drafts now and now it's down to a length of what would probably be in shooting time about four hours. We're at this point where we gotta lighten this boat. We gotta throw some people overboard. Who's expendable? . . . We tried to get rid of a couple of people and they didn't want to stay down. So that's where we are and we're trying to decide what to do next" (Underwood and Miller, *Feast* 161–162). The Romero-King collaboration efforts languished for over a decade, both men getting involved with different projects that kept distracting them, until King and ABC decided to resurrect *The Stand* into a four-part, four-night miniseries based on a four hundred–page teleplay written by King alone. As a miniseries, the problem of plot and character compression that had formerly hampered earlier efforts to transform *The Stand* into a theatrical release would no longer be an issue. Consequently, King's teleplay emerged as a close rendition of his novel, and none of the major characters was sacrificed. Moreover, director Mick Garris solicited the services of several foremost actors in film and television to play the leading roles.

The Stand is perhaps King's fiercest critique of modern technology; were this film not part of the made-for-television enterprise discussed in this chapter, I would have included it in chapter 6, as so much of the movie embodies the technological horrors present throughout King's work. Not only does the plague itself emerge as a consequence of unholy tinkering by government agents with the genetics of microbiology, but the aftermath that confronts the survivors of this devastation is cast in a distinctly technological context. Although Randall Flagg's evil is affiliated throughout the film with forces as diverse and ubiquitous as Satan and the wild creatures of the natural world (e.g., rats and crows), he is best represented in technological terms. As such, Flagg's role in this film provides another illustration of King's jaundiced perspective on modern America—a society that has comprised its moral integrity to the quest for synthetic productivity. Glen Bateman (Ray Walston) describes Flagg as a natural consequence and extension of the technological god worshipped prior to the plague, "the last magician of rational thought, gathering the tools of technology against us." Indeed, Flagg's vision of the future is conceivable only by resurrecting the tools of the past. And while we learn of his success at reconnecting the electric generators that return Las Vegas to its air-conditioned, pre-plague surreality, his ultimate goal is to reactivate the technologies of war—once again summoning the same lethal powers that were responsible for producing the plague—to fulfill his fantasy of worldly conquest.

Because Trashcan Man (Matt Fewer) echoes Flagg's tendency toward psychopathic behavior as well as his fascination with the potential destruction available in America's discarded technologies of war, it is not surprising that the two men gravitate toward one another. Trashcan Man emerges as Flagg's technological "id." He scours the desert in hopes of bringing to his master the ultimate power of fire—a nuclear device—that is emblematic of the "blind science" that guides both their mutual vision of technology and the pre-plague America that spawned such engines of destruction. Trashcan Man's madness, like that of Flagg, is symptomatic of the greater insanity that has led to the construction and deployment of America's lethal gadgetry. The apocalypse that Trashcan Man brings to Las Vegas under the misapprehended belief that he is serving Flagg's will—"My life for you" becomes his mindless mantra—merely underscores the essential distrust and inevitable potential for self-annihilation that King always affiliates with any attempt to harness the powers of technology.

At the end of this film, the Dark Man's Vegas empire is destroyed by the betrayal of technology, the inability to modify its energies and establish human control over it. In contrast, Mother Abigail and the Free Zone cling to a lifestyle that is rudimentary when compared to American existence in the pre-plague world and certainly to the comforts available in Flagg's Las Vegas. The Boulder community models itself, at least initially, on the precepts of Mother Abigail's primitive mysticism and unequivocal faith in God. The Free Zone resembles more her simple midwestern farm than Flagg's illuminated Vegas. When Mother Abigail requires greater power to aid her in guiding the community, she follows the examples of biblical prophets and religious mystics by wandering into the woods to seek correspondence with the unharnessed and nonhuman powers of the natural world. In turn, when the four members of the Free Zone who initiate the collapse of Flagg's dominion must journey over the mountains to confront him, they do so following Mother Abigail's instruction and example: Shunning automobiles and other machinery, weapons, and packaged food, they rely only on the faith that they are doing the will of a superior force that is greater than themselves. Thus, when Glen Bateman, Larry Underwood (Adam Storke), and Ralph Brentner (Peter Van Norden) are captured and brought to judgment in front of Flagg and his Vegas denizens, they are curiously unafraid and audaciously scornful of Flagg's oppressive regime. Their personal liberation is due in part to their collective confidence in Mother Abigail's prophetic abilities. But it also suggests that the Free Zone men are invested with a moral certitude that makes them superior to those who, in both the American government's handling of the plague and in the autocratic regime that follows in Las Vegas, have abdicated all moral responsibility.

Those characters genetically disposed against catching the plague that decimates 99 percent of the world's population are, to a greater or lesser degree, all detached from bourgeois society. Even Mother Abigail and Flagg are isolated from mainstream culture, she by virtue of her race, age, and sex; he by his very nature as an eternal drifter whose life centers around fomenting chaos and then taking personal advantage of the social vacuum that ensues. The main characters, whether good or evil or inhabiting a state of moral flux, have precisely the temperament required to live for at least a while without institutions and technology (Pharr, "Almost Better" 6). Nevertheless, the individuals who are drawn toward Las Vegas tend to desire more material comforts and social authority in their lives while those who head toward Boulder appear more predisposed toward democratic values and spiritualism. The film creates these demarcations and they are upheld in the specific choices and dreams that most of the characters encounter. Indeed, these oppositional distinctions help contribute to the telefilm as an allegory of good versus evil.

The Stand poses a Manichean dialectic of opposing principles at work in the universe, the clash of two elemental forces. Correspondingly, each major character has his or her counterfigure on the other side of the Rockies. In addition to viewing Las Vegas and Boulder as political and geographical opposites and Mother Abigail as Randall Flagg's philosophical contrary, Frannie Goldsmith, the post-plague world's Eve and helpmate to Adam, finds her dark opposite in Nadine Cross (Laura San Giacomo), the portrait of Eve as evil seductress who has saved her virginity to bear Flagg's infernal progeny. Trashcan Man's mental instability and penchant for violence is counterpointed by the mentally handicapped but sweetly innocent Tom Cullen (Bill Fagerbakke) and his best friend, Nick Andros (Rob Lowe), who likewise transcends his own physical handicaps in service to others. Lloyd Henreid (Miguel Ferrer) similarly emerges as Stu Redman's dark double; each of these men needed the plague to discover his full potential and to emerge as a figure of serious importance in its aftermath, as both their lives were going nowhere prior to the superflu disaster. It is possible to argue that Lloyd and Stu become the "political fathers" of the two post-plague societies: Stu becomes the chairman of the Free Zone Governing Committee and Lloyd leaves prison as Flagg's "first lieutenant," his chosen "eye" to oversee the entire Vegas operation. Stu is shaped by the social and religious insights of Glen Bateman and Mother Abigail respectively, while Lloyd becomes the loyal servant of Flagg's autocracy, continually repaying the "only one who ever had faith in me."

The two most interesting and morally complex dramatic foils in the film, however, are Harold Lauder (Corin Nemec) and Larry Underwood. In *The Stand,* more than any other King novel or film, free will and moral choice are solidly within the individual's purview; all of the major characters participate directly in determining their fates, and this is especially true with Lauder and Underwood. Underwood begins the film in flight to his mother's house in Queens in debt forty thousand dollars. His mother is hardly glad to see him, worried that Larry is doomed to follow in the path of his deadbeat father. But Larry is also on the verge of becoming famous as a popular rock star just at the moment that the plague changes American popular culture. Lauder likewise begins the film rebuffed by a woman he loves at the moment of his own personal triumph when he publishes a poem in a major literary magazine. Frannie Goldsmith, Lauder's not-so-secret love, comes to acknowledge his existence only after she realizes that he may be the only other person beside herself to have survived the plague. In the course of the movie, the paths of Underwood and Lauder parallel one another, intersect, and then sharply divide. Larry will head west out of New York City accompanied by Nadine Cross, who will eventually join forces with Harold (only to betray him as well) and then "cross" allegiances against the Free Zone in service to Flagg's will.

As Harold Lauder attempts to make a new life for himself in a new world, what he gains in confidence is diminished by his deepening resentment toward the romantic bond that Stu and Frannie establish; in fact, he becomes so obsessed with their union that all his subsequent actions appear motivated by his desire for revenge. Because he savors his bitterness and allows it to expand into an overreaction, it is easy to overlook that Harold's feelings of betrayal are somewhat justified, as Frannie makes the early mistake of encouraging his amorous attentions by kissing him and resting her head on his knee, while Stu reneges on his pledge when the two first meet that he will not come between Harold and Frannie: "That's the last thing in the world that I want." (Perhaps this failed promise to Harold and the uncomfortable bond they share through their mutual love of Frannie explains why Stu is the only one to experience telepathically Lauder's motorcycle accident and eventual suicide, as Stu is made to share "the taste of gun oil in my mouth." Moreover, Lauder's fate somewhat parallels his own, as shortly after Lauder's "accident," Stu is himself stranded in the Rockies with a broken leg and similarly forced to contemplate the viability of his own mortality.) In King's novel, Harold's obsession with revenge is allowed to stew slowly; through his devastating journal entries, the reader finds Lauder's effort to destroy the Free Zone an absolutely chilling illustration of his inability to manage his jealousy and rage. In the teleplay, however, Harold's corruption is not so convincingly developed. In the journey west, his facial acne magically clears, his attire becomes more macho, and he appears emboldened by his role as a survivor child on the verge of discovering his manhood. Even his body language becomes more complex and sinister as he grows into a morally conflicted being. But the miniseries, unlike King's novel, fails to portray adequately the missed potential that Harold surrenders in allowing Nadine and Flagg to seduce him over to the dark side. In King's book, Harold is presented a viable opportunity to escape the isolation that has characterized his past; he makes a deliberate choice to reject this opportunity. Lauder's decision to become Flagg's agent underscores his deliberate rejection of a social identity that is only dimly suggested in the film adaptation. In the novel, many members of the Free Zone have come to respect Harold's intelligence and contributions to the community; the Burial Committee even nicknames him "Hawk" because of his leadership skills. The miniseries supplies only the briefest passing insight to this thwarted personal potential when Lauder writes, "I'm sorry. I was misled" just before taking his life.

On the other hand, the film accurately follows the novel in its portrayal of Harold's death, which is the result of yet another act of treachery. Just as Harold betrays the Free Zone by planting a "surprise" bomb in Frannie and Stu's home, Nadine Cross and the Dark Man in turn deceive Harold. His suicide occurs appropriately in isolation on the side of a deserted mountain, where Harold is bereft of all human companionship and solace. Lauder's death is a final reflection of his self-absorption and decision to distance himself from others. Like the shattered bones in his ribs and leg that result from the motorcycle accident caused by Flagg, Harold exits a splintered character, doomed because of his inability to manage his destructive emotions toward Frannie and Stu and his ultimate decision to break away from what remains of the human community. Harold's fate reminds us of the Dantesque maxim that animates the whole of Stephen King's universe: "Those who have chosen the 'dark' side . . . pay for that choice in credible and proportionate ways, punished not so much for their sins as by them" (Bosky 124).

The post-plague world refines Larry Underwood's capacity for performing good to the same degree as it allows Harold the opportunity to indulge in evil. Harold's missed chances are not lost on Underwood, who matures and becomes more self-disciplined in the course of the film. The name "Underwood" is meant to evoke qualities that exist "under" the surface of Larry's personality that he desperately needs to uncover and bring forth. The plague allows him this opportunity. In his early interaction with his mother, Alice (Mary Ethel Gregory), the film suggests that Larry's meteoric rise to fame has brought with it several problems in self-indulgent behavior—drugs, debt, excessive pride, and the general inability to distinguish friends from manipulators, reality from illusion. But in the postplague world, Larry changes from hedonistic rock star into a man capable of respecting the commitment he shares with his girlfriend, Lucy Swann (Bridgit Ryan), and avoiding the seductive machinations of Nadine Cross. From the point when he rejects Nadine's sexual plea to the end of the film, Larry's personal ethics are never again in doubt. He has passed through the dark night of the soul and is entitled to a life with Lucy, who is pregnant with his child. Placed in a similar situation as Harold—both spurned by women who select other lovers—Larry chooses to react more positively, balancing his bruised feelings with self-control and the need to move on with his life. He later accepts his own self-sacrifice in Las Vegas as an action of free will that he performs for the people he has come to love in the Free Zone. In a movie that continually stresses the human propensity to avoid responsibility for choices that affect others, Larry exhibits qualities that underscore the human potential for unselfish acts of bravery. Both Harold and Larry die miserably at the end of this film, but the former remains a victim to his obsessive urge to annihilate whatever he cannot dominate, while Underwood demonstrates the capacity to rise above the limitations of his pre-plague self.

The rendering of *The Stand* into a television miniseries was the only option available for creating a viable cinematic adaptation of this ambitious novel. Accordingly, the project reflects the best and the worst of the genre. As a film, the whole of *The Stand* turns out to be greater than its individual parts. King's teleplay is a very accurate representation of the major issues and conflicts at work in his book. Filmed over a 104-day shooting schedule, *The Stand* features 125 speaking roles with more than 600 extras employed during the Las Vegas sequences alone (Jones 88). But there are also moments when the sheer scope of the teleplay works against its compelling plot. For example, in the second part entitled "Dreams," the dream sequences that feature characters from the Free Zone walking through Mother Abigail's unconvincingly plastic cornfield to receive from her essentially the same set of instructions tends to become tiresome and repetitive. The casting also suggests something about the mixed qualities of the miniseries. The film contains laudable efforts by Bill Fagerbakke as Tom Cullen and Gary Sinise as Stu Redman, but then disappoints in its selection of drab Molly Ringwald to play one of King's most dynamic female protagonists, Frannie Goldsmith (perhaps as serious a miscasting blunder as Kubrick's choice of Shelley Duvall in the role of Wendy Torrance). Similarly, there are moments of brilliant tension, as when Stu breaks his leg and must be left behind in the wilderness by his three conflicted friends who are destined to journey on to Las Vegas without him. Such an episode, rich in subtle emotion and depth, is sharply contrasted by the hyperbolic scene in Las Vegas when "The Hand of God" literally descends from the sky to detonate the nuclear device Trashcan Man has been permitted to drive into the center of town. Moreover, the atomic explosion itself is likewise unconvincingly staged, as it momentarily lights up the entire horizon in front of Tom and Stu, who sit watching it from afar, but then appears to dissipate into darkness seconds later.

THE SHINING (1997)

Since the release of Stanley Kubrick's *The Shining* in 1980, Stephen King has been neither politic nor objective in his criticism of this film. The anticipatory excitement over the heady honor of a young writer having his third published novel selected for cinematic adaptation by one of the twentieth century's most revered directors slowly began to sour when Kubrick rejected King's screenplay for the movie and, in collaboration with Diane Johnson, wrote his own. That collaboration produced a controversial narrative—borrowing heavily from King's novel one moment (the dialogue that transpires between Lloyd and Torrance in the two bar scenes, for example, is almost verbatim from the published text) and then, in the next, altering its plot so radically that the book's rescuer, Dick Hallorann, is killed before he even gets the chance to take off his winter parka. Although Kubrick's *Shining* is the product of an *auteur* director who understood the absolute legitimacy of his art as a wholly separate entity from its original source, King has begrudgingly admired the stunning photography, the use of the hedge maze as a metaphor for the Torrance family, and the various technical contributions of the Steadicam, but little else about Kubrick's interpretation:

> I think the problems are mostly with the scripting, not with the acting, per se, or the directing. There are weaknesses in the script, places where Kubrick and Diane Johnson apparently didn't think, or maybe where they thought too much. . . . I thought that Kubrick dealt with things sometimes in a way that was almost prissy. I wonder if he's ever seen *Dawn of Dead* or if he's ever seen *Alien?* If he's ever had a conversation with himself about primal terror? What I'm talking about is just going out and getting the reader or viewer by the throat and *never* letting go. Not playing games and not playing the *artiste.* Because horror has its own artistry, in that never-let-up sort of feeling. That's what's wrong with *The Shining,* basically . . . [t]he movie has no heart; there's no center to the picture. I wrote the book as a tragedy, and if it *was* a tragedy, it was because all the people loved each other. Here, it seems there's no tragedy because there's nothing to be lost. . . . Another big problem, the more I think about it, is that Jack Nicholson shouldn't have been cast as Jack Torrance. He's too dark right from the outset of the film. The horror in the novel comes from the fact that Jack Torrance is a nice guy, not

someone who's just flown out from the cuckoo's nest. People have said to me that Nicholson is crazy from the beginning of the film; there's never any progression. People impute that craziness to Nicholson because of other parts that he's played. Well, I'm concentrating on the negative here, but I got the impression more and more every time I saw the picture that Kubrick really did not know how to show a warm relationship between this father and his son. There's the scene in the bedroom where Jack takes Danny on his lap and tries to reassure the kid—"I'd never hurt you; I'd never hurt your mother." It's very cold and stilted, and you have the feeling that it's there because Kubrick knew that something had to be there at this point purely from a story perspective. (Underwood and Miller, *Feast* 85, 100–101)

Provoked each time he was asked by fans and interviewers to comment on Kubrick's opus, King's negative opinions hardened over the years; he became convinced that the story deserved to be filmed again, and this time more faithfully by employing the original screenplay he himself had composed. Following the previous commercial and critical triumph of *IT* and *The Stand*, ABC invited King to write the teleplay and produce *The Shining* as a three-night miniseries. Warner Brothers, the sponsoring production company, was forced to negotiate a substantial payment to Kubrick, who now owned the rights to *The Shining*, and part of the agreement was King's pledge that he would not discuss further Kubrick's film in any public forum. The filming of the second *Shining* took place between February and June 1996 at the Stanley Hotel in Estes Park, Colorado, the hotel that served as the actual inspiration for King's 1977 novel. Mick Garris, who successfully directed *The Stand*, was again King's choice to direct *The Shining*, which premiered on ABC from April 27 to May 1, 1997.

As indicated in the interview material just cited, King felt strongly about emphasizing different priorities than those found in Kubrick's adaptation. Thus, King's Jack Torrance (Steven Weber) progresses much more slowly into madness, while his relationship with the hotel and its nefarious history unfolds more erratically (and therefore is more convincing). As might be expected, the miniseries follows the novel closely—restoring, for example, the animated hedge animals that the Kubrick production was unable to bring to technological life—but since the miniseries format allotted the production more time, King's teleplay details *The Shining*'s major events much more extensively, and even includes additional material not present in the published book. As Garris viewed the crux of his efforts:

"The fact that we've chosen to go back to the book says nothing about Kubrick and what he did, other than we wanted to make the book" (Jones 110–111).

Kubrick's directorial focus is squarely on Jack Torrance, and he chose a Jack [Nicholson] as his first—and immediate—choice to play the role as soon as he finished reading King's novel. As already discussed in chapter 4, Jack not only receives more time on camera, but his mental status also centers the film. He often appears in mis-en-scènes by himself, alone at his desk typing the single line, or throwing the ball in a game of catch with the hotel wall. Whatever evil King located at the Overlook and its nefarious history is recentered by Kubrick in Jack himself, and the other characters become reactive agents, placed in situations where they are forced to respond to the tone that Torrance dictates. As King lamented in his interview with *Playboy,* "Kubrick just couldn't grasp the sheer inhuman evil of the Overlook Hotel. So he looked, instead, for evil in the characters and made the film into a domestic tragedy with only vaguely supernatural overtones" (Underwood and Miller, *Bare Bones* 29). The King teleplay, on the other hand, returns *The Shining*'s focus back to Danny Torrance (Courtland Mead), who centers the novel as well. Danny recognizes his importance after his encounter with the ghost woman in room 217: "It [the hotel] wants us, all of us. But most of all I think it wants me the most." The first half of the miniseries centers on Danny's telepathic powers, his relationship to his alter ego, Tony (Wil Horneff), and his private effort to cope with the preternatural forces at work in the hotel that appear, at least initially, to be far more interested in the child than his parents. Wendy (Rebecca De Mornay) and Jack begin the miniseries almost exclusively in the roles of supporting characters to their son, and the film shifts its concentration to the adult Torrances only when Jack's relationship with the hotel begins to displace his marriage.

While Steven Weber's portrayal of Jack Torrance is a much closer approximation to the character King envisioned in his novel than is Jack Nicholson's interpretation of the role, this does not necessarily mean that Weber provides a more memorable performance or that he triumphs as the "definitive" Jack Torrance. What is clear is that Weber followed a tour de force effort by Nicholson and therefore needed to play the character differently; after all, comparisons to Nicholson's acting would be inevitable. While it is true that Nicholson never physically harms either Wendy or Danny, in contrast to Weber's substantial and vicious use of the croquet mallet on Wendy's ribs and legs, Nicholson's range of expressive face and body language, his sense of unpredictability (in the bathroom with Grady, he moves from arrogant bravado to cringing cowardice in a single scene), and especially his ranting soliloquies offer a terrifying—as well as persuasive—depiction of insanity. As one critic of *The Shining* has argued in justifying Nicholson's over-the-top portrayal of Torrance, "The exceptional, rather than excessive vigor of [Nicholson's] performance, his overemphatic, malignly overeloquent acting, exaggerated by the Steadicam's intense accelerations as Nicholson pursues Danny through the maze, all serve to rush [Torrance] toward his own destiny; anything else would not be enough" (Walker 311).

King's strident effort to establish a systematic and virtually "rational" explanation for Torrance's mental collapse, in the end, makes the telefilm's Jack a less frightening character. The miniseries, far more than Kubrick's film, connects Torrance's character dissolution directly to his alcoholism; his marriage, his writing, and his relationship to Danny are all compromised by Jack's inability to break the cycle of his addiction. "Over half of its seven hours," as film critic Bob Haas points out, "is devoted to a dysfunctional marriage where alcohol is to blame" (Haas et al. 111). Early in the film, before we are even introduced to Wendy or Danny, the Overlook's manager, Stuart Ullman (Elliott Gould), expresses his reservations about placing "a drunk" in charge of his hotel for the winter. His misgivings are based exclusively on his belief that an alcoholic can never be rehabilitated and that the winter's isolation at the Overlook may push Jack once more "over the edge." Similarly, the viewer's introduction to Wendy features her memory of Jack breaking Danny's arm, an act caused by his drinking. The flashback ends with her threat that "this is the last time I'm going to an emergency room" and Jack's promise that he will begin attending AA meetings.

Reinforcing Wendy's early misgivings is a short but notable scene featuring Jack Torrance gazing longingly into the window of a Sidewinder bar. He is drawn to the window (the place is significantly named only *Tavern* on its sidewalk sign) by the sudden illumination of a green-and-red neon advertisement for ice-cold beer accompanied by a two-foot-high white martini glass bearing an oversized olive. Pressing his hand and face against the glass pane to peer inside, Jack's own face suddenly darkens as it is pulled out of the sunny Sidewinder afternoon and into the shadowy depths of the bar's interior lighting. This subtle sequence conveys to the viewer the nearly hypnotic pull alcohol (and even the setting for imbibing) exerts over a problem drinker. As Jack gazes inside, one of the patrons, as if on cue, turns around on his bar stool and toasts Torrance with a fresh glass of beer. On this occasion, Torrance elects not to enter into the tavern—he goes home to his family—but it is clear from the look on his face as he pulls himself away that he wishes desperately to be inside that darkened bar, and that he would be, if he were somehow released from his commitment to a family that will never understand the true nature of his addictive urge. Moreover, the illumination of the bar's neon sign immediately follows a frustrating and condescending telephone conversation that Jack has with his former drinking buddy and current benefactor, Al Shockley (Jan Van Sickle). All these events coupled with the bar patron's personalized foamy salute appear more than coincidental. These actions strike us as portentous, evidence that evokes the Overlook's ability to manipulate events, especially those associated with Jack's alcoholism. It is as if the bar itself is issuing a siren's call to Jack: Come on inside and get out of the glaring heat where your ice cream is melting. Sit down on the empty bar stool next to friendly Gus, and have a drink—in fact, have ten. In light of this tavern scene, it is especially interesting that Jack spends most of the third part of the miniseries inside the Overlook's Colorado Lounge and ballroom, carousing with alcoholic ghosts whom he comes to resemble closely (Garris offers several reflective head shots in barroom mirrors to reinforce this doubling effect) in their haggard expressions and pallid complexions.

What distressed King about Nicholson's projection of madness "right from the outset of the film" actually serves to create a certain level of confusion for the viewer that is unnerving and, therefore, ironically appropriate for illustrating the unstable nature of Torrance's psyche. Because Kubrick does not provide deep insight into Jack's relationship with the hotel, we have no idea what is happening to him until he begins to dialogue with Lloyd and Grady. And even then, as I have discussed in chapter 4, their surreal interactions are so fragmented and hallucinogenic that Kubrick is equivocal on the issue of whether these figures are "real" ghosts or projections of Jack's own haunted psyche. It is only when Jack escapes from the locked food pantry that we join Wendy in realizing that the Overlook's ghosts are palpable realities. In King's miniseries, however, the lines of demarcation are much more clearly wrought; everyone, including Wendy and Danny, understands that the hotel is responsible for enabling Jack's alcoholic recidivism. As a result, compared to Nicholson's unrestrained ferocity, Weber emerges as a less fractured and ultimately more sympathetic and comprehensible Jack Torrance.

At a press conference held shortly before the ABC telecast, Rebecca De Mornay was queried about her perspective on Wendy Torrance. "The [domestic abuse] subtext of the movie can and does happen to smart women, and not just to women who look and act like victims. I thought it was important to play her and give her the integrity and the intelligence that she deserves" ("At *The Shining*" 25). This point highlights one of the most dramatic differences that distinguish the two film interpretations of *The Shining:* The two versions of Wendy. King's teleplay and Garris's camera are extremely conscious of De Mornay's presence, in contrast to Kubrick's apparent lack of interest in his portrait of Wendy Torrance. Both films inspire audience sympathy for Wendy's character and the dire plight of her situation as a woman under siege in an abusive relationship—indeed, because of this we *want* to like her—but Kubrick erects several obstructions that end up pushing our response in the opposite direction: By the end of the film, the audience almost wants Jack to succeed in killing Wendy to get her off the screen. Shelley Duvall's lank hair, absence of makeup, disheveled appearance, and subordinate posturing complement her "endangered woman" stereotype and help to keep the viewer's interest always riveted on Nicholson. In contrast, whenever De Mornay is on the screen, she captivates our attention. She is a radiant contrast to her husband's mental and hygienic dissolution. But it is not just De Mornay's resplendent hair and other physical attributes that challenge Kubrick's interpretation of Wendy as a hapless victim; King's Wendy emerges as the clear heroine of the teleplay.

De Mornay restores much of the steely resiliency found in the female protagonist of King's novel, and this is particularly noteworthy when compared to Shelley Duvall's exaggerated portrayal of Wendy as Olive Oyl revisited: A simpering fatality of forces beyond her capacity to understand, much less surmount. Kubrick's Wendy leaves the audience impressed only with her abilities to scream and express hand-wringing distress—her terrifying encounter with Torrance's Johnny Carson parody, his murderous ax, and the splintered bathroom door that barely separates them is by far Duvall's most memorable moment in the entire film. Wendy's underdeveloped range of response undoubtedly contributed to the on-set acrimony between Duvall and Kubrick revealed so explicitly in Vivian Kubrick's documentary, *Making The Shining*. Contrastingly, as Torrance succumbs to his psychosis and the machinations of the Overlook, De Mornay's Wendy sustains her own distinctiveness from Jack and the powers at the hotel, even as she tries valiantly to aid him in his doomed struggle. When the hotel ghosts begin to address her directly, she utters a defiant "You can play with me all you want, but you're never taking my son." Her maternal bond with Danny remains resolute and should be measured against Jack Torrance's failings as his family's "caretaker." Watching nervously as Jack grows increasingly angry with Danny, blaming the child for many of the torments inflicted on him by the supernatural agency at work at the Overlook, Wendy is the only member of the Torrance family to remain calm. She continually endeavors to keep her husband lucid, taking the croquet mallet away from him before he goes in search of Danny in room 217, reminding him to "remember your temper—no matter what Danny has done." Eventually, when she recognizes that it is the hotel—and not just Jack—that is imperiling her and Danny, her response is to avoid panic and survive the situation. When Jack finally no longer responds to language or reason and begins to attack Wendy physically, she fights back. Even after he delivers a series of brutal blows from his croquet mallet, Wendy still manages to keep her wits about her and escapes him by throwing a croquet ball at his head and delivering a well-placed kick to his groin (in spite of her own severe leg injury). The viewer of both films cannot help but compare De Mornay's resiliency and self-protective assertiveness with Duvall's lame effort at defending herself on the stairs of the Overlook by jabbing at Jack with a baseball bat. It is little wonder that Nicholson's Torrance mocks her so relentlessly in this scene and refuses to view her as a serious threat.

De Mornay's portrayal reinvigorates Wendy into a formidable opponent with whom her sociopathic husband must contend, a character with multifaceted traits (e.g., she is a dedicated and talented artist) that were deliberately excluded in Kubrick's film, including a healthy sexual appetite that makes the dissolution of the relationship with her husband all the more painful to witness. In the second part of the miniseries, Wendy enters the hotel lobby resplendent in a white satin negligee. Danny is asleep in his bed, the hotel lobby is warmly lit in the glow of a romantic fire, outside the snow is melting in a temporary thaw, and Wendy appears determined to respond to the preceding scene where her son gently reprimanded her, "Sometimes Daddy doesn't think you love him." Although Wendy earnestly attempts to seduce Jack, he is clearly distracted—first by the proliferation of Danny's toys and dirty glasses and later by the boxes of Overlook memorabilia he has brought up from the basement. His obvious lack of interest in her invitation—"I've got something for you you're not going to find in any of those boxes, if you want it"—is really the first scene in the miniseries that signals Jack's psychic deterioration, his preference for the hotel in place of his wife. But rather than meekly accepting his diminished libido, as Duvall's Wendy is apparently content to do, De Mornay's Wendy demands to know what is happening to her husband. She asks, "Is stress the reason you don't want to make love to me anymore?" and concludes, "We have to leave this place. I don't know how I know that, but I do." Although Jack manages to convince his wife to stay at the Overlook, her instincts are right about the place. She chooses to remain because of her commitment to her marriage and her selfless wish to see her husband succeed as a writer. Rebecca De Mornay's characterization effectively links Wendy to the mother heroines discussed in chapter 3. The imminent threat to her child motivates her to action. And it is interesting to note how often in Stephen King's films the actions these mothers must take are against father husbands whose antipathy toward marriage turns them into monsters.

Jack is seduced by the information he is discovering about the Overlook's history: The titillating secrets lurking "between the lines" of the documents he is collating, and the hotel's registry of famous and infamous guests who appear, at least in his imagination, "as though they never checked out." All of this stimulates his dream to author "a publishable book" about the Overlook. As a writer, Jack is drawn to the stories of the rich and famous—and he yearns desperately to be part of this world; that is why he keeps assuring himself that the hotel wants him more than Danny. As he confesses to his wife, "I was meant to be here. Somehow my whole life has led up to this." Wendy, on the other hand, is interested only in what is best for her son and husband; the Overlook's nefarious history is important to her only insofar as it affects Jack. The spirits skew Jack's personal and professional priorities. In contrast, Wendy never wavers in her struggle to protect her family from the source of his delusions.

The Shining is an impressive miniseries. Until its finale, the film is one of the best made-for-television adaptations of any Stephen King novel. Indeed, the ballroom sequences that feature King himself as the band conductor of the Gage Creed Orchestra, the decadent costumes and makeup of the ghost partygoers, and the glowing iridescent bottles of alcohol perched on shelves above the bar in an art deco frieze present a dazzling visualization of the Overlook's deathless party ambiance that is highly evocative of Edgar Poe's influential tale "The Masque of the Red Death." Garris is particularly adept at using masks to generate a sensation of shamelessness and overindulgence associated with the guests at the Overlook. The perpetually masked phantom revelers—destined forever to remain in mid-party regalia, infinitely sinister at the same time that they are disturbingly enchanting—typify the atmosphere and the past of the hotel itself: hedonism without the attendant guilt. But costume masks are also employed to impart the seriousness of the actions that are occurring at the hotel, as they both disguise and reveal the essences of the hotel simultaneously. There is a complex physical language associated with the human face: Smiles, frowns, movement of the eyebrows, and twitches of the brow. While donning a mask, however, the face is reduced to a single frozen expression, be it the blankness of an elegantly made-up woman or the snarl of a wolf. Behind a mask, a person can assume the identity of someone or something else. Awakened one night as the ghosts begin to stir, Danny puts on a black cat's eye mask that Wendy discovers in the elevator so that he may "become someone else" to avoid the emotional distress of witnessing his parents arguing. A full head mask in the shape of a growling wolf that belongs to a party guest who at one point threatens to eat Danny is a constant presence in the hotel's barroom, perched atop its swinging entrance doors, as if guarding the lounge from Wendy's intrusion and then, later, hiding a bottle of whiskey from her view. The wolf's head is a mirror of sorts in which the audience can see Jack's identity paralleling the Overlook's, and perhaps this is why this particular mask is omnipresent in the last part of the miniseries. In addition to reflecting its wearer's nature—Wendy is repulsed each time she sees it or must touch it—this costumed head also reflects Torrance's own destiny. The wolf's head, frequently viewed without a ghost owner inside, is the face of a beast—snarling and feral—an invitation to Jack to pick up the mask and wear it, to assume the role of the beast that lurks within himself. At the same time, the mask is also a metaphor for the Overlook itself, the bestial spirit that resides just underneath the hotel's surface glamour and urbanity.

The conclusion of the teleplay, however, is not as consistent as the material that leads up to it. In the interview that begins this book, King acknowledges that he is "a sentimentalist at heart." This inclination curses the ending of *The Shining*. Faced with actually killing his son at the end of a hotel corridor, Jack abruptly rediscovers the paternal love he has allowed to erode. However, instead of simply permitting Danny to get away as Jack struggles against the force that is imposing itself over his mind, the scene turns into an emotionally contrived father-son reunion. The effort to allow Danny to escape is plausible, but coupling it with a restatement of the mawkish line "Kissin,' kissin,' that's what I been missin'" at this point in the film—uttered by a bloodied and psychotic man who just minutes before attempted to murder both Danny's mother and Hallorann (Melvin Van Peebles)—completely dilutes both the terror inherent in their confrontation and the audience's response to it.

The miniseries carefully traces the dissolution of Jack's familial and personal bonds as he gives himself over to the vampiric energies of the hotel. He devolves to the point where he exhibits absolutely no remorse during his assaults on either Wendy or Hallorann. Jack refrains from bringing his croquet mallet down in a final blow on Wendy's head only because the hotel's ghost owner, Horace Derwent (John Durbin), insists that

Danny's death is more immediately important. Thus, the production's credibility is strained once again when Torrance decides shortly thereafter to disobey the orders of "The Management" to dump the pressure on the hotel's boiler, and thereby enables his family and Hallorann to escape. The film's level of sentimentality reaches its own dangerous pressure point in *The Shining*'s penultimate scene when a nattily attired spectral vision of Jack appears on stage to blow Danny a kiss at his high school graduation and to repeat the "Kissin,' kissin,' that's what I been missin'" endearment a final time. These are regrettable indulgences in a production that other-wise redresses many of the major liabilities King has long lamented in Kubrick's adaptation. On the other hand, no film directed by Stanley Kubrick—and particularly *The Shining*—has ever been susceptible to the charge of maudlin excess.

STORM OF THE CENTURY (1999)

Unlike the other miniseries discussed so far in this chapter, *Storm of the Century* was originally conceived and written by King as a teleplay script, rather than adapted from a previously published novel. King worked on the narrative from December 1996 to February 1997, producing an epic critique of small-town life that closely resembles his portraits of Derry and Castle Rock found in earlier works of fiction and film. Eventually, his teleplay for *Storm* included sixty-five speaking roles and required a budget of $35 million, making it ABC's most expensive miniseries to that date. As King explained, " I like the length of television, the fact that you can expand a bit. I like the idea of a lot of characters and a lot of story" (Jones 122). Although King's initial choice to direct *Storm* was Mick Garris, he was unavailable to do the production and Craig R. Baxley received the assignment.

Filmed at a remote Maine locale, the fictitious Little Tall Island, which is also the secluded setting for *Dolores Claiborne, Storm* tells a simple tale set in 1989. Cut off from the rest of the world as a result of a violent snow-storm, the besieged inhabitants of this small community encounter an-other problem. A mysterious visitor, Andre Linoge (Colm Feore), has appeared with the first snowflakes to walk among them. He possesses ter-rible supernatural powers that enable him to reveal the darkest secrets of individual members of the town. Further, he also can make these citizens perform acts of violence to themselves and to their neighbors. Linoge's ar-rival at the onset of a massive snowstorm—"a winter's worth of snow in one storm"—links him directly to nature's fury and its indifference to man, although King's teleplay never answers the question of whether Linoge is responsible for the storm, or the storm is responsible for Linoge. In either case, as the storm picks up in its intensity, the sinful revelations of the town pile up like snowdrifts and Linoge's evil grows proportionately. Like Randall Flagg in *The Stand,* he is a force of mayhem and violence that walks among men, fomenting chaos and seeking to exploit the particular circumstances of social breakdown that coincide with human disasters. Like Leland Gaunt, the evil figure of supernatural manipulation in *Needful Things* (1994), Linoge possesses secret knowledge into the affairs of the Little Tall Island populace: "By and large," Linoge insists, "good is only an illusion, little fables folks tell themselves so they can get through their days without screaming." Individuals in each of these King communities are drawn to, and influenced by, the generated evil from which the plague of death emanates and spreads. In both Castle Rock and Little Tall Island, there exists some locus of decay that preys on the group will and social matrix of rural Maine life. As in one of King's favorite films, George Romero's *Night of the Living Dead* (1968), the afflicted townspeople—the drug traffickers, the sexually perverse, the amoral, the men and women most prone to violence, as well as those who appear to be the most chaste and decent citizens—become the walking dead who sacrifice their reason, vision, and morality. Both *Needful Things* and *Storm* have at their focus a demonic evil that descends on a small Maine town and reveals the respective town's vulnerability and penchant for violent self-destruction. As Burton Hatlen has suggested, "How many writers before King have so clearly delineated the hard, self-destructive streak that we find in so many Maine people? Edwin Arlington Robinson maybe—but I can't think of anyone else" ("Beyond the Kittery" 57).

Like the snowstorm itself that builds steadily over several days, the three-day miniseries, telecast on ABC over February 14, 15, and 18, 1999, eventually climaxes in the third part when Linoge reveals exactly what he wants before he will go away: "I want someone to raise and teach. Someone to carry on my work when I can no longer do it myself. I want a child." His pursuit of the town's children is a disturbing reminder of how vulnerable even a close-knit community remains to a man who preys on its weakest members. But instead of merely kidnapping a child, an action that would be heinous enough, Linoge demands that the town itself must select which child he should take. In return, Linoge will go away and spare the rest of the community. Selected by lottery, Ralph Anderson (Dyllan Christopher) becomes the chosen sacrifice. Even his mother, Molly (Debrah Farentino), accepts the group decision, and then represses the event, convincing herself over the years that "Ralph wandered away during the storm." Only Ralph's father, Mike Anderson (Timothy Daly), refuses to go along with the group's single-minded capitulation and refuses to forgive or to forget the betrayal of his friends and neighbors, thereby making him one of the few morally courageous father figures in King's films.

The situation poses a complicated set of ethical questions. On one hand, its citizenry selects a utilitarian course of action that benefits the greater good of the island: One child's sacrifice saves the remaining population in the town, including all the other children. As many of the islanders argue in the town hall discussion, and even Mike's wife concurs, "What choice do we have?" *Storm* is one of the most grim, Hawthorne-like moral fables that Stephen King has written. The decision to give Ralph to Linoge reflects an unspoken bond of corruption between Little Tall Island and its mysterious stranger, who is the dark alter ego of the town itself. The supernatural and horrific presence of Linoge is merely an extension of the town's general propensity for malevolence. Indeed, this is why Linoge expends so much time and energy exposing the various failings of the town's inhabitants: to make the entire community aware that its acts of evil are nothing new or particularly noteworthy and that therefore the sacrifice of single boy is merely just another in a long line of moral capitulations. In *Storm,* Dolores Claiborne's name is briefly invoked, and in many ways the same societal group-think that persecutes her in that film— from the teenagers who harass Dolores and Selena in their home to the police who pursue Dolores as Vera's murderer—is at work in Little Tall Island's inability to recognize the insidious nature of Linoge's demand. The island's decision to doom a child in place of taking the more difficult and potentially lethal stand against Linoge's manipulation is an indication both of its inability to rise above the personal limitations that Linoge continually exhorts and their collective unwillingness to undertake difficult moral choices.

The town employs a series of justifications to appease its guilt over sacrificing Ralph, and most of the inhabitants, including those parents whose children have been spared, soon go on with their lives as if they have done nothing wrong. Mike Anderson, however, sees beyond the island's collective effort to avoid culpability. He has learned that his fellow citizens are unable to think beyond their own personal safety or to entertain complicated ethical issues, and that when faced with a difficult challenge, his neighbors—like most of us—will opt for the expedient solution. In the interview that begins this book, King indirectly refers to Little Tall Island in his observation that all humans "are faced with situations in which we are tested. Generally it isn't until years later that we find out that we actually failed the test. We come to understand that our morals gave out a little here, or our sense of right and wrong slipped, or our misplaced sense of expediency got the better of our morality." The town's easy surrender to evil and efficiency, coupled with his own inability to cooperate with the community's dominant single voice, alienates Anderson from everyone, including his wife and his best friend, Hatch (Casey Siemaszko). Mike represents moral man in the face of overwhelming evil—a modern Abraham who is, however, unwilling to sacrifice his son even to appease a power greater than himself.

In Stephen King's best work, a bridge exists between the immediate and familiar landscape of contemporary America and the predominant concerns found in the tradition of nineteenth-century American literature. King's descriptions of his native Maine and the close scrutiny of character, tradition, and the clash between civilized values and the wilderness of nature find some of their closest points of comparison in the narratives of Nathaniel Hawthorne. King closely approximates Hawthorne's bifurcated vision of the regional merging into the transcendent, and the two writers also share a similar interest in posing individual characters in complicated moral predicaments. In Hawthorne's tales, it is always imperative that the main protagonist comes to recognize his bond with a universal evil—and thereby reconnects to "the magnetic chain of humanity"—by embracing the iniquity that exists within himself and those around him. Young Goodman Brown's "dying hour was gloom" because his innocence could not be reconciled with the fallen natures of the men and women he formerly idealized. In *Storm,* Mike Anderson is faced with a prototypical Hawthornian conundrum. Linoge may single out Anderson because he appears to be the only person on the entire island who has neither been corrupted by personal sin nor grown cynical in witnessing the sins of others. His innate goodness insulates him from Linoge's portrait of universal depravity. In the spirit of Hawthorne's most zealous idealists, Anderson clings stubbornly to a romantic faith in humanity, repudiating Linoge's negative assessments because "You see only the bad, none of the good."

While Mike has assiduously avoided passing personal judgment on the various foibles of his friends and fellow citizens highlighted periodically in Linoge's comprehensive survey of island sin, the events that unfold during the storm, because they involve him so intimately, finally force him to confront the universal depravity of human nature. As first his neighbors, whom he has so staunchly defended, and then his best friend and finally his wife desert him, Mike, like Hawthorne's Goodman Brown, wills himself into a pariah. Once Little Tall Island's central citizen—its constable, easy-credit grocer, voice of calm and rational reassurance, good Samaritan, and civic conscience—he moves to its periphery, unable to look his neighbors in the eye, unwilling to sleep in the same bed as his wife. Eventually, he uproots himself to the other side of the continent—to San Francisco—where he, like Andy Dufresne in *Shawshank,* begins a new life alone, in a new profession, in a new community next to an ocean devoid of "the same memories."

While his precipitous fall from grace finds parallels throughout Hawthorne's canon, Mike's inability to accept and to forgive the evil that he has experienced would produce disastrous consequences if he were one of Hawthorne's protagonists, isolating him as it does from human society and its community of sin. But in this instance at least, King breaks with his fellow New England allegorist in applauding Anderson's choice to separate himself from the corruption of Little Tall Island. Ironically, Anderson's moral idealism evokes the rebellious spirit of Henry Thoreau's "enlightened minority of one" rather than Hawthorne's maxim of sin's universal patrimony. Against the moral cowardice of the town itself, King views Anderson as a representative of the life force in his stubborn refusal to capitulate to evil's momentum. In this way, Anderson resembles King's other working-class heroes, although he is unable to save either the town or his son. The narrative belongs to Anderson; his weathered voice-over begins and ends the story. Moreover, he is the only (former) islander capable of revealing the town's darkest moment in its unrecorded history without the need to distort or to lie. In *Storm,* King insists that at the same time that the small-town Maine environment is sometimes capable of producing heroic individuals, most often it destroys others because of its pressure to conform and equivocal ethical standards.

All through King's cinematic universe, only individuals who separate from the single-minded corruption of the larger community attain possession of viable moral lives. Anderson may once have served as the fulcrum of Little Tall Island, but he cannot convince his friends and neighbors to act responsibly—"We don't give our kids away to thugs. How will we be able to live with ourselves?"—either when they are on the verge of storm hysteria while shopping in his store, or when they are faced with the choice of responding to Linoge's ultimatum. In the chapter 1 interview, King is right to link Mike Anderson to the Old Testament Job, but he resembles Lot as much as he does Job, for Anderson leaves a sinful place with his virtue intact. The town elects to doom a single child rather than to risk the mass destruction of its population. As in Shirley Jackson's "The Lottery," the tale that inspired the ancient stone lottery that helps to decide the fate of the town and its children, the men and women of the island sacrifice their collective soul in first appeasing Linoge and then hiding from all accountability for what they have done. As I note elsewhere in this book, it is only because of the maintenance of secrets in Stephen King's world that corruption sustains both its negative energies and the capacity for drawing others into its ethical morass. With the somber voice of a world-weary expatriate, Anderson posits that the inhabitants of Little Tall Island "can keep a secret when they have to. And the people who live there keep them still."*Storm of the Century* did not perform well in the Nielsen ratings. There are many possible explanations for this. Perhaps any miniseries broadcast in February that involved a three-day blizzard doomed itself demographically for at least half the nation. Perhaps the teleplay's bloated midsection—featuring a repetitive series of violent acts orchestrated by Linoge from his jail cell—needed more streamlining to sustain a television audience's restive attention. Perhaps the audience also could not summon sufficient patience when asked to wait for three nights before finally learning exactly what Linoge wanted before he would go away. Or maybe King's own analysis of network competition was the most trenchant interpretation of all: "I don't actually love starting against *The X Files* and finishing against *E.R.*" (Jones 123). Whatever reasons for America's failure to embrace *Storm,* it is important to note that evil prevails in this miniseries, and its conclusion is atypical both to King's oeuvre and to the American faith in our collective ability to resist and vanquish iniquity. From the Puritans and their obsession with sin, to our bloody campaign against the Nazis, to the current war on terrorism, Americans have always prided themselves on their capacity for resisting wickedness and pursuing its ultimate defeat. Stephen King suggests, at least in this miniseries, that evil is not so easily contained and that sometimes what we endeavor to destroy or to avoid we ultimately become. The unpredictable ending to *Storm* is as pessimistic a vision as any found in the films of Stephen King and therefore comes as a definite surprise. Perhaps not incidentally, the last hour of this miniseries is exceptional television drama, as good as anything the medium has ever broadcast. To have missed it in favor of an episode of *E.R.* may not only reflect America's general lack of patience, but also its reluctance to abide the triumph of evil.

ROSE RED (2002)

This telefilm was originally conceived as collaboration between King and director Steven Spielberg in the mid-1990s. The two men have long desired to work together on a movie project. Spielberg wanted to direct the "ultimate haunted house film" and asked King to write its script, but King's multiple revisions never meshed with Spielberg's artistic goals. According to King, "Steven [Spielberg] wanted a bigger, more positive kind of feeling than I wanted to go for. He wanted that whoosh thing and I wanted to scare the shit out of people. We finally got to a point where it just seemed like the best thing for me was to step away" (Jones 131). After several years elapsed, King returned to the concept with the intention of making it into a television miniseries. The teleplay became his primary writing project while convalescing from the serious automobile accident that hospitalized him for a month in 1999. ABC premiered the miniseries on the nights of January 27, 28, and 29, 2002.

Five men and eighteen women have disappeared in a rambling mansion named Rose Red. As these statistics indicate, the house appears to have a certain affinity for women. Besides being linked to the feminine in its name and throughout its well-apportioned interior decor, the house was originally constructed in 1909 as wedding gift to Ellen Rimbauer (Julia Campbell), whose ghost is the primary resident that the main characters in this miniseries hope to contact. In spite of his efforts to impress her with the mansion, Ellen's husband, an affluent banker and railroad executive, engendered his wife's antipathy because of his many illicit sexual liaisons. He infected her with a venereal disease that probably caused a birth defect in their daughter's left arm. The anger Ellen feels toward her wayward spouse appears to feed into Rose Red, which, in spite of its appetite for both genders, is far more violently disposed toward men than women (correspondingly, the ghosts who haunt the house are all female spirits). As Professor Joyce Reardon (Nancy Travis), a researcher in the field of parapsychology and the leader of an expedition of six psychics to probe the mysteries of the mansion, concludes, "In Rose Red's heyday, men didn't fare well." Ellen Rimbauer worked diligently at expanding the size of Rose Red, believing that as long as the house continued to grow she would never die. It is impossible to ascertain exactly how many rooms the structure contains because the number changes each time someone tries to count. After 1950, however, Rose Red, like a supernatural cancer, "began to grow on its own." But for the past thirty years, the house has become a "dormant cell." Reardon speculates that "with no psychic energy for the house to feed on, Rose Red seems to have fallen into sleep." Over a long Memorial Day weekend, Reardon and her hand-picked team of psychics visit Rose Red to discover some quantifiable evidence that the house still contains paranormal energies so that the professor's repu-

tation as a serious scientist (her academic tenure having been recently re-
voked) "will be secure for the rest of [her] life. Together, we can help to
legitimize a branch of psychology that has been treated as a poor relation
for too long."

Reardon emerges as a cunning and manipulating academic. She
sleeps with the last living relative of Rose Red in order to gain access to
the mansion before he intends to demolish it. She reminds him continually
not to undermine her authority on the history of the house, even though
he is the last living Rimbauer, and her interest in the house borders on
being pathologically obsessive. After witnessing sufficient evidence of
Rose Red's malign intentions, Reardon greets the reasonable suggestion
to vacate the premises as "cowardly" and perpetually finds excuses to justify "ignoring the probability of [the group's] demise." Unwilling to abandon her "scientific research" and her dream that the story of the Rimbauer
house will make her wealthy when she publishes a book about it, Reardon
is selfishly unaffected by the murders and disappearances of two members
of the psychic team. When one of the female psychics disappears mysteri-
ously during the first night of the group's visit to Rose Red, no one bothers
to look for her or mentions her name again for the remainder of the miniseries. As the house continues to feed off its new inhabitants, the professor
feeds her own distorted obsession with "checking the equipment" and encouraging the spirits of Rose Red to vent their wrath. Without even academic tenure to protect her any longer, at the end of the miniseries she
gets exactly what she not-so-secretly wishes when the ghosts of the house
claim her as one of their own. Reardon is the first to recognize that the
youngest member of her psychic team, Annie Wheaton (Kimberly
Brown), is the "key to awakening the spirits" that reside in the mansion.
Annie is a near-catatonic child with supernatural powers: the precognitive
abilities of Danny Torrance and the telekinesis of Carrie White. Annie's
weird innocence strangely complements Reardon's equally weird professional acumen. Together, these two females reawaken the coven of women
spirits who haunt Rose Red, but this turns out to be the only bond these
women share in the course of the drama.

On several occasions the cinematography allows us an aerial view of
the mansion. The farthest extension of the house nearly touches a multi-
lane expressway leading to and from downtown Seattle. Similarly, the
front door of Rose Red is located only several yards from the city's urban
heart, separated from a busy street by only a large iron gate. These juxtapositions are important to note, if for no other reason than for the contrast
Rose Red makes to the haunted house tradition. This is not a place that is

entirely typical to the genre, as Rose Red is neither located in the dank mists of a British moor nor perched atop a desolate hill or cliff. The mansion literally sits in the middle of the modern world; it brings together the turn-of-the-century rural American past with the urban pulse of contemporary life. The two worlds nonetheless do not interface very well. Rose Red's marble statuary, ivy and vine-covered façade, ornate wooden interior, and plethora of chimneys for multiple fireplaces are poised in sharp contrast to modern Seattle's huge concrete highways, speeding traffic, and cell-phone technology that intrude on the perimeters of the estate and its guarded history. In this miniseries, unlike many other haunted house stories, past and present do not merge, and the ghosts do not share much in common with the humans they haunt.

The primary difficulty with *Rose Red,* aside from its oppressive overreliance on special effects, is that the miniseries spends an excessive amount of time dramatizing the shocking and horrific displays of the house's reanimation and not nearly enough effort examining why any of these displays are relevant to a larger purpose. Following a very promising opening installment, in which the history of the house is explored and the viewer is introduced to motley cast of psychic mercenaries, the second and third parts degenerate into a horrorscape of zombie dream girls, ghostly garden statuary, and panic-stricken mortals fleeing spectral horrors. The effect is to take the viewer into an elaborate carnival hall of mirrors in which no object is ever sentient or stable. Rose Red's corridors and rooms suddenly change configuration and flip their interiors upside-down, the library's mirrored floor turns liquid, and a statue of Ellen Rimbauer in the garden removes her marble face from the rest of her skull. Like Robert Wise's black-and-white classic, *The Haunting* (1963), much of the terror ride in *Rose Red* is to be found in the architecture itself—specifically, the surreal geometry of bizarre angles, vertigo elongations, undulating floors. Running from room to room, floor to floor, by the third installment Reardon and her hyperventilating crew are no longer trapped in a haunted house, but rather in "a house that has gone insane." While the film's superannuated Halloween tricks are often visually and technically stunning, they also tend to weaken the seriousness of *Rose Red*'s storyline and dominate it at the expense of character development. The reasons behind Ellen Rimbauer's efforts to "design a house to break hearts, as hers was broken" apparently revolve around her husband's frequent sexual betrayals, but his libidinous forays, especially in light of his wife's choice to murder him by tossing him through the stained glass tower window, seem somehow a woefully insufficient cause for the grotesquely elaborate feminine fury that continues over the years unabated. A film about an explicitly feminist supernaturalism is a compelling concept, especially in the hands of the writer who gave us *Gerald's Game, Dolores Claiborne,* and *Rose Madder* (yet another *Rose* responding to a nightmare marriage). But for this to work in *Rose Red,* the haunted Rimbauer marriage would need to have been more centrally featured—essentially displacing the house and its infernal biology as the subject matter of the narrative text—much as the ghosts at the Overlook remain a secondary focus to Jack Torrance and his family in *The Shining.* The feminine bond that potentially exists among the resident vampires of Rose Red, Joyce Reardon, and the female psychics she brings into the house requires development that the miniseries does not provide.

Last, because of overreliance on phantasmagoria, there are few characters in the miniseries that we care about—and certainly no one to inspire the heroic imagination, as does Wendy Torrance in the miniseries version of *The Shining* or Mike Anderson in *Storm.* For example, the viewer is never certain about Professor Reardon's enigmatic motivations. Is the central character's disturbing quest merely for professional gain, or is it an unconscious death wish to join the spirits she so desperately yearns to contact? In either case, she appears to have much in common with house's vampires prior to becoming one. As obsessed with obtaining spectral evidence as Ellen Rimbauer is with avenging her brokenhearted misery, the professor is willing to sacrifice anyone and anything to gain these data. In the end, she is so distracted by her need to record the existence of paranormal activity that she misses many opportunities to witness dramatic evidence of what she seeks. While the ghosts of Rose Red relentlessly torment the psychics she has delivered, Reardon wanders around empty rooms with a video camera and microphone or plays with Annie and the dollhouse replica of Rose Red, anxiously awaiting the spirits that are actively engaged elsewhere in the mansion. Thus, while the film's camerawork is unnervingly beautiful and the house itself an imposing structure of decadent dread, *Rose Red* finally shares the same flaw that King himself found in Kubrick's direction of *The Shining:* It is a picture that "has no heart, no center" (Underwood and Miller, *Feast* 85). When King wrote *The Shining,* he "discovered about halfway through that I wasn't writing a haunted-house story, that I was writing about a family coming apart. It was like a revelation" (Underwood and Miller, *Bare Bones* 105). The main problem with *Rose Red* is that there is no similar "revelation"; in the absence of a family with which viewers identify or care about, the "haunted-house story" is all that there is to this miniseries, and it's just not enough.

So, where are we left by way of an overall critical assessment of the Stephen King miniseries? In comparison to other made-for-television films written by other authors and dealing with topics as mundane as the disease of the month, the struggle and triumph of single parenthood, or another recalcitrant father's teary reconciliation with his prodigal child, King's television productions represent a refreshing, if macabre, change of pace in network programming. In the more than three decades in which the genre of the miniseries has impacted American television, very few have been either sweeping or lasting. Generally, they are productions that may begin with good intentions, but quickly descend into noncontroversial and predictable exploitations of mawkish story lines. I think most Americans would be hard-pressed to name five miniseries titles not associated with Stephen King's name.

Perhaps it is the length and scope of the typical broadcast miniseries, or the priorities of television itself, or a combination of both, but the emphasis in most miniseries—and King's are no exception—is almost exclusively on plot. Simply encompassing the story line of a book the size of *The Stand* or *IT* is no doubt an exhaustive enterprise, leaving very little space and time for imaginative digressions. In his excursions into fantastic realms, King's teleplays radically transform the landscape of the familiar (*The Stand* and *Storm*) while also bringing us to supernatural places where the surreal is made manifest (*The Shining* and *Rose Red*). To transport the viewer into a universe that never was and is not likely ever to be, the narrative itself must be of paramount concern. Moreover, the eternally restive nature of the television audience must always be taken into account; the entertainment and emotive value of the subject itself must supercede all other aesthetic and artistic considerations.

Still, we are left with the abiding question: How do King's broadcast narratives compare with Hollywood's feature-length films made from his work? In this writer's judgment, the made-for-television movies are approximate in quality to most of Hollywood's adaptations—functioning on the level of, say, *Hearts in Atlantis* or *Christine;* that is, they engage us as popular entertainment, but do not necessarily qualify as art of a very high order. And furthermore, these telefilms all fall considerably short of the more memorable and sustained excellence of theatrical feature work such as *Shawshank Redemption, The Dead Zone,* and Kubrick's *The Shining,* which distinguish themselves as highly accomplished examples of cinematic art.

The Shining may here serve as an illustrative case in point, as it is currently the only interpretation of a King novel that has been produced as both a televised miniseries and a major theatrical release. In the end, Kubrick's variation offers us a more complex rendition of the world, even as Wendy in the ABC teleplay triumphs over Kubrick's misuse of her character. Kubrick's cinematic interpretation is an evocative reminder that film can be a highly textured art form that rewards multiple viewings, as is evident from the diverse and prolific critical bibliography that the movie has generated over the past twenty years. Kubrick was preoccupied, in the opinion of Alexander Walker, "with finding 'the moment' in every scene—the revelatory detail, be it a gesture, a look, the way a word was said, even an inanimate object, that electrified the effect of the playing" (Walker et al. 22). In contrast, the Shining miniseries simply does not inspire or reward in a similar manner; it is not a film that stresses, as does Kubrick's, the complexity of forces that affect the actions of an individual and those around him. Garris's frequent efforts to employ mirrored reflections of the spirits in the Colorado Lounge and ballroom, for example, only remind us of how much more successful Kubrick was in applying his own various mirrored spectral images to create an atmosphere of symbolic layering and ambiguity. Similarly, while Garris possessed the computer expertise necessary to animate King's hedge animals—expertise that was unavailable to Kubrick in 1980—they do not add a great deal to the teleplay, even by way of heightening an ambiance of terror. And certainly their usage pales when compared to Kubrick's substitution of the hedge maze, a device that suggests the tortured confinement of Jack Torrance's psyche as well as posing a microcosmic parallel to the labyrinths of corridors and dark recesses of the hotel's interior design. Once more the emphasis in The Shining miniseries is on plot enhancement—the hedge animals exist primarily to chase after Danny and Jack and explode into fire as the interior of the hotel is destroyed. Kubrick's maze, on the other hand, is never so easily dissected—its symbolic value, its quality as an idea, increases as we come to appreciate that the maze is really an organic metaphor for the entire movie.

In the "The Making of *Rose Red*" section of the DVD edition, Stephen King says this: "ABC has been very good for me, and I have been good for ABC." This is a more complex statement than it first appears. It addresses television's bottom line as a corporate business, but likewise its potential as a medium for producing valuable programming. Television, King goes on to note in this same interview, has allowed him the opportunity to indulge his own stylistic tendency toward "expansive" writing: "I'm more of a 'putter in' than a 'taker-out.' And for that reason the miniseries format is perfect. It gives me a chance to tell novels in a different medium, and to reach a different audience." I take this to mean, as this chapter has already noted, that the miniseries format has made available King projects that, because of their thematic scope, would never have been produced as conventional Hollywood theatrical releases. Without the made-for-television genre, seminal works from King's canon such as *IT, The Stand,* and *Storm of the Century* would probably not have appeared in celluloid—and that would have been a loss to both King's fans and to fans of quality television. The miniseries genre has become for King the equivalent of a small-screen version of the episodic thriller or cliffhanger story that was popular in the 1950s and occupies such an important metatextual position in *Misery.* King's narrative and filmic texts are often set in this era (when he himself was an adolescent attending the movies), and his fascination with the serial format for telling stories is evident in *The Green Mile,* which was originally published in several installments, and *The Dark Tower* books, which have appeared periodically over the years. The televised miniseries, stretching over a three-night period, ideally imitates the same type of deliberate narrative buildup and anticipation in the audience that is a distinguishing feature of the cliffhanger tale.

On the other hand, perhaps the most trenchant criticism repeated over the years by reviewers and critics writing about King's novels is that they are too self-indulgent—indeed, too expansive. No less a luminary in the fields of fantasy and horror art than Harlan Ellison (who also authored the twenty-minute teleplay for the King story *Gramma,* which premiered on CBS in 1986) has concluded that Stephen King is "one of the most accomplished storytellers the twentieth century has produced." This accolade notwithstanding, Ellison goes on to recognize that all of "King's novels with the possible exception of maybe *IT* or the *Dark Tower* books could have been told just as well as a novella. This is to me the main flaw in Stephen's work" (qtd. in Beahm 147). I think this insightful evaluation holds true for most of the movies that have been adapted from Stephen King's fiction as well. Notwithstanding King's own self-evaluations that his work requires more space rather than less, arguably the best films that Hollywood has produced, for either the small screen or the large, have tended, ironically, to emerge from the shortest and most concise of his fictional texts: *Rita Hayworth and the Shawshank Redemption, The Body, Misery, Apt Pupil, Dolores Claiborne,* and *Carrie.*

FILMS CITED

Alien. Dir. Ridley Scott. Screenplay by Dan O'Bannon and Ronald Shusett. Perf. Sigourney Weaver. Twentieth Century Fox and Brandywine Productions, 1979.

American Graffiti. Dir. George Lucas. Screenplay by George Lucas and Gloria Katz. Perf. Richard Dreyfuss, Ron Howard, Suzanne Somers. LucasFilm, The Coppola Company, Universal Pictures, 1973.

Animal House. Dir. John Landis. Screenplay by Harold Ramis and Douglas Kenney. Perf. John Belushi and Tom Hulce. Universal Pictures, 1978.

Artificial Intelligence [A. I.]. Dir. Steven Spielberg. Screenplay by Ian Watson. Perf. Jude Law and William Hurt. Amblin Entertainment, Dream Works, Stanley Kubrick Productions, Warner Brothers, 2001.

Apt Pupil. Dir. Bryan Singer. Screenplay by Brandon Boyce. Perf. Ian McKellen and Brad Renfro. Phoenix Pictures, Canal+DA, Bad Hat Harry, TriStar, 1997.

Blade Runner. Dir. Ridley Scott. Screenplay by Hampton Fancher and David Peoples. Perf. Harrison Ford, Rutger Hauer, Sean Young. Blade Runner Partnership and The Ladd Company, 1982.

Carrie. Dir. Brian De Palma. Screenplay by Lawrence D. Cohen. Perf. Sissy Spacek, Piper Laurie, Amy Irving. United Artists Corporation, 1976.

Children of the Corn. Dir. Fritz Kiersch. Screenplay by George Goldsmith. Perf. Peter Horton and Linda Hamilton. Angeles Cinema Group, Gatlin, Inverness, Roach, 1984.

Christine. Dir. John Carpenter. Screenplay by Bill Phillips. Perf. Keith Gordon, John Stockwell, Alexandra Paul. Columbia Pictures, Polar Film, Columbia-Delphi Productions, 1983.

A Clockwork Orange. Dir. Stanley Kubrick. Screenplay by Stanley Kubrick. Perf. Malcolm McDowell. Hawk Films, Polaris Productions, Warner Brothers, 1971.

Crash. Dir. David Cronenberg. Screenplay by David Cronenberg. Perf. James Spader and Holly Hunter. Alliance Communications Corporation, Recorded Picture Company, The Movie Network, Telefilm Canada, 1996.

Creepshow. Dir. George A. Romero. Screenplay by Stephen King. Perf. Hal Holbrook, Ted Danson, Ed Harris, Leslie Nielsen, E. G. Marshall. Laurel Show, United Film Distribution Company, Warner Brothers, 1982.

Cujo. Dir. Lewis Teague. Screenplay by Don Carlos Dunaway and Lauren Currier. Perf. Dee Wallace, Christopher Stone, Daniel Hugh-Kelly. Sunn Classics Pictures, The Taft Entertainment Company, Warner Brothers, Republic Pictures, 1983.

The Dark Half. Dir. George A. Romero. Screenplay by George A. Romero. Perf. Timothy Hutton, Amy Madigan, Michael Rooker. Orion Pictures Corporation, 1992.

Dawn of the Dead. Dir. George A. Romero. Screenplay by Dario Argento and George A. Romero. Perf. David Emge, Ken Foree, Gaylen Ross. Laurel Group, 1978.

Dead Ringers. Dir. David Cronenberg. Screenplay by David Cronenberg and Norman Snider. Perf. Jeremy Irons. Mantle Clinic II, Morgan Creek Productions, Telefilm Canada, 1988.

The Dead Zone. Dir. David Cronenberg. Screenplay by Jeffrey Boam. Perf. Christopher Walken, Brooke Adams, Martin Sheen. Dino De Laurentiis Corporation, Paramount Pictures, 1983.

Dolores Claiborne. Dir. Taylor Hackford. Screenplay by Tony Gilroy. Perf. Kathy Bates, Jennifer Jason Leigh, Christopher Plummer. Castle Rock Entertainment, Columbia Pictures, 1995.

Dracula. Dir. Tod Browning. Screenplay by Garrett Fort, Louis Bromfield, Tod Browning. Perf. Bela Lugosi. Universal Studios, 1931.

Dreamcatcher. Dir. Lawrence Kasden. Screenplay by William Goldman. Perf. Morgan Freeman and Jason Lee. Castle Rock Entertainment, NPV Entertainment, SSDD Films, Village Roadshow Productions, 2003.

Dr. Strangelove, or How I Learned to Stop Worrying and Love the Bomb. Dir. Stanley Kubrick. Screenplay by Stanley Kubrick, Terry Southern, Peter George. Perf. Peter Sellers and George C. Scott. Hawk Films, 1964.

The English Patient. Dir. Anthony Minghella. Screenplay by Anthony Minghella. Perf. Willem Defoe, Kristen Scott Thomas, Ralph Fiennes. Miramax Films, 1996.

Eyes Wide Shut. Dir. Stanley Kubrick. Screenplay by Stanley Kubrick and Frederic Raphael. Perf. Tom Cruise and Nicole Kidman. Hobby Films, Pole Star, Warner Brothers, 1999.

The Exorcist. Dir. William Freidkin. Screenplay by William Peter Blatty. Perf. Ellen Burstyn, Linda Blair, Jason Miller. Hoya Productions and Warner Brothers, 1973.

The Exorcist II: The Heretic. Dir. John Boorman. Screenplay by William Goodhart. Perf. Linda Blair and Max von Sydow. Warner Brothers, 1977.

Fast Times at Ridgemont High. Dir. Amy Heckerling. Screenplay by Cameron Crowe. Perf. Sean Penn and Jennifer Jason Leigh. Refugee Films and Universal Pictures, 1982.

Firestarter. Dir. Mark L. Lester. Screenplay by Stanley Mann. Perf. Drew Barrymore, Martin Sheen, George C. Scott. Universal City Studios, Dino De Laurentiis, 1984.

Firestarter 2: Rekindled. Dir. Robert Iscove. Teleplay by Philip Eisner. Perf. Marguerite Moreau and Malcolm McDowell. USA Films, Traveler's Rest Films, USA Cable Network, 2002.

The Fly. Dir. David Cronenberg. Screenplay by David Cronenberg, George Langelann, Charles Edward Pogue. Perf. Jeff Goldblum and Geena Davis. Brooksfilms, 1986.

Friday the 13th. Dir. Sean S. Cunningham. Screenplay by Victor Miller. Perf. Ari Lehman. Georgetown Productions Pictures, Sean S. Cunningham Films, 1980.

Full Metal Jacket. Dir. Stanley Kubrick. Screenplay by Gustav Hasford and Michael Herr. Perf. Matthew Modine. Natant and Warner Brothers, 1987.

The Godfather II. Dir. Frances Ford Coppola. Screenplay by Frances Ford Coppola. Perf. Al Pacino, Diane Keaton, Robert De Niro. Paramount Pictures and The Coppola Company, 1974.

Gramma [*The Twilight Zone*]. Dir. Bradford May and Harlan Ellison. Teleplay by Harlan Ellison. Perf. Barret Oliver and Frederick Long. CBS Entertainment Productions, Persistence of Vision, MGM-UA, CBS-TV, 1986.

The Green Mile. Dir. Frank Darabont. Screenplay by Frank Darabont. Perf. Tom Hanks, Michael Clarke Duncan, David Morse. CR Films, Castle Rock Entertainment, Darkwoods, Warner Brothers, 1999.

Halloween. Dir. John Carpenter. Screenplay by John Carpenter and Debra Hill. Perf. Jamie Lee Curtis. Compass International Pictures and Falcon Films, 1978.

The Haunting. Dir. Robert Wise. Screenplay by Nelson Gidding. Perf. Julie Harris and Claire Bloom. Argyle Enterprises and Metro-Goldwyn-Mayer, 1963.

Hearts in Atlantis. Dir. Scott Hicks. Screenplay by William Goldman. Perf. Anthony Hopkins, Antn Yelchin, Hope Davis. Castle Rock Entertainment, Warner Brothers, Village Roadshow Pictures, NPV Entertainment, 2001.

Hellraiser. Dir. Clive Barker. Screenplay by Clive Barker. Perf. Clare Higgens and Oliver Smith. Cinemarque Entertainment, Film Features, Rivdel Films, 1987.

Interview with the Vampire. Dir. Neil Jordon. Screenplay by Anne Rice. Perf. Tom Cruise and Brad Pitt. Geffen Pictures, 1994.

Kingdom Hospital. Dir. Craig R. Baxley. Teleplay by Stephen King. Columbia TriStar Television, Touchstone Television, ABC-TV, 2003.

The Lawnmower Man. Dir. Brett Leonard. Screenplay by Brett Leonard and Gimel Everett. Perf. Jeff Fahey and Pierce Brosnan. Allied Vision, Lane Pringle, Fuji Eight Company, New Line Cinema, 1992.

The Lost Boys. Dir. Joel Schumacher. Screenplay by Jeffrey Boam, Janice Fischer, James Jeremias. Perf. Kiefer Sutherland, Corey Feldman, Jason Patric, Corey Haim. Warner Brothers, 1987.

Making The Shining. Dir. Vivian Kubrick. Perf. Jack Nicholson, Shelley Duvall, Danny Lloyd, Scatman Crothers. Eagle Film SS, 1980.

The Mangler. Dir. Tobe Hooper. Screenplay by Tobe Hooper, Stephen Brooks, and Peter Welbeck. Perf. Robert Englund and Ted Devine. Investec Bank Limited, Distant Horizon, Filmex, Allied Film Productions, New Line Cinema, 1994.

The Masque of the Red Death. Dir. Roger Corman. Screenplay by Charles Beaumont and R. Wright Campbell. Perf. Vincent Price. Alta Vista Productions, American International Pictures, 1964.

Maximum Overdrive. Dir. Stephen King. Screenplay by Stephen King. Perf. Emilio Estevez. Dino De Laurentiis Productions, 1986.

M. Butterfly. Dir. David Cronenberg. Screenplay by David Henry Hwang. Perf. Jeremy Irons and John Lone. Geffen Pictures and Miranda Productions, 1993.

Misery. Dir. Rob Reiner. Screenplay by William Goldman. Perf. Kathy Bates and James Caan. Castle Rock Entertainment, Nelson Entertainment, Columbia Pictures, 1990.

Naked Lunch. Dir. David Cronenberg. Screenplay by David Cronenberg. Perf. Peter Weller and Roy Scheider. Film Trustees, Naked Lunch Productions, Nippon Film Development, Recorded Picture Company, Telefilm Canada, 1991.

Needful Things. Dir. Fraser C. Heston. Screenplay by W. D. Richter. Perf. Ed Harris, Max von Sydow, Bonnie Bedelia. Castle Rock Entertainment, New Line Cinema, Columbia Pictures, 1993.

The Night Flier. Dir. Mark Pavia. Screenplay by Mark Pavia and Jack O'Donnell. Perf. Miguel Ferrer, Julie Entwisle, Michael H. Ross. New Amsterdam Entertainment, Stardust International, Medusa Film, Home Box Office, New Line Cinema, 1997.

Night of the Living Dead. Dir. George A. Romero. Screenplay by George A. Romero and John A. Russo. Perf. Duane Jones. Image Ten and Laurel, 1968.

Nightmare on Elm Street. Dir. Wes Craven. Screenplay by Wes Craven. Perf. Robert Englund and Heather Langenkamp. Media Home Entertainment, New Line Cinema, Smart Egg Pictures, 1984.

Nosferatu: A Symphony of Terror. Dir. Friedrich Wilhelm Murnau. Screenplay by Henrik Galeen. Perf. Gustav von Wangenheim and Max Schreck. Prana-Film (Germany), 1922.

Pearl Harbor. Dir. Michael Bay. Screenplay by Randall Wallace. Perf. Ben Affleck and Josh Hartnett. Jerry Bruckheimer Films and Touchstone Pictures, 2001.

Pet Sematary. Dir. Mary Lambert. Screenplay by Stephen King. Perf. Dale Midkiff, Fred Gwynne, Denise Crosby. Paramount Pictures, 1990.

Pet Sematary Two. Dir. Mary Lambert. Screenplay by Richard Outten. Perf. Edward Furlong, Anthony Edwards, Clancy Brown. Paramount Pictures, Columbus Circle Films, 1992.

Peyton Place. Dir. Mark Robson. Screenplay by John Michael Hayes. Perf. Lana Turner and Hope Lange. Twentieth Century Fox, 1957.

Porky's. Dir. Bob Clark III. Screenplay by Bob Clark III. Perf. Dan Monahan, Mark Herrier, Wyatt Knight. Astral Bellevue Pathe, Melvin Simon Productions, 1981.

The Pit and the Pendulum. Dir. Roger Corman. Screenplay by Richard Matheson. Perf. Vincent Price and Barbara Steele. Alta Vista Productions, American International Pictures, 1961.

Psycho. Dir. Alfred Hitchcock. Screenplay by Joseph Stefano. Perf. Anthony Perkins and Vera Miles. Shamley Productions, 1960

Quicksilver Highway. Dir. Mick Garris. Teleplay by Mick Garris. Perf. Christopher Lloyd and Matt Frewer. Twentieth Century Fox, National Studios, Fox Television Network, 1997.

The Rage: Carrie 2. Dir. Katt Shea and Robert Mandel. Screenplay by Rafael Moreu. Perf. Emily Bergl. Red Bank Films, United Artists, 1999.

A Return to 'Salem's Lot. Dir. Larry Cohen. Screenplay by Larry Cohen. Perf. Michael Moriarty. Larco Productions, 1987.

The Running Man. Dir. Paul Michael Glaser. Screenplay by Steven E. De Souza. Perf. Arnold Schwarzenegger, Jessie Ventura, Richard Dawson. Taft Entertainment, Keith Barish Productions, Home Box Office, TriStar Pictures, 1987.

'Salem's Lot: The Movie. Dir. Tobe Hooper. Teleplay by Paul Monash. Perf. David Soul, James Mason, Lance Kerwin. Warner Brothers, CBS-TV, 1979.

The Shawshank Redemption. Dir. Frank Darabont. Screenplay by Frank Darabont. Perf. Tim Robbins, Morgan Freeman, Bob Gunton. Castle Rock Entertainment, Columbia Pictures, 1994.

The Shining. Dir. Stanley Kubrick. Screenplay by Stanley Kubrick and Diane Johnson. Perf. Jack Nicholson, Shelley Duvall, Danny Lloyd. Warner Brothers, The Producer Circle Company, Peregrine, 1980.

Sometimes They Come Back . . . Again. Dir. Adam Grossman. Screenplay by Guy Riedel and Adam Grossman. Perf. Michael Gross, Alexis Arquette, Hilary Swank. Trimark Pictures, Vidmark, 1995.

"The Sorcerer's Apprentice." *Fantasia.* Dir. James Algar and Samuel Armstrong. Screenplay by Joe Grant and Dick Huemer. Walt Disney Pictures, 1940.

Stand By Me. Dir. Rob Reiner. Screenplay by Raynold Gideon and Bruce E. Evans. Perf. Wil Wheaton, River Phoenix, Corey Feldman, Kiefer Sutherland. Columbia Pictures, Act III Productions, 1986.

Star Wars. Dir. George Lucas. Screenplay by George Lucas. Perf. Mark Hamill, Harrison Ford, Carrie Fisher. Lucasfilm, 1977.

Stephen King's Golden Years. Dir. Kenneth Fink (Episode 1), Allen Coulter (Episodes 2, 4, 6), Michael G. Gornick (Episodes 3, 7), Stephen Tolkin (Episode 5). Perf. Keith Szarabajka, Frances Sternhagen, Ed Lauter. Laurel-King, CBS-TV, Republic Pictures, 1991.

Stephen King's IT. Dir. Tommy Lee Wallace. Teleplay by Lawrence D. Cohen and Tommy Lee Wallace. Perf. Harry Anderson, John Ritter, Annette O'Toole, Richard Thomas, Tim Curry. Lorimar Television, The Konigsberg-Sanitsky Company, Green-Epstein Productions, Warner Brothers, ABC-TV, 1990.

Stephen King's Rose Red. Dir. Craig R. Baxley. Teleplay by Stephen King. Perf. Nancy Travis and Robert Blanche. Greengrass Productions, Victor Television Productions, Mark Carliner Productions, 2002.

Stephen King's Silver Bullet. Dir. Daniel Attias. Screenplay by Stephen King. Perf. Gary Busey, Corey Haim, Megan Follows. Famous Films, Dino De Laurentiis, Paramount Pictures, 1985.

Stephen King's Sleepwalkers. Dir. Mick Garris. Screenplay by Stephen King. Perf. Brian Krause and Alice Krige. Columbia Pictures, Ion Pictures, Victor & Grais, 1992.

Stephen King's Sometimes They Come Back. Dir. Tom McLoughlin. Teleplay by Lawrence Konner and Mark Rosenthal. Perf. Tim Matheson and Brooke Adams. Paradise Films, Dino De Laurentiis, CBS-TV, Trimark Home Video, 1991.

Stephen King's Storm of the Century. Dir. Craig R. Baxley. Teleplay by Stephen King. Perf. Tim Daly, Colm Feore, Debrah Farentino. Greengrass Productions, Mark Carliner Productions, Walt Disney Television, ABC-TV, 1999.

Stephen King's The Shining. Dir. Mick Garris. Teleplay by Stephen King. Perf. Rebecca De Mornay, Steven Weber, Courtland Mead. Lakeside Productions, Warner Brothers Television, ABC-TV, 1997.

Stephen King's The Stand. Dir. Mick Garris. Screenplay by Stephen King. Perf. Gary Sinise, Molly Ringwald, Rob Lowe, Jamey Sheridan, Ruby Dee. Greengrass Productions, Laurel, ABC-TV, 1994.

Stephen King's The Tommyknockers. Dir. John Power. Teleplay by Lawrence D. Cohen. Perf. Jimmy Smits and Marg Helgenberger. Konigsberg-Sanitsky Productions, K&S II Partnership, ABC-TV, Vidmark, 1993.

2001: A Space Odyssey. Dir. Stanley Kubrick. Screenplay by Stanley Kubrick and Arthur C. Clarke. Metro-Goldwyn-Mayer and Polaris, 1968.

The Talented Mr. Ripley. Dir. Anthony Minghella. Screenplay by Anthony Minghella. Perf. Matt Damon and Gwyneth Paltrow. Mirage, Miramax, Paramount Pictures, Timnick Films, 1999.

The Terminator. Dir. James Cameron. Screenplay by James Cameron and Gale Anne Hurd. Perf. Arnold Schwarzenegger, Linda Hamilton. Cinema 84, Euro Film Fund, Hemdale Film Corporation, Pacific Western, 1984.

Terminator 2: Judgment Day. Dir. James Cameron. Screenplay by James Cameron and William Wisher. Perf. Arnold Schwarzenegger, Linda Hamilton, Robert Patrick. Carolco Pictures, Le Studio Canal, Lightstorm Entertainment, Pacific Western, 1991.

The Texas Chainsaw Massacre. Dir. Tobe Hooper. Screenplay by Tobe Hooper and Kim Henkel. Perf. Marilyn Burns and Gunnar Hansen. Vortex, 1974.

Thinner. Dir. Tom Holland. Screenplay by Michael McDowell and Tom Holland. Perf. Robert John Burke, Michael Constantine, Lucinda Jenney. Spelling Films, Paramount Pictures, Republic Pictures, 1996.

Titanic. Dir. James Cameron. Screenplay by James Cameron. Perf. Leonardo Di Caprio and Kate Winslet. Twentieth Century Fox, Lightstorm Entertainment, Paramount Pictures, 1997.

Top Hat. Dir. Mark Sandrich. Screenplay by Alexander Farago, Alodar Laszlo, Karoly Noti, Alan Scott, Dwight Taylor. Perf. Fred Astaire Ginger Rogers. RKO Radio Pictures, 1935.

Trucks. Dir. Chris Thomson. Teleplay by Brian Taggert. Perf. Timothy Busfield and Brenda Bakke. Trucks Productions, USA Pictures, Trimark Pictures, Leider-Reisberg, Credo Entertainment, USA Network, 1997.

True Lies. Dir. James Cameron. Screenplay by James Cameron. Perf. Arnold Schwarzenegger, Jamie Lee Curtis, Thomas Arnold. Twentieth Century Fox, Lightstorm Entertainment, Universal Pictures, 1994.

Unfaithful. Dir. Adrian Lyne. Screenplay by Alvin Sargent. Perf. Diane Lane, Richard Gere, Oliver Martinez. Epsilon Motion Pictures, Fox 2000 Pictures, Intertainment, New Regency Pictures, 2002.

Videodrome. Dir. David Cronenberg. Screenplay by David Cronenberg. Perf. James Woods and Debbie Harry. Famous Players, Filmplan, Guardian Trust Company, Canadian Film Development Corporation, Universal Pictures, 1983.

The Word Processor of the Gods [*Tales from the Darkside*]. Dir. Michael Gornick. Teleplay by Michael McDowell. Perf. Richard Hagstrom. USA Television Network, 1984.

WORKS CITED

Allen, Dick, ed. *Science-Fiction: The Future.* New York: Harcourt Brace Jovanovich, 1983.

Anderson, Linda. "'OH DEAR JESUS IT IS FEMALE': Monster as Mother/Mother as Monster in Stephen King's *IT.*" *Imagining the Worst: Stephen King and the Representations of Women.* Eds. Kathleen Margaret Lant and Therese Thompson. Westport, Connecticut: Greenwood Press, 1998. 111–126.

"At *The Shining* Press Conference." ABC Television Network. 9 Jan. 1997. Cited in *Phantasmagoria* 5 (April 1997): 24–32.

Barker, Clive. "Surviving the Ride." *Kingdom of Fear: The World of Stephen King.* Eds. Tim Underwood and Chuck Miller. New York: New American Library, 1986. 55–63.

Barry, Dan. "Death as a Constant Companion." *New York Times* 11 September 2002, natl. ed: 37–39.

Beahm, George. *The Stephen King Companion.* Kansas City: Andrews and McMeel Publishing, 1989.

———. *Stephen King from A to Z: An Encyclopedia of His Life and Work.* Kansas City: Andrew McMeel Publishing, 1998.

Biddle, Arthur. "The Mythic Journey in *The Body.*" *The Dark Descent: Essays Defining Stephen King's Horrorscape.* Ed. Tony Magistrale. Westport, Connecticut: Greenwood Press, 1992. 83–97.

Bosky, Bernadette. "Choice, Sacrifice, Destiny, and Nature in *The Stand.*" *A Casebook on The Stand.* Ed. Tony Magistrale. Mercer Island, Washington: Starmont House, 1992. 123–142.

Brown, Royal S. "Considering De Palma." *American Film: Journal of Film and Television Arts* 11 (1977): 54–61.

Burns, Gail E., and Melinda Kanner. "Women, Danger, and Death: The Perversion of the Female Principle in Stephen King's Fiction." *Sexual Politics and Popular Culture.* Ed. Diane Raymond. Bowling Green, Ohio: Bowling Green State University Popular Press, 1990. 158–172.

Carvajal, Doreen. "Who Can Afford Him? Stephen King Goes in Search of a New Publisher." *New York Times,* 27 October 1997, natl. ed: D1+.

Casey, Susan. "On the Set of 'Salem's Lot." *Fangoria* (February 1980): 38–42.

Cheever, John. *The Stories of John Cheever.* New York: Random House, 1947. 1981.

"Christopher, Saint." Entry in *Encyclopedia Britannica.* Chicago: William Benton, 1959 ed.

Clover, Carol. *Men, Women, and Chainsaws: Gender in the Modern Horror Film.* Princeton, New Jersey: Princeton University Press, 1992.

Collings, Michael R. *The Films of Stephen King.* Mercer Island, Washington: Starmont House, 1986.

Conner, Jeff. *Stephen King Goes to Hollywood.* New York: New American Library, 1987.

Creed, Barbara. *The Monstrous-Feminine: Film, Feminism, and Psychoanalysis.* New York: Routledge, 1993.

Dickinson, Emily. *The Complete Poems of Emily Dickinson.* Ed. Thomas H. Johnson. Boston: Little, Brown and Company, 1960.

Edgerton, Gary. "The American Made-for-TV Movie." *TV Genres: A Handbook and Reference Guide.* Ed. Brian G. Rose. Westport, Connecticut: Greenwood Press, 1985. 151–180.

Egan, James. "Technohorror: The Dystopian Vision of Stephen King." *Stephen King: Modern Critical Views.* Ed. Harold Bloom. Philadelphia: Chelsea House Publishers, 1998. 47–58.

Ferreira, Patricia. "Jack's Nightmare at the Overlook: The American Dream Inverted." *The Shining Reader.* Ed. Anthony Magistrale. Mercer Island, Washington: Starmont House, 1991. 23–32.

Figliola, Samantha. "Reading King Darkly: Issues of Race in Stephen King's Novels." *Into Darkness Peering: Race and Color in the Fantastic.* Ed. Elisabeth Anne Leonard. Westport, Connecticut: Greenwood Press, 1997. 143–158.

Foucault, Michel. *Discipline and Punish: The Birth of the Prison.* Trans. Alan Sheridan. New York: Vintage Books, 1977, 1995.

Freeland, Cynthia A. *The Naked and the Undead: Evil and the Appeal of Horror.* Boulder, Colorado: Westview Press, 2000.

Haas, Bob, and Lynda Haas and Mary and Donald Pharr. "Sit and Shine." *Discovering Stephen King's The Shining.* Ed. Tony Magistrale. San Bernardino, California: The Borgo Press, 1998. 107–122.

Hawthorne, Nathaniel. *Tales and Sketches.* New York: Viking Penguin, 1987.

Hatlen, Burton. "Beyond the Kittery Bridge: Stephen King's Maine." *Fear Itself: The Horror Fiction of Stephen King.* Eds. Tim Underwood and Chuck Miller. New York: Signet, 1985. 45–60.

———. "Good and Evil in *The Shining.*" *The Shining Reader.* Ed. Tony Magistrale. Mercer Island, Washington: Starmont House, 1991. 81–104.

Hohne, Karen, A. "In Words Not Their Own: Dangerous Women in Stephen King." *Misogyny in Literature.* Ed. Katherine Anne Ackley. New York: Garland, 1992. 327–345.

Horsting, Jessie. *Stephen King at the Movies.* New York: Starlog Press/ New American Library, 1986.

Jackson, Shirley. *The Lottery and Other Stories.* New York: Farrar, Straus, 1949.

Jameson, Fredric. *Signatures of the Visible.* New York: Routledge, 1990.

Jones, Stephen. *Creepshows: The Illustrated Stephen King Movie Guide.* New York: Billboard Books, 2002.

Kent, Brian. "Stephen King and His Readers: A Dirty, Compelling Romance." *A Casebook on The Stand.* Ed. Tony Magistrale. Mercer Island, Washington: Starmont House, 1992. 37–68.

King, Stephen. *Apt Pupil. Different Seasons.* New York: Viking, 1982.

———. *Bag of Bones.* New York: Scribner's, 1998.

———. *The Body. Different Seasons.* New York: Viking, 1982.

——. "The Bogeyboys." Keynote Address, Vermont Library Conference. June 1999. www.vema.together.com/king.htm.

——. *Carrie.* New York: Doubleday, 1974.

——. *Christine.* New York. Viking, 1983.

——. *Cujo.* New York: Viking, 1981.

——. *Cycle of the Werewolf.* Westland, Michigan: Land of Enchantment, 1983.

——. *Danse Macabre.* New York: Berkley Publishing, 1981.

——. *The Dark Half.* New York: Viking, 1989.

——. *The Dead Zone.* New York: Viking, 1979.

——. *Dolores Claiborne.* New York: Viking, 1993.

——. *Dreamcatcher.* New York: Simon and Schuster, 2001.

——. *Firestarter.* New York: Viking, 1980.

——. *Four Past Midnight.* New York: Viking, 1994.

——. *Gerald's Game.* New York: Viking, 1992.

——. *The Green Mile.* New York: New American Library, 1996.

——. *Hearts in Atlantis.* New York: Scribner's, 1999.

——. *Insomnia.* New York: Viking, 1994.

——. *IT.* New York: Viking, 1987.

[Richard Bachman, pseud.]. *The Long Walk.* New York: New American Library, 1979.

——. "The Mangler." *Night Shift.* New York: Doubleday, 1978.

——. *Misery.* New York: Viking, 1987.

——. "The Night Flier." *Prime Evil: New Stories by the Masters of Modern Horror.* Ed. Douglas E. Winter. New York: New American Library 1988.

——. *On Writing: A Memoir of the Craft.* New York: Pocket Books, 2001.

——. *Pet Sematary.* New York: Doubleday, 1983.

[Richard Bachman, pseud.]. *Roadwork.* New York: New American Library, 1981.

——. *Rose Madder.* New York: Viking, 1995.

[Richard Bachman, pseud.]. *The Running Man.* New York: New American Library, 1982.

——. *'Salem's Lot.* New York: New American Library, 1975.

——. *The Shawshank Redemption. Different Seasons.* New York: Viking, 1982.

——. *The Shining.* New York: Doubleday, 1977.

——. *The Stand.* New York: Doubleday, 1978; rev and unexpurg. New York: Doubleday, 1990.

[Richard Bachman, pseud.]. *Thinner.* New York: New American Library, 1984.

——. "Trucks." *Night Shift.* New York: Doubleday, 1978.

——. "Word Processor of the Gods." *Skeleton Crew.* New York: G. P. Putnam's Sons, 1985.

King, Stephen, and Peter Straub. *The Talisman.* New York: Viking and G. P. Putnam's Sons, 1987.

Kroll, Jack. "Stanley Kubrick's Horror Show." *Newsweek,* 26 May 1980: 96–99.

Lant, Kathleen Margaret. "The Rape of Constant Reader: Stephen King's Construction of the Female Reader and Violation of the Female Body in *Misery.*" *Journal of Popular Culture* 30 (1997): 89–114.

Lant, Kathleen Margaret, and Teresa Thompson. "Introduction." *Imagining the Worst: Stephen King and the Representations of Women.* Eds. Kathleen Margaret Lant and Therese Thompson. Westport, Connecticut: Greenwood Press, 1998. 3–8.

Leibowitz, Flo, and Lynn Jeffres. *"The Shining." Film Quarterly* 34 (Spring 1981): 45–51.

Lindsey, Shelley Stamp. "Horror, Femininity and Carrie's Monstrous Puberty." *The Dread of Difference: Gender and the Horror Film.* Ed. Barry Keith Grant. Austin: Texas University Press, 1996. 279–295.

Lloyd, Ann. *The Films of Stephen King.* New York: St. Martin's Press, 1993.

Magistrale, Tony. *Stephen King: The Second Decade, Danse Macabre to The Dark Half.* New York: Twayne, 1992.

Manchel, Frank. "What About Jack? Another Perspective on Family Relationships in Stanley Kubrick's *The Shining.*" *Discovering Stephen King's The Shining.* Ed. Tony Magistrale. San Bernardino, California: The Borgo Press, 1998. 82–94.

Matheson, Richard. *I Am Legend.* New York: Fawcett, 1954.

Marx, Karl. *Capital.* Volume 1. London: Harmondsworth, 1966.

Montag, Warren. "A 'Workshop of Filthy Creation': A Marxist Reading of *Frankenstein.*" *Mary Shelley's Frankenstein: Case Studies in Contemporary Criticism.* Ed. Johanna M. Smith. Boston: Bedford/St. Martin's Press, 2000. 384–395.

Mulvey, Laura. "Visual Pleasure and Narrative Cinema." *Screen* 16 (1975): 6–18.

Mussell, Kay. *Fantasy and Reconciliation: Contemporary Formulas of Woman's Romance Fiction.* Westport, Connecticut: Greenwood Press, 1984.

Nelson, Thomas Allen. *Kubrick: Inside a Film Artist's Maze.* Bloomington, Indiana: Indiana University Press, 1982.

Pharr, Mary. "'Almost Better': Surviving the Plague in Stephen King's *The Stand.*" *A Casebook on The Stand.* Ed. Tony Magistrale. Mercer Island, Washington: Starmont House, 1992. 1–20.

———. "Partners in the Danse: Women in Stephen King's Fiction." *The Dark Descent: Essays Defining Stephen King's Horrorscape.* Ed. Tony Magistrale. Westport, Connecticut: Greenwood Press, 1992. 19–32.

Rodley, Chris, ed. *Cronenberg on Cronenberg.* London: Faber and Faber, 1992.

Senf, Carol A. "Donna Trenton, Stephen King's Modern American Heroine." *Heroines of Popular Culture.* Ed. Pat Browne. Bowling Green, Ohio: Bowling Green State University Popular Press, 1987. 91–100.

———. *"Gerald's Game* and *Dolores Claiborne:* Stephen King and the Evolution of an Authentic Female Narrative Voice." *Imagining the Worst: Stephen King and the Representations of Women.* Eds. Kathleen Margaret Lant and Therese Thompson. Westport, Connecticut: Greenwood Press, 1998. 91–110.

Simpson, Philip. *Psycho Paths: Tracing the Serial Killer Through Contemporary American Fiction and Film.* Carbondale: Southern Illinois University Press, 2000.

Steinbeck, John. *Of Mice and Men.* 1937. New York: Penguin, 1994.

Stoker, Bram. *Dracula.* 1897. New York: W. W. Norton, 1997.

Thoens, Karen. *"IT,* A Sexual Fantasy." *Imagining the Worst: Stephen King and the Representations of Women.* Eds. Kathleen Margaret Lant and Therese Thompson. Westport, Connecticut: Greenwood Press, 1998. 127–142.

Thompson, G. R. "Introduction: Romanticism and the Gothic Tradition." *The Gothic Imagination: Essays in Dark Romanticism.* Pullman: Washington University Press, 1974. 1–10.

Twitchell, James B. *Carnival Culture: The Trashing of Taste in America.* New York: Columbia University Press, 1992.

Underwood, Tim, and Chuck Miller, eds. *Bare Bones: Conversations on Terror with Stephen King.* New York: McGraw-Hill, 1988.

————. *Feast of Fear: Conversations with Stephen King.* New York: Carroll and Graf, 1989.

Verniere, James. "Screen Previews: *The Dead Zone.*" *Twilight Zone Magazine* (November/December 1983): 52–55.

Walker, Alexander, Sybil Taylor, and Ulrich Ruchti. *Stanley Kubrick, Director.* New York: W. W. Norton, 1999.

Warren, Bill. "The Movies and Mr. King: Part II." *Reign of Fear: The Fiction and Films of Stephen King.* Ed. Don Herron. Lancaster, Pennsylvania: Underwood-Miller, 1988. 123–148.

Williams, Tony. *Hearths of Darkness: The Family in the American Horror Film.* Madison, New Jersey: Fairleigh Dickinson University Press, 1996.

Winter, Douglas E. "The Night Journeys of Stephen King." *Fear Itself: The Horror Fiction of Stephen King.* Eds. Tim Underwood and Chuck Miller. New York: Signet, 1985. 205–252.

————, ed. *Prime Evil: New Stories by the Masters of Modern Horror.* New York: New American Library, 1988.

————. *Stephen King: The Art of Darkness.* New York: New American Library, 1984.

Wood, Robin. "The American Nightmare: Horror in the 70s." *Horror: The Film Reader.* Ed. Mark Jancovich. London and New York: Routledge, 2002. 25–32.

————. "Cat and Dog: Lewis Teague's Stephen King Novels." *Action 2* (1985): 39–45.

Yarbro, Chelsea Quinn. "Cinderella's Revenge—Twists on Fairy Tales and Mythic Themes in the Work of Stephen King." *Fear Itself: The Horror Fiction of Stephen King.* Eds. Tim Underwood and Chuck Miller. New York: New American Library, 1982. 45–56.

INDEX

ABOUT THE AUTHOR

Tony Magistrale is professor of English at the University of Vermont. He has been teaching courses in writing and American literature at the university since 1983, when he returned to the United States after a Fulbright post-doctoral fellowship at the University of Milan, Italy. He obtained a Ph.D. at the University of Pittsburgh in 1981. Magistrale's most recent books include: *Stephen King: The Second Decade; Poe's Children: Connections between Tales of Terror and Detection;* and *The Student Companion to Edgar Allan Poe.* In 1997 Magistrale received the Kroespsch-Maurice Award for Excellence in Teaching at the University of Vermont; in 2001 he was presented the university's George V. Kidder Outstanding Faculty Award; in 2003 he was named the Dean's Lecturer for the college of Arts and Sciences.